Although some children read aloud with apparent fluency, they fail to understand fully or remember connected discourse. Most research on reading has focused on problems at the word-recognition level and less attention has been given to comprehension difficulties. Teachers usually monitor reading ability by listening to children read aloud, or by using reading tests that concentrate on word-recognition skills. Thus, comprehension problems may go unnoticed.

The authors provide an introduction and an overview of adult and child text comprehension. They then describe their own research on children who have a specific comprehension deficit. Such children have difficulties in making inferences from text, in using working memory to integrate information into a coherent model and in reflecting on their own comprehension. The authors relate these findings to educational practice and make suggestions for comprehension improvement.

Cambridge Monographs and Texts in Applied Psycholinguistics

Children's problems in text comprehension

Cambridge Monographs and Texts in Applied Psycholinguistics

General Editor: Sheldon Rosenberg

Books in the series

Ann M. Peters *The units of language acquisition*
Sheldon Rosenberg, Editor *Advances in applied psycholinguistics, Volume 1: Disorders of first-language development*
Sheldon Rosenberg, Editor *Advances in applied psycholinguistics, Volume 2: Reading, writing, and language learning*
Nicola Yuill and Jane Oakhill *Children's problems in text comprehension: an experimental investigation*
Frank R. Vellutino and Donna M. Scanlon *Reading and coding ability: an experimental analysis* (in preparation)

Children's problems in text comprehension

An experimental investigation

NICOLA YUILL
Lecturer in Psychology, School of Cognitive and Computing Sciences, University of Sussex

and

JANE OAKHILL
Lecturer, Laboratory of Experimental Psychology, University of Sussex

CAMBRIDGE UNIVERSITY PRESS

Cambridge
New York Port Chester
Melbourne Sydney

CAMBRIDGE UNIVERSITY PRESS
Cambridge, New York, Melbourne, Madrid, Cape Town, Singapore,
São Paulo, Delhi, Dubai, Tokyo

Cambridge University Press
The Edinburgh Building, Cambridge CB2 8RU, UK

Published in the United States of America by Cambridge University Press, New York

www.cambridge.org
Information on this title: www.cambridge.org/9780521125796

First published 1991
This digitally printed version 2009

A catalogue record for this publication is available from the British Library

Library of Congress Cataloguing in Publication data

Yuill, Nicola.
Children's problems in text comprehension: an experimental
investigation/Nicola Yuill and Jane Oakhill.
p. cm. – (Cambridge monographs and texts in applied
psycholinguistics)
Includes bibliographical references.
ISBN 0 521 35324 6
1. Reading comprehension. 2. Learning, Psychology of. 3. Reading
disability. I. Oakhill, Jane. II. Title. III. Series.
LB1573.7.Y85 1991
372.4′1–dc20 90-24682 CIP

ISBN 978-0-521-35324-3 Hardback
ISBN 978-0-521-12579-6 Paperback

To Alan Cutting and Alan Garnham

Contents

Preface

Our main aim in writing this book has been to bring together research we have carried out over several years with children whose comprehension of text is unexpectedly poor, given their ability to read the words fluently. Although we have published some of our results in research papers (see References for a list of these), we were only able to give part of the story in each one. In some respects, writing this book has been like assembling a jigsaw puzzle: we could see clearly what was represented by each of the pieces, but had to think hard about how they fitted together.

Our motivation was in some respects rather personal: we wanted to make sense of the problems of a particular group of children. However, we also hope that the book will stimulate critical and constructive thought in researchers working in related areas. Our research has spanned several areas of psychology – memory, language, reasoning and educational applications – and we hope that it will be of interest not only to psychologists carrying out research into reading, but also to researchers in education, educational psychologists and teachers.

We would like to thank Alan Garnham for reading and providing comments on the manuscript. At Cambridge University Press, Penny Carter, ably followed by Marion Smith and Judith Ayling, encouraged us, gave useful advice and reminded us of deadlines. This book has survived several disruptions to our lives: in the course of its many drafts, one of us moved to Cambridge and back, and the other became a mother. The numerous changes in computer systems it has survived were eased by the computing and secretarial staff at Sussex, particularly Sylvia Turner. Our task was also made easier by the helpful staff and excellent facilities of Sussex University Library.

The work began with Jane Oakhill's D.Phil research at the Laboratory of Experimental Psychology, Sussex University, funded by the then Social Science Research Council (UK) and supervised by Phil Johnson-Laird, whose contribution to this preliminary work is gratefully acknowledged. The bulk of the research described in this book was funded by a project grant (Reference no.

C00232053) over four years from the Economic and Social Research Council, and we would particularly like to acknowledge the interest and support of Alan Parkin, who has collaborated on some of the work we report here. Many other people were involved in the research, in planning and carrying out studies as student projects – Sharon Bridgman, Trish Joscelyne (who also ably carried out and analysed the experiments on the extension of our grant), Shelagh Madden and Sima Patel, in testing subjects – Frances Aldrich, Sally Payne and Bea Smith, and in helping to score and analyse data – Tushar Robins and Deborah Yuill. We are also very grateful to the staff of the schools, too numerous to mention here, but acknowledged separately in our other publications, who so willingly provided the facilities for our research. The whole enterprise could not, of course, have taken place without the children who were unfailingly eager to take on the many tasks that we set them. Finally, we would like to thank our respective Alans for the many ways in which they have supported our work.

1 The nature of poor comprehension

Introduction

One of the main tasks facing children in their early years at school is learning how to read. In the initial stages at least, reading instruction usually has a strong emphasis on decoding. Considerable resources have quite rightly been devoted to helping children in this task, and the majority of children manage to attain a reasonable level of fluency. However, fewer resources in teaching and assessment are devoted to the application of reading skills in understanding what is read. In many cases, the concentration on decoding rather than comprehension does not seem to matter: once children have 'cracked the code', they can use their reading skills and knowledge of spoken language to read and understand text. If comprehension skills are taught, it is at a later stage, in secondary or further education, and instruction usually involves relatively high-level skills of library-use, note-taking, etc. Younger children may be given tasks that require such skills, in project work or in standard 'comprehension' exercises, for example, but rarely is there any overt instruction in how to develop basic comprehension skills. Furthermore, theoretical accounts of reading often stress decoding, rather than comprehension.

Despite the apparent ease with which most children develop comprehension skills as they learn to decode print, we have clear evidence that fluent reading does not always go hand in hand with comprehension. Consider the following two transcripts of young children, reading a short story from a reading test (the Neale Analysis of Reading Ability, 1966). A sequence of dots shows hesitation or failure to read the following word, and words in parentheses show help or corrections given by the tester.
First Lianne:

John and Ann were fishing. Sunday -no- Frid- Saturday (suddenly) suddenly they heard a... (splash). A... (woodman) woodman had fallen into the... log (lake) lake. He could not swim for he was... (hurt) hurt. The children tr- tried to pull him out (ashore) ashore. He was too hurt (heavy) heavy. Then John and... John had the (held) held - no, hang on - John held the man's hand (head) head against (above) above the above water - doesn't make sense, above water, oh yeah it does - and Ann ran for help.

Lianne's reading is painfully slow and stilted, in comparison to 8-year-old Natalie, who has few difficulties:

John and Ann were fishing. Suddenly, they heard a splash. A woodman has found (fallen) into the lake. He could not swim for he was hurt. The children tried to pull him a...shore. He was too heavy. Then John heard (held) the man's head above the water and Ann ran for help.

Which child is the better reader? Clearly, Natalie is fluent: she could read smoothly, with appropriate intonation, and showed little hesitation. Lianne, on the other hand, read more than twice as slowly: decoding each word seemed such an effort that it would seem very difficult for her to consider the meaning of each word, or to connect the words to make sense of the passage. Natalie made only two errors, Lianne made ten. After completing the entire test, Natalie showed a reading age one month above her chronological age, while Lianne's reading age was six months below her age.

After reading the passage, the text was removed and the two children were asked questions about what they had just read. The questions, together with the children's responses, are shown in Table 1.1.

The responses to the questions show quite a different picture from the results for accuracy: despite her halting pronunciation, Lianne gives an acceptable answer for all but one question. Natalie's fluency is deceptive: although she remembers some details of the story - what the children were doing, and why they could not pull the man out - her other answers are either failures to remember, or confused confabulations mixed with repetitions of fragments of the wording. For the whole test, her comprehension age, based on the number of questions correct for two passages she read, is sixteen months below her chronological age. Lianne's comprehension age is just above the average for her age, and well above her reading age. Clearly, we would want to revise our ideas about which is the better reader, or at least specify more precisely what constitutes 'good' reading.

This book is about children who, like Natalie, are fluent readers, but who show little evidence of understanding what they read. We argue that this type of comprehension deficit cannot be explained in terms of difficulties in decoding. There are several clues in the above examples as to how we might characterise the features of poor comprehension. Firstly, Natalie does not *remember* so much about what she has read. On two occasions, she can give no answer at all, unlike Lianne, who gives an answer to every question. Secondly, when Natalie does use information from the text in her answers, she fails to *integrate* it appropriately. She combines information in idiosyncratic and incorrect ways: for example, she seems to have picked the word *ran* (using it in a syntactically

Table 1.1. *Two children's responses to questions in 'fishing' story*

Question	Natalie's answers	Lianne's answers
1. What were John and Ann doing?	Fishing	Er-fishing
2. What noise did they hear?	Umm ... ah ... (remember?) No	A splash
3. What had happened?	Um they were fishing and um the man come along and they um ... (anything else?) er they ... they ... he put the man's head in the water, above the water	The woodman had fallen in the water – the lake
4. Why could the man not swim ashore?	Because ... um ... can't remember	Cos he couldn't swim (any reason why?) No
5. What did the children try to do?	They tried to ran (sic) and catch him	Tried to pull him out
6. Why were they unable to pull him ashore?	Because ... um ... he was too heavy	Cos he was too heavy
7. How did John help the man?	Because ... um ... John tried to get him out but he couldn't (anything else?) No, that's all	By holding his head above the water
8. How did Ann help?	Well ... um ... Ann helped by um ... She tried to help him get out but she couldn't because she was um ... they they was trying to run and catch him but he was in the water before they got there	By getting help

inappropriate way) and associates it with the idea that the children are trying to catch the man. Thus, she has brought her outside knowledge to bear on the story, but in a way that does not bring any coherence to it. Similarly, her answer does not make clear whether the children put the man's head in or above the water, a crucial distinction for seeing the main theme of the story as cooperative rather than antagonistic. Lianne has clearly understood the coordination of the children's actions to help the man: one of them keeps the man from drowning while the other gets help. A third way in which the children differ is shown by Lianne's comments to herself as she reads the story. She obviously *monitors her comprehension* as she reads. At first she cannot understand the phrase 'held the man's head above water', as her explicit comment shows, but having repeated it, she realises what it means and accepts it. This checking procedure allows her to skip back in the text and to clarify misunderstandings as they arise. Even when Natalie does realise that she has forgotten something, it is only because the tester poses a question, and by then it is too late for her to refer back to the text. Furthermore, she is unable to derive the answer from her memory of the text. This is perhaps not surprising, given her apparently confused ideas about what is happening in the story. Lianne gives correct answers without hesitation, whereas Natalie can give no answer for some questions, even when she read the text perfectly.

Previous research on good and poor comprehenders has focused mainly on differences at the word decoding level. (For a summary, see Perfetti, 1985.) Implicit in this approach is the idea that reading is essentially a process of translating printed symbols into spoken language, and then relying on the abilities already developed to understand spoken language to take over. The idea that poor comprehenders have some more general deficit, at the level of text integration, which would also be manifest in their comprehension of the spoken word, is rarely considered. The 'decoding sufficiency' viewpoint stresses instead the importance of fast and accurate word recognition because, when decoding is automatic, it will not use up too much processing capacity. Thus, attention can be focused on the processes, such as deriving meaning, that reading shares with the understanding of spoken language. Claims that there are children who are good decoders but poor comprehenders (e.g. Cromer, 1970) have been vigorously attacked, largely on the grounds that such children do in fact have difficulties in speed or automaticity of decoding (e.g. Calfee, Arnold and Drum, 1976). We discuss such criticisms in more detail, and in relation to our own work, in Chapter 3. Although inefficient word recognition may often be a corollary of poor comprehension, there is no evidence that the relation is causal. The work we describe in this book suggests that other comprehension difficulties exist that have nothing to do with the recognition of individual words. This conclusion is also supported by the existence of 'hyperlexia' (Healy, 1982; Huttenlocher and Huttenlocher, 1973; Mehegan and Dreifuss, 1972; Silverberg and Silverberg, 1967). Hyperlexic children show 'unusual and premature talent in reading against a background of generalised failure of development, or marked impairment, of other language functions' (Mehegan and Dreifuss, 1972, p. 1106). Unlike our poor comprehenders, hyperlexic children may also have a range of more general behavioural, intellectual and emotional problems, such as hyperkinesis, mental retardation or autism. However, the existence of such children suggests that good decoding can coexist with poor comprehension.

Our approach differs from some earlier research on comprehension failure, which describes and analyses the *products* of poor comprehension, using psychometrics and factor analysis (e.g. Davis, 1972; Spearitt, 1972), rather than seeking to examine the *processes* which lead to the poor performance illustrated by Natalie. Recent work on reading comprehension in adults has explored comprehension processes, although it has been focused primarily on normal comprehension, rather than on assessing differences in comprehension skill. Our work combines an interest in processes of comprehension with a concern to explain and treat comprehension failure. As in other areas of investigation, the best way of finding out how something works is often to examine what happens when it goes wrong. Our two interests are complementary: poor comprehension reveals aspects of normal comprehension that we may fail to see when the process runs smoothly, and recent research on normal comprehension in adults is an invaluable source of techniques and hypotheses.

The focus of our discussion so far has been on *reading* text, but as we have already hinted, children who have a reading comprehension problem are frequently also poor at understanding spoken language (see Rubin, 1980, for a review). For example, Smiley et al. (1977) found that seventh- grade poor readers also had a listening comprehension problem, and that reading and listening comprehension were highly correlated. Townsend, Carrithers and Bever (1987) provide evidence from several sources to argue that listening and reading involve a single set of comprehension processes. Furthermore, the relation between reading and listening skills becomes closer as children develop their reading skills. Curtis (1980) found that listening comprehension was a more important factor in reading comprehension skill for older and better readers than for less-skilled and younger children. Many of the studies we will discuss in subsequent chapters have shown differences in ability between good and poor comprehenders in listening as well as reading tasks. Thus, we are claiming that, although slow decoding may contribute to problems with reading comprehension, at least in the initial stages of learning to read, it is unlikely to be their only, or even their main, cause.

Subject selection

Poor readers are sometimes treated as a homogeneous group, and so-called 'poor comprehenders' identified in the literature are often also poor at decoding, at least relative to the good comprehenders with whom they are compared. However, studies of poor comprehenders who are also poor readers cannot establish whether comprehension problems are due simply to difficulties in decoding. If children cannot decode a text they read, they can hardly be expected to be able to answer comprehension questions about it. Some researchers have endeavoured to study children with problems specifically in comprehension (e.g. Isakson and Miller, 1976; Levin, 1973). Cromer (1970) identified two types of poor reader: 'deficit' poor readers, who are poor at comprehension because they lack decoding skills or vocabulary knowledge, and 'difference' poor readers, who have the skills needed for decoding, but lack the ability to work out meanings and interrelations of ideas in text.

Our methodology

Our approach separates comprehension from decoding by looking at poor comprehenders who are matched with good comprehenders on decoding and vocabulary skills. This procedure holds decoding skill constant while using existing variations in comprehension skill to assess differences between good and poor comprehenders. Most of the studies we report in this book share a common design: good and poor comprehenders, matched on decoding skill, are given tasks that vary in level of difficulty. The tasks differ in one crucial element that is hypothesised to be an important aspect of comprehension skill. For example, one version of the task may impose a load on memory, or require a particular inferential skill, while another version does not. If the two skill groups differ only on one of the tasks, then we can infer that the critical component is implicated in the less-skilled comprehenders' poor performance, rather than some incidental feature such as attention or motivation. Methods of selection in previous research have varied, but we have been able to select groups of children by a single set of criteria, thus facilitating comparisons between our studies.[1]

We selected children by first testing entire year-groups of 7–8-year-olds on the Gates–MacGinitie Primary Two Vocabulary test (Gates and MacGinitie, 1965). This test requires children to look at each of forty-eight pictures and to circle one of four printed words that goes with the picture. We used this test as a gauge of children's knowledge of the meanings of printed words, and also as a way of excluding exceptional readers (very poor or very good) from the more time-consuming procedure of individual testing on selected children.

The next stage was to administer our main selection instrument, the Neale Analysis of Reading Ability (Neale, 1966), to children selected on the basis of their performance on the vocabulary test. In the Neale Analysis children read aloud a series of short passages which increase in length and difficulty. After each one, they are asked questions to answer from memory. The passage we quoted above, comparing performance by Lianne and Natalie, is the second passage in Form B of the test. The tester pronounces a word if a subject hesitates for more than about four seconds, and that word is scored as an error. Testing stops when the child makes a prescribed number of reading errors. The Neale test yields two separate scores, both of which can be expressed relative to age: reading accuracy, based on the number of reading errors, and reading comprehension, based on the number of questions answered correctly. Although the test is rather old, and no recent normative data are available, it was the only British test we could find at the time we began the research that gave separate, independently standardised scores for accuracy and comprehension. Also, we were less concerned with the absolute performance of our subjects relative to norms than with their relative performance on accuracy and comprehension. In

Table 1.2. *Sample means (in years; months) and standard deviations (in parentheses) of characteristics of 7–8-year-olds in our research*

	n	Chronological age	Neale Accuracy age	Neale Comprehension age
Less-skilled comprehenders	96	7;9 (0·36)	8;3 (0·36)	7;3 (0·55)
Skilled comprehenders	96	7;9 (0·46)	8;2 (0·61)	8;9 (0·80)
Others	372	7;9 (0·44)	8;0 (1·06)	8;0 (1·07)
Total	564	7;9 (0·43)	8;1 (0·93)	8;0 (1·03)

addition, the Neale test is widely available thus ensuring that comparable groups of readers to those used in the present studies may be readily identified. A revised version of the Neale Analysis has since been produced (Neale, McKay and Childs, 1986), but was not available at the time we performed most of our studies.

From the results of these tests, we selected two groups of children to take part in each series of experiments. The groups were matched for vocabulary and word-recognition skills, but differed in comprehension ability. Because of the nature of the Neale test, adequate word-recognition scores are not compatible with *very* low comprehension scores: children who can read the words in a story can usually answer some of the comprehension questions. The 'poor' comprehenders therefore showed an average discrepancy between accuracy and comprehension of about one year. In some other studies, 'poor comprehenders' are described as being *several grades* below the average (e.g. Isakson and Miller, 1976; Maria and MacGinitie, 1987). However, in such studies, good and poor comprehenders are not precisely matched on word-recognition skills: poor comprehenders are generally described as being 'at grade level' in word-recognition skill. Our selection procedure is more stringent. We matched the poor comprehenders with a group of skilled comprehenders for chronological age and accuracy age. The matching on accuracy scores was based on the regressed scores of the two groups, as this procedure takes into account the possibility that the two skill groups were derived from populations that differ in word-recognition ability. If this were so, then the groups might be found to differ in accuracy scores on re-testing, due to regression towards the mean scores of the populations from which they came (McNemar, 1962). We computed the regressed scores making the most unfavourable assumption (that the mean Accuracy score of the population from which the poor comprehenders were taken is equal to their Comprehension age, and similarly, that the mean Accuracy age of the good comprehenders was equal to their Comprehension age). Again, this is considerably more stringent a criterion than in previous studies, in which regression effects are not taken into account. Our groups were also matched on the Gates–MacGinitie vocabulary test, to ensure that the less-skilled comprehenders' ability to read aloud was not purely a decoding skill that did not entail knowledge of word meanings.

The groups of less-skilled children all conformed to the following specifications:

> – reasonable accuracy for their age: reading accuracy age no more than five months below chronological age (C.A.), although in most cases it was above C.A.
>
> – comprehension well below accuracy: comprehension age at least six months below accuracy age, although in most cases it was about one year behind.

Children selected in this way also showed an average lag of about six months between their chronological age and their comprehension age, although we did not exclude children who showed comprehension ages more commensurate with their real ages, because we considered the lag between accuracy and comprehension to be more relevant to our concerns. Table 1.2 shows typical characteristics of subjects in the two groups.

Overall, we tested children from about twenty different schools in the Brighton area, representing a fairly wide range in terms of social class and teaching methods used in the schools. We carried out our experiments on different groups of subjects in each school term, and each group took part in three to six experiments during the term in which they had taken the reading tests used for selection. The two skill groups included roughly equal numbers of children of each sex and from each school. We also performed a few studies with older children (8–9-year-olds), but unless explicitly stated, all the children in our own experiments reported here are 7–8-year-olds, and were selected as we described above.

In order to give some idea of how poor comprehenders compare with the other children we tested, we present in Table 1.2 characteristics of 564 children, comprising all the children given the Neale Analysis in the three years from 1983 to 1986. This sample represents about 66% of children given the initial Gates–MacGinitie test in the thirty-six classes we visited in that period. The children not given the Neale test were generally those who were absent, very high or very low scorers on the vocabulary test, or who had some other characteristic that made them unsuitable as subjects for our research (e.g. children who were not native English speakers, or who had some notable learning difficulty identified by their teacher). The table shows separately the characteristics of the ninety-six less-skilled comprehenders who participated in our studies during the relevant time-period. As it shows, the average discrepancy for this sub-group between accuracy and comprehension ages was over eleven months, and the discrepancy ranged from six months, our cut-off point, to thirty-seven months.

It is also possible to compare this group of less-skilled comprehenders to the other children who took the Neale test, whose characteristics are also given in Table 1.2. The poor comprehenders were slightly above the average of this group in their reading accuracy. This pattern highlights an important point: problems experienced by poor comprehenders may often go unnoticed if reading skill is indexed by tests of accuracy, as it often is. It is true that reading accuracy is highly correlated with comprehension skill: for the data shown in the table, we found a correlation of $r(562) = .77, p < .001$. This correlation masks the fact that for some children, there is a wide discrepancy between accuracy and comprehension. The less-skilled children in our sample were on average almost a year behind the rest of the children in reading comprehension scores. The meaning of poor comprehension in terms of performance is illustrated by the contrast between Natalie and Lianne.

We also found an unexpected sex difference in our sample: less-skilled comprehenders were more often girls than boys (22% versus 11% of children tested, chi squared $(1) = 11.25, p < .001$, taking into account the greater absolute number of girls in the sample). This difference probably arises partly because children have to attain a basic level of reading skill to read texts on which comprehension questions can be asked, and in our sample, boys tended to have lower accuracy scores (mean accuracy age in months = 95.8 for boys and 97.6 for girls, $t(532) = 1.78, p < .075$) and so some boys had not reached the stage at which reading comprehension could be realistically assessed.

General intelligence

A potential confounding factor in comparing good and poor comprehenders is their intelligence: it could be argued that poor comprehenders are simply less intelligent. However, attempting to control for this possibility by matching the groups on IQ might eliminate the very differences that are important in explaining why the groups differ in comprehension skill, or conversely, magnify the importance of a relatively minor causal factor (see also Perfetti and Lesgold, 1977; McClelland and Jackson, 1978). Hunt (1977; Hunt et al., 1975) found that verbal IQ is related to speed of information processing in a variety of tasks involving scanning and selecting information from short- and long-term memory, and argued that subjects with high verbal IQ may acquire more knowledge because they are faster at information processing, rather than the reverse. Analogously, if comprehension is viewed as a progression through interdependent subskills, children may perform better on the higher-level processes because they are more efficient at executing the lower-level ones. Thus, ability to perform higher-level processing during comprehension and performance on verbal IQ tests may be highly correlated, but this observation provides no information about the *reasons* for such a correlation. The information that good comprehenders are good because they have high IQs may be true, but is essentially useless. An intelligence test provides no way of telling us which of a number of potentially relevant processes are responsible for the deficiencies observed. Also, the knowledge that less-skilled children perform poorly on verbal IQ tests does not help in discovering how to improve poor comprehension. However, if we can identify some of the components that contribute to poor comprehension, there is some possibility of developing ways of improving comprehension deficits. The purpose of our studies has been to identify some of these components and, as we shall see later, attempts at remediation have shown some success.

In fact, we have assessed the IQ of a number of our groups of subjects, but the results have been equivocal as to whether the poor comprehenders generally have lower IQs. To some extent the conclusions depend on the type of IQ test used. In some cases we have found evidence that the groups differ on a verbal, but not a non-verbal IQ test, and in other cases they have not been shown to differ on either.

Motivation

Anyone mindful of the wider meaning and purposes of reading might be wondering whether our 'cognitive' approach to the problem is too restrictive. Perhaps poor comprehension is a result of some broader misunderstanding on the part of the child about the purposes of reading, or perhaps it is a problem of motivation: the Neale test, and many of our experimental materials, could hardly be called 'ripping yarns', and some children might have been happier reading (and understanding) comics in the playground, or the instructions for a new game or toy. Furthermore, children who seem inarticulate and 'slow' at school often show remarkable fluency and sophistication when observed in other contexts (see e.g. Tizard and Hughes, 1984). As we have described above, though, our experimental method consists of comparing skilled and less-skilled comprehenders on tasks that are similar except for one crucial variation. If poor comprehenders were not motivated to perform well, or failed to understand a task, then their performance on both versions of the task should be reduced.

The cognitive approach does not, of course, rule out the possibility that good and poor comprehenders differ in their attitudes towards reading. In fact, many of the poor comprehenders seemed to revel in their ability, often precocious, to decode long and complicated words, despite never having encountered them before. For example, Natalie, who was just seven, read with ease a passage containing words such as *apparently*, *familiar*, *territory*, *skirted* and *subsequently*, but gave not a single correct answer to the eight comprehension questions. Lianne, on the other hand, was a good comprehender, but was painfully aware of her inadequacies in decoding, and had to be encouraged before reading each story. It may seem surprising from an adult perspective that anybody could enjoy reading something they could not understand, but for children who have just mastered some of the regular spelling-to-sound correspondences, it can be an interesting and challenging task, which also gains ready praise from adults.

Overview of the book

Compared to the amount of research on the components of reading comprehension in adults, and in children who are poor at reading in general, there is little research looking specifically at children's difficulties in comprehension. This book focuses on poor comprehension in children, although we think that our research also contributes to the understanding of comprehension processes in general. We begin by describing briefly what is already known about how adult skilled readers make sense of what they read and review what work there is on comprehension development, and poor comprehenders in particular. Then we address our main question: why do some children fail to understand text? The most obvious answer, which we examine (and find wanting) in Chapter 3, is that they have some hidden difficulty in decoding, not apparent from the reading tests we use. Perhaps they read more slowly, or they might have trouble accessing the meanings of individual words. After looking at low-level processes such as reading and understanding single words and basic memory capacity, in Chapter 4 we describe research demonstrating specific aspects of text comprehension in which less-skilled children are deficient: inference and integration skills that research with adults show to be important in text comprehension. There is ample evidence in this and the preceding chapter that poor comprehenders may show verbatim memory skills equal to those of their skilled counterparts, suggesting that their comprehension deficits cannot be accounted for simply in terms of memory capacity. In Chapter 5, we propose that one source of the difference between groups lies in the more dynamic *working-memory* system. We support this view with an account of our work on children's 'on-line' processing of text. By measuring how long children take to read particular pieces of text, we can build up a picture of how they are allocating their mental resources in the complex task of decoding words and concurrently constructing a representation of the text. This account is followed in Chapter 6 by an investigation of higher-level processes, such as the way in which children use their knowledge of text during comprehension. The allocation of resources can be consciously controlled by a reader – if something is puzzling, or hard to remember, the reader can skip back, re-read part of the text, or seek outside help. But deliberate strategies can only be used if readers are aware of their own level of understanding, and have a repertoire of strategies for dealing with comprehension problems. Of course, comprehension is not entirely a function of the reader's skill: it is also influenced by characteristics of the text. There are many linguistic means of signalling and clarifying links that are to be made between different parts of a text. Chapter 7 describes studies comparing skilled and less-skilled comprehenders' abilities to benefit from these signals, particularly as reflected in their ability to produce cohesive discourse. The penultimate chapter describes the work we have done to investigate how poor comprehension can be improved. The motivation for this work is twofold: it has the theoretical aim of testing our ideas about the causes of poor comprehension, and the practical aim of producing specific suggestions for teaching comprehension. Finally we return to the broader issues associated with our work, bringing together the results of our empirical work and outlining the wider implications of the research.

2 Background: reading, remembering and understanding

What is involved in skilled reading?

Before considering the background to our own work on children's reading comprehension problems, we need to consider how skilled adult readers understand text. It is difficult to give a succinct account of this ability because competent adult readers obviously have a variety of skills that contribute to their fulfilling the ultimate goal of reading – extracting the meaning from the text – and they probably use different skills at different times, and for different types of text. One way of viewing the process of understanding, and one which we will return to frequently in the course of this book, is to say that the reader builds a *mental model* of the situation described in a text – a representation of the world (real or imaginary) that the text describes. For such a representation to be derived, however, the reader must engage in numerous lower-level processes: identifying letters, recognising words, and holding information in memory while deriving the structure of sentences. These lower-level processes are obviously important because, unless they take place, the higher-level comprehension processes will not be able to occur either. We will start this chapter, therefore, with a brief consideration of some important lower-level processes. We have restricted our discussion to those processes on which work with children, and good and poor readers in particular, has been carried out. We will not discuss, for example, some equally important lower-level processes, such as the control of eye movements during reading, because we have not done any work on their relation to individual differences in children's comprehension. (For a recent review of eye-movement research and its relation to reading skill see Kennedy, 1987.) Although we have divided this part of the chapter into sections, and have dealt with 'lower-level' processes first, this does not mean that we believe that the processes involved in reading occur serially and sequentially. The subprocesses of reading may interact: indeed whether and how they do is an active area of research.

Lower-level processes: word recognition and syntactic analysis

There is a considerable amount of research on word recognition in adults, but the details of this research are not important here. One area that is relevant to our research, however, is the question of whether adults are able to recognise a word and access its meaning purely visually or whether the word has to be *recoded* to a phonological form to access the mental lexicon.

Beginning readers often identify printed words that they do not immediately recognise by sounding them out, and identifying the sound that they have thereby produced as a word in their spoken vocabulary. Skilled readers could, of course, use the same procedure – converting the written form into a spoken form by applying conversion rules, and then using the spoken word to access the lexicon. It is sometimes assumed that such *phonological recoding* is an important part of skilled reading because we often seem to 'hear' what we are reading in our heads. However, such evidence does not indicate whether the phonological form of the word becomes available *before* it is recognised and is an essential part of the recognition process, or only afterwards, because such information is associated with the lexical entry. In fact, there is extensive evidence that adults and even beginning readers can access the lexicon directly, without using phonological recoding (Barron, 1978; Barron and Baron, 1977; Coltheart et al., 1986). We will discuss the research into the use of phonological recoding in beginning readers briefly here because it is relevant to the more general issues of its use in skilled word recognition.

Since the sight vocabularies of beginning readers are relatively under-developed in comparison with their aural vocabularies, phonological recoding might be an important skill for these readers to develop in order to retrieve the meanings of words that have been heard but never before encountered in print. The ability to identify words that are not in their sight vocabulary by converting the graphemic representation to its spoken counterpart may be useful even if reading at a more advanced level requires more than grapheme-to-phoneme conversion. While recoding may not be *necessary* for retrieving the meaning of words, some evidence has suggested that younger children do seem to make relatively more use of phonological coding in reading for meaning than do older ones. Doctor and M. Coltheart (1980) present data which, they argue, show that young children encode words phonologically when reading for meaning. However, more recently, V. Coltheart and her colleagues (1986) have argued that the effects found by Doctor and Coltheart were due to post-lexical phonological coding (i.e. the phonological form is derived from the lexicon), rather than being used to access the word. Coltheart et al.'s findings suggest that visual (direct) access develops first, and that grapheme–phoneme conversion skills are comparatively late in developing (see also Jorm and Share, 1983). They found that all nine-year-olds used direct access, and it was only the best readers who had well-developed grapheme–phoneme conversion skills. Other studies (Barron, 1978; Snowling, 1980) have also shown that better readers tend to make greater use of phonological coding to access word meanings.

Whether or not phonological recoding is used in word recognition, it might have a useful memory function in skilled reading. As Huey (1908/1968) suggested, a phonological representation is more durable than a visual one for storing the early part of a sentence in memory while the rest of it is being read. Thus, even if phonological recoding plays no part in lexical access, it might be important in comprehension. For example, though a task which is assumed to interfere with the generation of a phonological code (simultaneous subvocalisation) does not affect the comprehension of single words, it does affect the comprehension of continuous prose in adults (Kleiman, 1975). Levy (1978) qualified this conclusion by showing that the effect of subvocalisation only occurs when the precise wording of the text has to be retained in order to understand it. Although there are some problems in the interpretation of both Kleiman's and Levy's experiments, Baddeley and his colleagues (Baddeley and Lewis, 1981; Baddeley, Eldridge and Lewis, 1981) have found similar results using sentence verification tasks, and appropriate control conditions. For example, Baddeley, Eldridge and Lewis (1981) showed that suppressing articulation substantially impaired subjects' ability to detect anomalies in passages of prose (produced by changing the order of two words), but simultaneous tapping did not lead to a decrement in performance. They conclude that being free to subvocalise while reading may be important in relatively complex comprehension tasks.

Once the words in a sentence have been recognised, the structure of the sentence as a whole (its syntax) has to be worked out. *Parsing* a sentence to derive a syntactic structure is often a precursor to deriving the meaning. Sometimes the meaning of a sentence can be understood without doing a full syntactic parse. For instance, if one reads a sentence about watering, a girl and some flowers, a good bet would be that the sentence is about a girl watering some flowers – the meanings of the words allow for only one sensible interpretation, whatever the precise details of the syntax. However, in other cases the syntactic structure is crucial to the understanding of a sentence. For example, if you knew only that a sentence was about shouting, a boy and a girl, then there would be various sensible interpretations and exactly who was talking to whom could only be established by using the syntactic information.

Inferences and text integration

Even simple texts often require a number of inferences for their interpretation. For example, to understand the following sentence in a meaningful way:

Mary lent her umbrella to Jill because she didn't want to get wet.

it is necessary to bring to bear many aspects of general knowledge. You need to know that umbrellas can keep people dry under certain circumstances, and that *she* in the second clause probably refers to Jill, because she is the recipient of the umbrella and a likely reason for borrowing one is to keep dry. A less certain inference would be that it is raining at the time and that Jill intends to leave some sheltered place and go into the rain. We could also make numerous other plausible inferences about the characters, based on what we know about people who lend items to others, people who are unprepared for changes in the weather, and so on. In fact, an infinite number of inferences can be made from any one text, though only a limited number are likely to be useful for comprehension, and making too many could actually hinder the process. In the section on necessary and elaborative inferences, below, we will consider the sorts of inferences that are made *during the course of* the comprehension process.

The importance of inference making during text understanding became apparent to psychologists in the early 1970s, who realised that the predominant view of the 1960s – that the mental representations of sentences correspond to their linguistic representations – was inadequate. The new approach resulted from a revival of interest in the work of Bartlett (1932). Bartlett's experiments revealed many distortions in people's recall of prose, and he demonstrated that precise recall is the exception, rather than the rule. Bartlett argued that meaning is not inherent in a text, but must be *constructed* by the reader. His ideas have been influential in stimulating research into the role of inferences in text comprehension. Bransford and his colleagues in particular (e.g. Bransford, Barclay and Franks, 1972) have stressed the importance of inference making, and have characterised comprehension as a constructive and integrative process. In this section, we will deal in turn with these two aspects of text processing.

Numerous studies of adults have demonstrated that they spontaneously make inferences and integrate information from separate sentences in a text, rapidly forgetting the syntax of the original sentences once the meaning has been extracted. The effects of these constructive processes can be detected by testing people's memory for sentences or passages of prose (e.g. Bransford and Franks, 1971; Bransford et al., 1972). The essence of the constructive approach is that comprehension requires the subject to go beyond the information explicitly presented, in order to derive the *significance* of the text (Johnson-Laird, 1977). The *mental models* theory of text comprehension (see, e.g. Johnson-Laird, 1983) has built on this approach. Johnson-Laird argues that the relatively automatic processes of encoding words and sentences in a text may be followed by more deliberate constructive processes, including the addition of implicit information, which results in a *mental model* of the state of affairs described in the text. Understanding is not the passive reception of information, but the active composition of a message, using information from several sources. Since no two individuals have the same experiences, there will be differences in both the quantity and the quality of their prior knowledge that is relevant to the interpretation of a particular discourse. In the following sections, before going on to studies of text integration, we will discuss some further research on inferences that will be important for our later discussion of good and poor readers.

Necessary versus elaborative inferences Garnham (1982) has suggested that two kinds of inference can be made in understanding a text: those that are *necessary* to provide a coherent overall interpretation, and those that are merely *elaborative*. For example, in the sentence *The milkman had been bitten as he delivered the milk*, an elaborative inference would be that the milkman had been bitten by a dog. This inference is not necessary to an understanding of the sentence, although it might become so later in the text, to form a link between two sentences, if reference is made to a dog.

Since necessary inferences are, by definition, required to understand a text fully, they must typically be made as the text is read, and there are several sources of evidence that this is the case. In one early study by Haviland and Clark (1974) subjects read simple, two-sentence passages, such as:

We took the beer out of the trunk.
The beer was warm.

We checked the picnic supplies.
The beer was warm.

Andrew was especially fond of beer.
The beer was warm.

To understand the second of these passages, it is necessary to infer that the beer was an item in the picnic supplies, since it was not explicitly mentioned in the first sentence. Haviland and Clark found that the second sentence in this text took longer to read than the same sentence in the first passage, where beer *has* been mentioned. Passages of the third type were included to check that the effect was not simply due to the repetition of *beer* in the first passage. The second sentence was read comparatively slowly in this third type of passage, despite the repetition of *beer*, because there is no specific antecedent for *the beer*. These data, then, demonstrate that necessary inferences are made as a text is read.

Other experimental evidence suggests that at least some elaborative inferences are also made during reading. For instance, Johnson, Bransford and Solomon (1973) claimed to have shown that elaborative inferences are encoded into the memory representation of the sentence. One problem with such a conclusion is that it is difficult to predict which inferences readers will make, out of the very large number of possible ones. Since inferences are time-consuming, and many elaborative inferences that could be drawn will not be necessary in understanding subsequent text, it is not parsimonious to assume that readers make large numbers of elaborative inferences. In addition, subsequent experimental work, by Corbett and Dosher (1978) showed that the effects found in earlier studies could be explained by processes arising at the time of retrieval from memory, and not because elaborative inferences were included in the initial encoding of a text. Garnham (1982) proposed the *omission* hypothesis to explain the data on elaborative inferences. This theory proposes that inferable information (even when it is explicit) is left out of a representation of the text. If it is subsequently needed, it will be inferred from the text representation. Presumably, this strategy is more efficient than making and storing large numbers of possible inferences which may prove to be unnecessary.

Text cohesion and anaphora Inferences play an important role, more generally, in the linking of the different parts of a text into a coherent whole. In a conversation, speakers can take advantage of a great variety of ways of establishing cohesion: although the conversants may differ in knowledge, background, and so on, they have a great deal in common. They are in the same place at the same time, and they can point or otherwise refer to things around them to show what they are talking about. But communication via text does not have these advantages. Although a text does refer to something outside itself, much of the cohesion is carried by links within the text. Comprehension of cohesive devices is therefore particularly important for building up an integrated model of a text.

The interconnections in a text can be described both at the global level – its *macrostructure*, and at a local level – its *microstructure*. The macrostructure of a text refers to the way that the separate episodes in the text relate to one another. Knowledge about how things usually happen in the world will often be helpful in determining these global links.

The microstructure of a text is signalled by linguistic devices that link items within and between sentences. *Anaphoric* devices, such as pronouns, ellipsis and word substitutions are an important means of maintaining cohesion within and between sentences. (Halliday and Hasan, 1976, refer to such devices as *cohesive links*.) An important aspect of text comprehension is the identification and understanding of anaphora. Anaphoric expressions take their meaning from a part of the text that usually precedes them – the *antecedent*. In the simplest cases, anaphors have the same meaning as their antecedents. For example, in the text:

Betty went to the shop on the corner.
She bought some chocolate.

the pronoun *she* means the same as *Betty*. Other anaphors have the same meaning as their antecedents in a different sense. For example, in the sentence:

Fay has a red jumper and I want one too.

the indefinite pronoun *one* refers not to the red jumper owned by Fay but to another jumper of the same kind. Although readers usually understand anaphoric expressions without conscious effort, the process of interpretation can be quite complex. A pronoun, for example, can often refer to a number of things. In the text:

John left the window and drank the wine on the table.
It was brown and round. (Wilks, 1975)

there are four possible 'things' in the text to which the pronoun, *it*, could refer (*John*, *the wine*, *the table* and *the window*). It is unlikely that the pronoun refers to *John*, because pronoun and antecedent do not match in gender. It is most likely to refer to the table, rather than the window or the wine, because our knowledge of the world tells us that tables are more likely to be described as brown and round (but cf. Hirst, 1981, who argues that the sentence is ill-formed). The use of such knowledge in the interpretation of pronouns takes longer than resolving them on the basis of syntactic cues, such as gender (Garnham and Oakhill, 1985). For example, in passages containing an anaphoric pronoun, such as:

Trish sold her car to Carol
because she had decided to take up cycling.

where there are two antecedents that match in gender (Trish and Carol), the second clause takes longer to read than in passages where there is only one syntactically matching antecedent for the pronoun, such as where *Carol* is replaced by *Tom*. In the first version, it is only possible to decide who *she* refers to by using knowledge of the world to work out that a person who takes up cycling may decide to sell their car, and/or that a person who's taken up cycling is unlikely to want to buy a car.

Definite noun phrases are another class of anaphoric expressions that depend on world knowledge for their interpretation. Not all such phrases are anaphoric, but many are, and their antecedents need not be explicit in the text. For example, in the passage of Haviland and Clark's, given above, the first sentence was about picnic supplies, and the mention of *the beer* in the second sentence can only be understood by inferring that the picnic supplies must have included some beer. This example is one of a variety of cases that Clark (1977) terms *bridging inferences*.

As we discussed earlier, knowledge about the world is important in establishing global links between different parts of a text and establishing how the ideas as a whole *cohere*. Constructing a mental model of a text will be made easier if the text is *referentially continuous*. The prototypical case of a referentially continuous text is one in which each sentence or clause always contains a reference to something mentioned in the preceding sentence or clause. Evidence that such texts are easier to understand than discontinuous ones is provided by Garnham, Oakhill and Johnson-Laird (1982), Ehrlich and

Johnson-Laird (1982) and Oakhill and Garnham (1985). Referentially continuous texts are presumably easier to understand because they make fewer demands on working memory (see the next section).

Some theories of text comprehension that aim to characterise the global structure of text have tried to assign it a hierarchical analysis (e.g. Meyer, 1977). The idea that texts have a structure other than as a series of episodes has also resulted in proposals for text grammars (e.g. van Dijk, 1972) and story grammars (e.g. Rumelhart, 1975). Such grammars attempt to describe the structure of stories in the same way that sentence grammars are aimed at describing the structure of sentences. However, there are numerous problems with such proposals (see Black and Wilensky, 1979; Garnham, 1983). Garnham suggests that the hierarchical structure of goals and subgoals described by such grammars is simply another way in which knowledge about the world is used in understanding. Such knowledge is not specific to stories and, therefore, there is no need to postulate any special procedures for implementing knowledge in text understanding though, of course, as we have already seen, good readers need to have access to a rich fund of world knowledge to aid their story understanding.

Working memory in text understanding

As we have stressed, the main goal of the text understander is to derive a coherent and integrated representation (or *mental model*) of the text as a whole. However, we have also pointed out that such a representation will include not only information that is explicit in the text, but will incorporate inferences and knowledge about the world. In this section, we will consider how memory limitations might hinder the construction of a mental model.

Although studies have not shown a strong relation between standard short-term memory tasks (digit span) and verbal comprehension skill in adults (e.g. Hunt, Lunneborg and Lewis, 1975), there is increasing evidence (see, e.g. Daneman, 1987, for a review) that text comprehension depends on having an efficient *working memory* – a system for temporarily storing and processing information before it is transferred to long-term memory. For example, short-term retention of information in an immediately available form is important in the parsing of complex syntactic structures, where parts of the sentence may need to be held in memory while the overall structure is worked out. It is also important in integrating information from neighbouring sentences in a text. More generally, if the reader fails to recall the immediately preceding text, it will be difficult to link the current word or sentence with previous, related, information. Working memory capacity is known to be strictly limited, and texts that impose heavy demands on it will be difficult to understand.

The most complete account of working memory is that developed by Baddeley and his colleagues (see, e.g. Baddeley, 1986). These ideas have been incorporated into theories of text comprehension by, for example, Kintsch and van Dijk. Their model of text comprehension includes a limited capacity buffer, of the type described by Baddeley, as a temporary store for integrating information from different propositions (Kintsch and van Dijk, 1978; van Dijk and Kintsch, 1983). According to this theory, readers process text in cycles of a few propositions, or meaning units, at a time and, in order to derive a coherent representation for the text, they must relate the propositions in one processing cycle to those in preceding cycles. This integration can be achieved most easily if earlier relevant propositions are still in working memory, otherwise they must be reinstated from long-term memory. Daneman and Carpenter (1980, 1983) present empirical work which showed that working-memory efficiency is related to text-comprehension skill in adults. They reasoned that, since comprehension involves both storage and processing, a test that utilises both these components of working memory should be sensitive to differences in comprehension skill. They developed such a test, the reading span test, and showed that performance on it correlated with various measures of reading comprehension in college students. Interestingly, they were able to show that working memory has a role in specific comprehension processes: their measure correlated with how easily pronouns could be understood when their antecedents occurred earlier (up to seven sentences) in the text. However, as its name suggests, the reading span test involves reading: as Daneman and Tardif (1987) acknowledge, the test can be criticised precisely because it is too much like reading comprehension itself. We will have more to say about this issue in Chapter 5.

Children's text understanding and comprehension problems

We have argued that the successful comprehension of text requires the production of a *mental model* of what the text is about, and that a number of reading skills are needed to build such a model. Readers must be able to recognise individual words, understand the grammatical and semantic relations between the words, and integrate the ideas in the text, making inferences to aid this integration, or to fill in implicit information, where necessary. We will now turn to the development of these skills in children and, where it is available, we will discuss the research on good and poor comprehenders.

Research into children's comprehension problems has focused on three main theoretical approaches to comprehension deficit. The first is that comprehension problems are really word-recognition problems in disguise. The second is that poor comprehenders have difficulty in the syntactic and semantic analysis of text, and cannot make use of the structural constraints of language. The third, which we favour, is that poor comprehenders have difficulty with making inferences from text and integrating the ideas in it. We will introduce each of these main hypotheses in a little more detail.

Perfetti (e.g. Perfetti and Lesgold, 1979) has shown that good comprehenders recognise words more rapidly than poor comprehenders. He argues that because decoding in poor comprehenders is less automatic than that of good comprehenders, a 'bottleneck' is created in working memory. As a consequence, poor comprehenders have less working memory space available for comprehension processes than do good comprehenders – not because they have smaller working memories, but because they make less efficient use of them.[1] Perfetti and Lesgold (1977) propose that good and poor readers differ in what they call 'functional' capacity – i.e. what is left over for temporary storage once the computational or processing requirements of the task have been met. The second view is that of Cromer (1970) who argues that comprehension problems lie at a higher level of processing. His work has shown that poor comprehenders fail to make use of the syntactic constraints in text, and tend to read word-by-word, rather than processing the text in meaningful units. Our own emphasis is on processes at a higher level still. We argue that poor comprehenders have difficulty at the level of inferences and integration of information (failing to make even *necessary* inferences from text), and that they differ in their ability to monitor their comprehension and deal with failures (even in the presence of adequate word-recognition and syntactic skills). Each of these views might be correct to some extent – each may characterise the problems of a particular *group* of poor comprehenders, or each might contribute to the problem, without being a whole answer in itself. We will be discussing each of the three main views of comprehension failure further in the remainder of this chapter.

Our survey of children's comprehension skills will concentrate on four main areas. First, we will discuss reading skills at the single-word level: vocabulary, decoding speed and automaticity, and semantic access. Although our work is concerned with comprehension problems, and not word-decoding problems, as we explained above, much recent research has suggested that the two are inextricably interrelated. Second, we will consider children's knowledge of the semantic and syntactic constraints of language. Third, we will consider how children's text-comprehension skills are related to the capacity of their short-term and working memories, and how the efficiency of such memory systems might relate to the skills of inference and integration of information in text. In the fourth section, we will consider the relation between comprehension skill and metacognitive skills – the ability to monitor one's own comprehension, to recognise problems, and to deal with them as they arise.

It is often difficult to interpret the findings of studies on good and poor comprehenders because the subjects are usually selected using a very general measure of reading comprehension skill – one that depends on both decoding and comprehension (see Chapter 1). The 'comprehension' problems of the children in these studies may, therefore, arise because they cannot decode the words on which the comprehension questions are based. It is also difficult to compare the results of studies because some match the comparison groups for 'vocabulary' and some include children with severe word-recognition problems. Where subjects' decoding skills have been taken into account, we say so explicitly. Research that has investigated the problems of poor comprehenders has usually contrasted a group of poor comprehenders with a group of good comprehenders of the same age. The groups are compared on tasks that are believed to reflect important components of text understanding. Many of the studies we will describe, including our own, have used this methodology. However, it must be borne in mind that if a difference is found between good and poor comprehenders in some skill, it cannot be concluded that the skill is *causally* related to comprehension difficulty.[2] Ehri (1979) distinguishes between four possible relations that can account for such a difference. First, the skill may be a *prerequisite*: a skill that is essential for reading development, and which must be acquired before it can take place. Second, it may play the role of *facilitator*: a skill that may speed progress in reading development, but which is not essential to it. Third, it may be a *consequence* of learning to read: a skill that develops through practice in reading, rather than *vice-versa*. Lastly, there may be no direct link at all between a skill and reading ability – they may be correlated simply because each is also related to some other factor, such as verbal intelligence. It should always be kept in mind that if good and poor comprehenders are shown to differ on some skill, that can usually only be taken as evidence that the skill and comprehension ability are correlated, and not that they are causally related. One way to distinguish between some of these relations is to use training studies. Because there is always a variety of possible explanations for a relation between a particular skill and reading comprehension, the effect of training a skill may vary according to the nature of the relation. Training will only be useful if a skill is either a prerequisite to or a facilitator of skilled reading. If training in the skill in question can be shown to improve the reading comprehension of the poor comprehenders, then this would provide some evidence that the skill has a causal role in comprehension. We will have more to say about the various possible outcomes of training studies, their problems, and what can be inferred from them, in Chapter 8.

Problems at the level of single words

There are at least four ways in which problems at the word level could influence comprehension: children may not know the meanings of words that they can decode, they may decode words, or access their meanings, so slowly that comprehension is hampered, or they may fail to make appropriate use of context in word recognition. We will deal with each of these possibilities in turn.

Vocabulary An obvious explanation of poor comprehension (and one that has often been suggested to us by teachers) is that children who have comprehension difficulties, although they are skilled at *pronouncing* words, do not understand the meanings of the words that they read. It is clearly possible, given some knowledge of spelling-to-sound rules, to pronounce regularly spelled words without knowing their meanings. Skill at reading aloud, therefore, may be a poor predictor of text comprehension. In our own studies, we have always matched our groups on vocabulary as well as word recognition, and have shown that comprehension problems cannot be accounted for in terms of vocabulary size. However, it would be true to say that, for most children, reading-comprehension skill can be predicted quite well from vocabulary size, perhaps because both are related to general linguistic skill (see Rosenshine, 1980, for a review; Perfetti, 1985, p. 83). We will, therefore, give a brief account of the research in this area.

Beck, Perfetti and McKeown (1982) showed that difficult vocabulary directly affects text comprehension – 9-year-old children found texts easier to remember if they knew the meanings of the words in them. Beck et al. also showed that vocabulary instruction can improve comprehension. However, other research has not supported this finding. Pany, Jenkins and Schreck (1982) have shown that such instruction has only limited effects. The procedures used that were successful in increasing children's vocabularies improved their comprehension of single sentences, but not of passages. In any case, a poor vocabulary cannot be a complete explanation of comprehension problems because children can fail to understand texts that are comprised only of very familiar words (Perfetti, 1985, p. 97).

Problems with word-decoding speed and automaticity As we have seen in Chapter 1, reading fluency is not necessarily a good guide to comprehension skill. The existence of good comprehenders who are not fluent readers (see our example in Chapter 1) shows that fluency is not a *prerequisite* for good comprehension. However, in general, the *rate* at which words can be recognised and their meanings accessed is closely related to comprehension skill – efficient comprehension depends on reasonably fast and automatic word identification. This is because, in a system of limited capacity, processes compete, and readers who have to allocate more processing resources to decoding words and accessing their meanings will have less capacity available for other important processes in text comprehension than more efficient readers (who can decode words quickly and automatically).

Perfetti's *verbal efficiency* or *bottleneck* hypothesis stresses the importance of fast and automatic processing at the word level (see Perfetti, 1985, for a recent account). LaBerge and Samuels' (1974) shared capacity theory is based on similar arguments. These theories assume that decoding and comprehension processes are in competition for a limited amount of space in short-term memory, and that this competition has two main consequences. First, if a process is slow (or otherwise inefficient), then there will be less capacity left over for other processes to operate simultaneously. Second, since the contents of short-term memory decay rapidly, slow and inefficient processing will mean that fewer of the products of such processes are still available in memory when they are needed.

This idea of a trade-off between processing and storage in short-term memory explains why word-level processing might affect comprehension. The relatively automatic decoding and semantic access processes of skilled readers are more efficient in their use of available memory space, and leave more capacity available for other, higher-level, processes than do those of less-skilled comprehenders. In addition, since information is rapidly lost from short-term memory, very slow decoding may mean that the early part of a sentence is no longer available in memory before the final part has been decoded and can be integrated with what has gone before. Beginning readers sometimes use a strategy to cope with this problem: they concentrate on decoding the words as they read through a sentence for the first time and then re-read the whole more rapidly, to get the meaning of the sentence.

There are numerous sources of evidence that poor comprehenders are slow at decoding. For example, Perfetti and Hogaboam (1975a) found large differences between good and poor comprehenders (third and fifth grade[3]) in the time taken to name single words. There were differences for words of both high and low frequency, but the poor comprehenders were particularly slow for the low-frequency words. The groups also differed in the speed with which they could decode word-like nonwords (*pseudowords*). Although Perfetti and Hogaboam did not *match* their groups for decoding accuracy, this could not provide an explanation of the differences between the groups since the poor comprehenders were significantly slower even at naming common words which they could identify and whose meanings they knew. Similar results have also been shown for older children by Frederiksen (1978).

Since Perfetti and Hogaboam used naming time, one trivial explanation of their results would be that poor comprehenders are not slower in decoding words, but are simply slower at saying their names. However, this potential explanation was ruled out in an experiment by Perfetti, Finger and Hogaboam (1978). They showed that there were no differences between good and poor comprehenders in the speed with which they could name colours, numerals and pictures. Furthermore, the word-naming difference between good and poor comprehenders was shown to increase as the words got longer, whereas there was no such effect for the other sorts of stimuli. Further work by Perfetti and his associates has shown that measures other than *naming* time also distinguish between good and poor comprehenders. For example, good comprehenders are faster on tasks that require a manual response, such as pressing a button, rather than a verbal response (see Perfetti, 1985, p. 95). However, other work, by Hess and Radtke (1981), suggests that it is certainly not the case that individual variation in comprehension skill can be accounted for in terms of coding differences alone. They showed, using multivariate analyses, that comprehension skill differences can arise through ability differences at *two* independent levels: processing speed and memory.

Despite the existence of a general relation between decoding efficiency and reading comprehension, there is no good evidence that the relation is *causal.* Children who are good decoders at the early stages of learning to read usually turn out to develop good comprehension skills but, at any particular stage of reading development, as we illustrated from the case studies in Chapter 1, it is relatively easy to find exceptions to this general rule – good decoders who are poor comprehenders and vice-versa. For example, Cromer (1970) identified two groups of readers who differed in comprehension skill, even though they were matched for IQ, vocabulary and word-recognition ability.[4] Furthermore, if fast decoding did have a causal role in comprehension, then training in rapid decoding would be expected to improve comprehension. However, studies that have explored this hypothesis have met with little success. Perfetti and Hogaboam (1975b) found that such training was successful in reducing the difference in decoding speed between good and poor comprehenders, but that it had little effect on comprehension ability. In addition, Fleisher, Jenkins and Pany (1979) found that training fourth- and fifth-grade poor readers to recognise words and phrases as rapidly as good readers increased their decoding speed, but did not improve their comprehension, even though the passages on which they were tested comprised exclusively the practised words. In Chapter 8 we will be discussing an experiment of our own which showed that training in rapid decoding had a minimal effect on children's comprehension skill.

From these findings, it would appear that slow and laboured decoding cannot provide a complete explanation of children's comprehension problems. Perfetti and Lesgold (1979) have suggested that, in fact, the relation between word recognition and comprehension may arise much more indirectly: perhaps because good readers have more practice at reading, they are also more likely to develop decoding facility (they term this alternative to their bottleneck hypothesis the *by-product* hypothesis). However, some more recent data contradicts this idea. A study by Lesgold, Resnick and Hammond (1985) showed that, whereas there was a clear relation between early proficiency at word recognition and later skill at comprehension, the converse relation did not hold: early comprehension skill was *not* associated with later proficiency at word recognition. Thus, their data suggest that word recognition skills *do* facilitate the development of comprehension skills, and not vice-versa. Perhaps fast and automatic decoding has only an indirect effect on comprehension – allowing it to develop, rather than influencing it directly. It certainly seems that training in decoding fluency alone cannot be relied on to improve comprehension skills. Moreover, our own experiments have shown that many children have comprehension problems, even in the absence of any detectable decoding difficulties.

In summary, although children with comprehension problems frequently have decoding problems too, there is probably no direct link between the two skills. In addition, fast and automatic decoding is usually associated with accurate decoding, and with having a large vocabulary. Once these additional factors are taken into account, decoding speed may not be such a good predictor of comprehension skill.

Use of context in word recognition Qualitative differences in the decoding errors of good and poor comprehenders have also been shown. Weber (1970) found that poor comprehenders not only make more reading errors than good ones, but that their errors are more often contextually inappropriate, and that they are less likely to correct themselves even when their errors make nonsense of the text. This finding is hardly surprising – poor comprehenders, since they are, by definition, having difficulty in understanding, will be less likely to notice that what they produce is not sensible. Such deficiencies may be related to their poorer metacognitive skills – their ability to monitor and assess their understanding – about which we will have more to say later in the chapter.

Weber's findings suggest that good comprehenders make greater use of context in reading, to help them decipher words. However, a distinction needs to be made between use of context in this sense – to prevent or correct errors – and the use of context to speed word recognition. In general, good comprehenders are better at using context in tasks that require them to make or check predictions about what the next word in a text might be – i.e. guessing from context and using context to monitor their comprehension (Perfetti, Goldman and Hogaboam, 1979; Bowey, 1985), but they do not make so much use of context as do poor comprehenders to speed word recognition. We will not go into details of the work in this area, as our own work has not examined this aspect of comprehension skill. A detailed survey of the area can be found in Stanovich (1982) who reviewed twenty-two studies, using a variety of different paradigms, all of which failed to show that good readers make more use of context to aid word recognition than do poor readers. If anything, the reverse pattern seems to hold – poor readers make *more* use of context in such tasks. Thus, it would seem that skilled comprehenders are more *sensitive* to context, but are less *dependent* on it to aid word recognition, because their decoding is too fast and automatic for context to have an effect.

Problems in accessing the meanings of words The modest amount of work that has been carried out on the development of speed of semantic access has shown that both speed of semantic access, and ability to make use of information about the semantic categories of words, increases with age (Gitomer, Pellegrino and Bisanz, 1983; Chabot, Petros and McCord, 1983). In this section we will examine the evidence concerning ease of semantic access in good and poor comprehenders. As in the case of decoding, semantic access may be more or less fast and automatic, and the consequences of slow and laboured access should be similar to those associated with slow and laboured word decoding.

An (unpublished) experiment by Perfetti, Hogaboam and Bell (cited by Perfetti and Lesgold, 1979, p.66) showed that good and poor comprehenders did not differ in the speed with which they could match spoken words with printed words or pictures. However, Perfetti et al. argued that such tasks demand only low-level feature matching. In a *categorisation* task, in which the subjects had to make use of semantic information to decide whether a given word or picture belonged to a particular category (e.g. apple – fruit?) there were differences between the groups – the good comprehenders were faster. Perfetti and Lesgold conclude from these results that semantic information may not be automatically retrieved during the process of lower-order decoding in less-skilled readers. Work by McFarland and Rhodes (1978) has also shown that good and poor readers differ in their semantic encoding of individual words presented auditorially. The groups differed in memory for word lists when they had to rate semantic attributes of the words, but not when they had to produce rhymes for the words, or deliberately try to memorise them.

The automaticity as well as the speed with which word meanings can be accessed has been investigated more directly by Golinkoff and Rosinski (1976). They explored the relations between decoding, semantic access and comprehension in a picture–word interference task. Their results showed that semantic access is no more automatic in good than in poor comprehenders. In this experiment, as in many we have described, reading comprehension was confounded with word recognition skill, so the implications of the results for skilled comprehension are not clear. In Chapter 3, we will describe a replication of Golinkoff and Rosinski's experiment in which we used groups of subjects who were *matched* for decoding ability, and we will be discussing their experiment in more detail in relation to our own experiment.

In summary, poor comprehenders do not seem to have any problem in accessing the meanings of common printed words, though they may not be able to access rich and detailed semantic descriptions as readily as good comprehenders.

Syntactic and semantic knowledge

Once the words in a text have been identified, and their meanings accessed, readers have to use their knowledge of semantic and syntactic categories, and of the rules of grammar, to derive the meanings of the sentences. Although children have mastered the basic syntactic structures of their language by the age of 5, there are still specific areas where their knowledge is incomplete, and knowledge of syntax develops well into the school years (for an overview, see

Oakhill and Garnham, 1988, Chapter 3). For example, Chomsky (1969) found that it was not until about 8 that children could reliably understand the *easy to see* construction, and that children of this age were still confused about complement constructions with verbs such as: *ask*, *promise* and *tell*. Differences between good and poor readers' understanding of such constructions have also been found. Byrne (1981) showed that poor readers of 7–8 years misinterpreted sentences such as *the bird is easy to bite* more often than did good readers of the same age. Goldman (1976) showed that skilled comprehenders were more likely than poor comprehenders to understand the distinction between sentences such as:

Bill promised John to leave.
Bill told John to leave.

Reading-comprehension skill was a better predictor of the children's ability to understand such sentences than was age or IQ. These results suggest that it is plausible that an inadequate grasp of syntax may have an adverse effect on the comprehension ability of some children: difficulties in understanding certain sentence constructions could impose a 'processing bottleneck' at a higher level.

Even if children can understand sentences in a spoken form, they might not understand them in their written form (even assuming adequate decoding). In spoken language, there are prosodic cues to guide understanding – stress, intonation etc. – that are not available in written language. Obviously, some information can be conveyed in written language by the use of punctuation, but young children are typically not very good at using such cues in their reading and writing. If children have difficulty in identifying the syntactic constituents in a text, both their understanding of, and their memory for, the text is likely to suffer.

Cromer and his associates have investigated the idea that poor comprehenders have difficulty in making use of syntactic information in text (Cromer, 1970; Steiner, Wiener and Cromer, 1971; Oakan, Wiener and Cromer, 1971). As mentioned earlier, Cromer identified two groups of (college-level) poor comprehenders. One group, who had poor vocabulary and decoding skills, as well as poor comprehension skills, he termed the 'deficit' group. The 'difference' group, on the other hand, had a comprehension problem, even though their vocabulary and decoding skills were commensurate with those of good comprehenders of the same age. Thus, the 'deficit' group had a general reading problem, whereas the 'difference' group had a specific comprehension problem. In this respect, the subjects in Cromer's difference group were very similar to the less-skilled comprehenders with whom we will be concerned in this book. The distinction made by Cromer reinforces our argument that both single-word decoding skill and comprehension skill need to be taken into account when assessing children's comprehension.

In Cromer's original experiment, the subjects were presented with texts in one of four modes: as whole sentences, segmented into meaningful phrases (e.g. the cow jumped/over the moon), in fragmented phrases (e.g. the cow/jumped over the/ moon), and as single words. After each text, the children were asked a series of questions about the text and, overall, the poor comprehenders answered fewer questions correctly. However, the 'difference' group performed as well as the good comprehenders in the meaningful phrase condition. In addition, the 'difference' group's scores were the same for the normal sentence, single-word and fragmented-phrase conditions, whereas the good comprehenders' performance was better in *both* the normal sentence and meaningful phrase conditions than in the single-word and fragmented-phrase conditions. These results suggest that the 'difference' group normally reads word-by-word, so they are not affected by the disruptive conditions (by comparison with normal sentences), but chunking the sentences into meaningful units aids their comprehension. The 'deficit' group, on the other hand, was not helped by division of the sentences into meaningful phrases. Their problem does not arise simply from inefficient text organisation. The finding that the good comprehenders were not helped when the text was chunked into meaningful phrases, but were disrupted in the fragmented phrase and single-word modes, suggests that they normally organise text into phrase-like units – unlike poor comprehenders, they use sentence structure to aid their comprehension.

A further experiment by Steiner, Wiener and Cromer (1971) supports this conclusion. They reasoned that an advance summary of a text might help poor readers to read for meaning. Groups of good and poor readers (10-year-olds) read texts out loud, either with or without summaries. The texts were sometimes presented one word at a time, and sometimes in paragraphs. An analysis of reading errors showed that the good readers made more errors when given an advance summary as opposed to no summary – they paid less attention to word detail. However, the poor readers' error rate remained unchanged whether they were given a summary or not – even with a summary, they continued to read in a word-by-word manner. This style of reading is similar to the list-like intonation described as characteristic of poor readers by Clay and Imlach (1971).

In a few studies, the relation between comprehension skill and sensitivity to syntactic structure has been investigated more directly. Weinstein and Rabinovich (1971) looked at children's memory for spoken 'sentences' comprised of nonsense words, which either did or did not conform to syntactic constraints. Examples of their sentences are:

All the rak ibnu lurmed and wabed elirly (structured)
And all rak elirly, wabed ibnu the lurmed (unstructured)

They found that 9-year-old good and poor comprehenders performed equally poorly at recalling the unstructured sentences. However, the good readers found the structured strings easier to memorise than the unstructured strings. This pattern of results was found even when IQ differences between the groups had been taken into account. Although the groups were not matched for word decoding skill, this factor could not have accounted for the results, since the sentences were spoken.

However, an experiment by Mann, Liberman and Shankweiler (1980) failed to show any effect of syntactic structure on good and poor readers' ability to repeat spoken sentences. The discrepancy between the results may be due to the fact that Weinstein and Rabinovich asked their subjects to *learn* the sentences, whereas Mann et al. required immediate repetition.

Another experiment, by Isakson and Miller (1976) showed that poor comprehenders are less sensitive to both semantic and syntactic cues in text. We will be discussing this experiment in more detail in Chapter 3, as it relates very closely to one of our own.

In summary, there is some evidence that good comprehenders are more sensitive than poor comprehenders to both syntactic and semantic constraints, and use this information to guide their segmentation of text.

Text-level processes

Obviously, understanding the individual sentences in a text does not constitute understanding the text as a whole – the sentences need to be linked together. This integration of information depends on several skills: appreciating the structure of the text and the main ideas, making appropriate inferences to link up the ideas, and monitoring the comprehension process as it proceeds. We will look at the research on each of these aspects below. Most of this work has been done on children of different ages, rather than on good and poor readers, but will, nevertheless, provide an idea of the capabilities of children at different stages.

Understanding the structure of a text The ability to decide what the main topic of a text is, and to group sentences from a text according to topic increases from second to sixth grade (Otto and Barrett, cited by Yussen 1982; Danner, 1976). Work by Yussen and his associates (see Yussen, 1982) has shown that the ability to select a statement to convey the main idea of a picture story sequence improved between second and eighth grade.

Interestingly, although young children are poor at classifying the ideas in a text according to their level of importance, their recall is related to the level of importance as rated by adults (Brown and Smiley, 1977). This work suggests that even quite young children (the youngest they tested were 8) do pay attention to the important ideas in a text, even though they are unable to make judgements about relative importance.

To some extent, too, children's ideas about what *types* of information are most important in stories change with age. Stein and Glenn (1979) showed that, whereas first graders usually rated the consequences of actions as the most important elements in a text, fifth graders selected the goals of the main characters. Their experiment suggests that even first graders may have clear ideas about what is important in a text, but that their ideas may differ markedly from those of older children and adults.

Another important aspect of comprehension is understanding how the ideas in a text are related. One way of assessing children's understanding of the logical structure of stories is to get them to tell, or retell, stories themselves. Like adults, children show that they expect certain types of information to occur in a well-formed story and, when those aspects are missing, they are often added in retelling, so that the story conforms more closely to what was expected (see, e.g. Stein, 1979; Baker and Stein, 1981). As they get older, children are more likely to reorder a poorly structured story to make it better (Baker and Stein, 1981).

Children also become increasingly able to understand the use of connectives to mark relations between parts of a text explicitly. Stenning and Michell (1985) looked at the productions of 5–10-year-olds, and found that there was a substantial increase in the use of connectives after 7. They also found that the use of referring expressions (e.g. *he*, *the man*) became more appropriate between 5 and 7. Both these developments reflect an increase in ability to use linguistic devices to mark text *cohesion*. Karmiloff-Smith (1980) has also shown that children's use of cohesive devices continues to change even after they have mastered pronominalisation, as they become concerned with cohesion beyond the sentence level. We will be discussing our own research related to some of these issues (understanding the main point and hierarchical structure of a story and understanding and producing cohesive devices) in Chapters 4, 6 and 7.

In summary, even quite young children are sensitive to the hierarchical and logical structure of a text, but the ability to make this knowledge explicit develops only gradually throughout the primary school years. However, the concept of what makes a good story probably develops even before children start to read.

Inference and integration In the first part of this chapter, we discussed the important role of integration and inference in text comprehension. In order to understand a text, the ideas that are expressed must be connected, and this process often involves making inferences to fill in information that is only implicit in the text. As we argued earlier, only a very small proportion of all possible inferences are made as a text is read, and which particular inferences are made will be guided by the reader's *mental model* of the text. In this section we will only give a very brief account of the relevant research as much of it is very directly related to our own and is, therefore, discussed much more fully in later chapters.

Paris and his associates have carried out numerous studies of the development of children's inferential processes as they understand text, based on the work of Bransford and his co-workers, which we discussed earlier. For instance, Paris and Carter (1973) showed that both 7- and 10-year-olds used inferential processes, and remembered meaning-based representations of texts, rather than the specific words or sentences. This experiment, and associated findings, will be discussed in more detail in relation to our own experiments on inferential processing in Chapter 4.

Paris and Lindauer (1976) used a different, cued recall, procedure to investigate whether children (they tested first, third and fifth graders) would routinely infer highly probable instruments (e.g. a knife for cutting steak) that were not explicitly mentioned in a text. For each sentence, there were two versions, one in which the instrument was explicitly mentioned and one in which it was not, for example:

The workman dug a hole in the ground (with a shovel).

The words in parentheses were included only in the explicit version. After the children had heard several such sentences, the names of the instruments (implied or explicit) were given as cues to the recall of the sentences. Paris and Lindauer found that recall was better with explicit than with implicit cues in the first and third graders, but that for the fifth graders cue type did not have any effect on recall. The finding that the explicit and implicit cues were equally effective for older children indicates that those children were better able to make the inferences that enabled them to use the implicit retrieval cues. However, even the 6-year-olds could choose the appropriate instrument almost all the time in a subsequent test where they were questioned directly. The results of this second test suggest that even the youngest children *can* make such inferences when it is clear to them what they have to do, but that they did not *spontaneously* infer the instruments, either when they first heard the sentences, or when they were given the cue words. In a related study, Paris, Lindauer and Cox (1977) extended the technique to assess children's ability to make inferences about the consequences of events. They compared the performance of 8- and 12-year-olds and college students when given a noun as a cue that was either explicitly mentioned or was an implicit consequence. The difference in the effectiveness of the two cues again decreased with age. In a second experiment, they showed that inferential processing and better recall could be induced in 6-year-olds by asking them to make up stories related to the sentences. These results again support the idea that younger children can make the same inferences as older children, but may not do so spontaneously.

These experiments on implied instruments have much in common with what Anderson and his colleagues have termed *instantiation*, where the interpretation of a word is made more specific by the context in which it occurs. This type of inference has been studied fairly extensively in adults, though there is also some related work with children. For instance, an experiment by Merrill, Sperber and McCauley (1981) has shown that less-able readers are less likely than skilled ones to select the contextually most appropriate interpretation of a word. Work of our own has also investigated such differences between skilled and less-skilled comprehenders. This work will also be discussed in Chapter 4.

If poor comprehenders make fewer inferences than good comprehenders, one must always ask: is it because they have deficient inferential skills (a problem that may be exacerbated by deficiencies in working memory), or because they simply cannot remember the information in the text on which the inference is based? This question is particularly important because many measures of text comprehension impose demands on memory, so 'poor comprehenders' as identified by such tests, may simply have poor memory for text. Some experiments that address this issue will be described in Chapter 4.

We have argued above that both memory for information in the text and working memory are important in making inferences, but there could also be a relation in the opposite direction – the very fact that more inferences are made may facilitate text recall. For instance, Paris and Upton (1976) showed that making inferences helps children to remember stories. In one experiment, children aged 5–11 were read a series of short stories and, immediately after listening to each story, they were asked questions about it. Half of the questions required memory for the wording of the story, and half could only be answered if an inference had been made. The results showed that accuracy on both sorts of question increased with age, but that the developmental changes in ability to understand and remember inferences did not appear to result from changes in memory capacity alone. Indeed, Paris and Upton suggest that making inferences may help in the encoding of text into memory – attempting to infer additional information may aid comprehension of and memory for the original information. However, the connection between inference making and recall has been questioned. For instance, Omanson, Warren and Trabasso (1978) showed that an experimental manipulation that increased the number of inferences made by children did not increase recall. Whether or not inference making aids recall remains uncertain.

Earlier in the chapter we mentioned the important role of anaphoric devices in establishing how the ideas in a text are connected in skilled reading. Little work has been done to compare good and poor readers' understanding of anaphoric expressions but, in general, children seem to find them quite difficult. For instance, Bormuth, Manning, Carr and Pearson (1970) report that only 77% of anaphoric expressions were understood by a group of 9-year-old average readers. In another study, skill-deficient fourth graders, even after training in pronoun resolution, still showed an accuracy rate of only 57%, although this was greater than the 31% accuracy rate of untrained subjects

(Dommes, Gersten and Carnine, 1984). As we have mentioned above, some individual differences research with adults (Daneman and Carpenter, 1980; 1983) has shown that comprehension skill is related to working-memory ability which, in turn, is correlated with ability to resolve pronouns (though they did not test the relation between comprehension skill and pronoun resolution directly).

Although several studies have looked at children's ability to resolve pronouns, little is known about how they deal with other types of anaphor, or about differences between good and poor comprehenders. In our own work, we have explored differences between skilled and less-skilled comprehenders in understanding a variety of different types of anaphoric expression. These studies will be discussed in Chapter 4.

The role of memory in text integration In most recent theories of skilled reading, various types of memory play an important part. As we mentioned earlier, working memory is needed for the temporary storage and integration of information, and a link has been shown between working memory and comprehension skill in adults. Long-term memory serves as a source of relevant background knowledge which will be important in understanding text and making inferences, and problems will arise if children do not or cannot use information from long-term memory to help them make sense of the text.

Short-term and working memory in text comprehension. As we outlined earlier, the short-term retention of information in a text is important in parsing, and in integrating information from the current sentence with preceding sentences.

A number of studies have shown that good and poor readers differ on memory-span tasks, and that these differences can be accounted for primarily in terms of differences in the efficiency of phonetic recoding in working memory, which are independent of general intellectual ability (see Stanovich, 1986; Wagner and Torgesen, 1987). However, such differences between good and poor readers are by no means the rule. For instance, Perfetti and Goldman (1976) failed to find differences using their 'probe-digit' task, which also requires memory for lists of digits. It may be that differences in short-term memory only appear when readers who differ widely in ability are compared. In any case, few studies have addressed the question of whether children with a specific comprehension problem, as opposed to some more general reading problem, have deficient short-term memories. Our own work, which we will discuss in the next chapter, addresses this issue.

Although short-term memory span has been shown to increase with age, this increase appears to reflect children's developing ability to encode information in an efficient way, rather than changes in the capacity of short-term memory itself (Chi, 1976; Huttenlocher and Burke, 1976). An increase in memory span could occur through a decrease in the proportion of space that is devoted to basic operations, so that the *available* resources could increase even if the total capacity remains constant (see Case, Kurland and Goldberg, 1982). Thus, it may be that good and poor comprehenders differ in the efficiency of their *encoding* strategies, rather than in their memory capacity *per se*. This is an issue we will address in Chapter 5.

Although the research findings on the relation between standard measures of short-term memory skill (e.g. digit span) and comprehension ability are equivocal, there is stronger evidence that good and poor readers differ in their ability to remember recent parts of continuous text. Goldman et al. (1980) used a probe memory task (analogous to the 'probe-digit' task, mentioned above) to explore short-term retention of text. In the reading version of this task, reading was interrupted at intervals, and a word that had appeared earlier in the text was presented. The child's task was to say what word (the target) had followed the probe word in the text. Goldman et al. varied the distance between the target and the re-presentation of the probe word, and the structure of the intervening text. Although both skilled and less-skilled readers were able to recall more words from the sentence they were reading than from the preceding sentence, skilled readers were better at recalling words from the previous sentence than were the less-skilled ones. These differences are not specific to reading – Perfetti and Goldman (1976) found comparable differences in a listening task, with subjects from the third and fifth grades. They also found that the difference between skilled and less-skilled comprehenders was much larger for two-clause than for one-clause sentences, especially when the probe was very recent. These data indicate that the ability to integrate information in text may be a source of comprehension problems, even when short-term memory span, as measured by a comparable probe-digit task, is not. Similarly, Townsend (personal communication) found that middle-school children (11–13-year-olds) who differed in reading-achievement scores did not differ in digit span, but did differ in sentence span. They also showed that the groups differed in sensitivity to structural properties of sentences, such as clause boundaries and subordination, in both reading and listening tasks: the high reading achievement group was more sensitive to structural properties of sentences. Perfetti and Lesgold (1977) suggest that individual differences in text memory might be found in the absence of differences in digit span and related tests, because the task demands of discourse processing – the rapid shifting of attention among coding operations – are more considerable than those required in standard digit-memory tasks.

Digit-span tasks have traditionally been used as measures of short-term memory. Within the working-memory framework, such tasks are thought of as largely dependent on only one of the subsystems (the articulatory loop), whereas text processing relies on other aspects of the working-memory system as well, in particular the central executive (a more general limited-capacity system for temporary storage and processing). Therefore, digit-span tasks may not be a good measure of those aspects of working memory required in text processing. We mentioned previously that performance on tests of working-memory skill, which require simultaneous storage and processing of information, have been shown to be related to text comprehension in adults (Daneman and Carpenter, 1980, 1983; Baddeley, Logie, Nimmo-Smith and Brereton, 1985). There is also some evidence for a link between working memory and reading in children. Siegel and Ryan (1989) showed that reading-disabled 7–13-year-olds performed more poorly on both a sentence-span and a counting-span task. Kail et al. (1977) provided indirect evidence for a relation between working memory and comprehension in children. They asked their subjects to read a text, and then to say whether a series of sentences were true of the text that they had heard. The better comprehenders were able to make judgements about the sentences that were true inferences more quickly than were the poorer ones. Kail et al. argue that this difference cannot be explained simply by differences in the ability to retain information, and neither can it be explained in terms of differences in coding efficiency, since reading time was controlled. They argue, rather, that it reflects the facility with which good comprehenders are able to manipulate and integrate information in working memory. This conclusion is consistent with that of Hess and Radtke (1981) who showed that skilled comprehenders of elementary school age are more efficient at scanning the contents of working memory than are poor comprehenders. We have some further evidence that skilled and less-skilled comprehenders differ in the efficiency of their working memories, and that this may be one source of differences in comprehension skill between them. This work will be discussed in Chapter 5.

Metacognitive skills and comprehension monitoring

The main cognitive skills used in reading are those of decoding and comprehension. Metacognitive skills are those involved in reflecting on the operation and outcomes of the cognitive skills and, like the cognitive skills, may also be constrained by the limitations of working memory.

Some idea of children's metacognitive abilities can be gleaned from interviews, although their responses should be treated with caution as they may be limited by the children's ability to express what they know about reading. One finding from such interviews that is relevant in the present context is that younger children tend to think that decoding, rather than comprehension, is the main point of reading (see, for example, Canney and Winograd, 1979; Myers and Paris, 1978). Myers and Paris (1978) found that, although younger children (8-year-olds) knew that familiarity with the content of a text and strategies such as rereading are helpful, they had fewer ideas about how to deal with difficulties such as unknown words or difficult sentences.

An important metacognitive skill in relation to comprehension is that of *comprehension monitoring*. If skilled readers fail to understand part of a text, they take action, such as re-reading, to overcome the problem. However, young children often fail to realise that they have not adequately understood a text, or know what to do about it if they do realise (see, e.g. Baker and Brown, 1984; Garner, 1987; Markman, 1981). For instance, Markman (1977) assessed children's ability to detect that instructions for how to play a game or how to perform a magic trick were inadequate. The younger children (first graders) usually failed to realise that there was anything missing from the instructions until they tried to carry them out, whereas the older children (third graders) were more likely to point out that the instructions were incomplete.

In another study, Markman (1979) used texts that were logically inconsistent. If an adequate text model is to be derived, then any inconsistencies in a text must be noted and, if possible, resolved. However, Markman showed that young children are poor at spotting even gross inconsistencies, such as those in the following passage:

Ants

Everywhere they go they put out a special chemical from their bodies. They cannot see this chemical, but it has a special odor. An ant must have a nose in order to smell this chemical odor. Another thing about ants is they do not have a nose. Ants cannot smell this odor. Ants can always find their way home by smelling this odor to follow the trail.

The children (third, fifth and sixth graders) were asked what, if any, changes would be needed to make the texts easier to understand. Although there was some improvement with age in ability to detect the inconsistencies, a substantial proportion of the passages were judged fully comprehensible by even the oldest children. Subsequent work by Markman and Gorin (1981) showed that these results could be explained partially by children's reluctance to criticise written material, and by the standards they use to evaluate texts. The children were given one of three sorts of instruction: they were told simply to look for problems, or were told to look specifically for falsehoods or for inconsistencies in texts that contained both. The specific instructions increased the children's ability to detect the type of problem mentioned, especially in the case of the older children.

In summary, children's ability to monitor their own comprehension increases during the primary school years and the instructions they are given can sensitise them to potential problems in a text.

Another type of metacognitive skill that has recently gained prominence as an important aspect of reading is metalinguistic skill. Various terms (e.g. linguistic awareness, metalinguistics, metalinguistic awareness) have been used to describe a set of related abilities including the knowledge of linguistic terms (e.g. word, letter), the awareness that language is made up of phonemes and lexical items, general beliefs about reading (e.g. Downing, 1984), and the ability to think about language apart from its communicative function. Metalinguistic skill involves the awareness of the form of language, in contrast to linguistic skill, which is the ability to use language. There is growing evidence that children's awareness of language, and their knowledge of the purposes of reading, contribute to success in acquiring reading skills (e.g. Downing, 1984; Forrest-Pressley and Waller, 1984; Tunmer and Bowey, 1984). Studies showing how linguistic awareness increases with age and reading experience are too numerous and diverse to review here (see Downing and Valtin, 1984; Sinclair, Jarvella and Levelt, 1978; Tunmer, Pratt and Herriman, 1984), but the general message of this work is that children become increasingly able to reflect on linguistic form, as well as meaning. We will now turn to what is known about the relation between comprehension ability and metalinguistic and metacognitive skills.

Good comprehenders seem to have a better awareness of their own comprehension (Golinkoff, 1975–76), and there is some evidence that poor comprehenders fail to make use of monitoring strategies. Olshavsky (1976–77) showed that, although both good and poor tenth-grade readers described themselves as using similar comprehension strategies, the good readers reported using them more frequently.

Garner (1980) has also shown that poor comprehenders are less good at comprehension monitoring. In her study, good and poor comprehenders from the seventh and eighth grades read passages that contained obvious inconsistencies in some sections. The children were asked to say how easy each section of the passage was to understand, and to explain why some sections were difficult. The results showed that the good comprehenders classified the inconsistent sections as harder to understand than the consistent ones, and that their comments showed that they were aware of the source of their problems. Poor comprehenders, by contrast, did not differentiate between the consistent and inconsistent sections and, even when they reported a comprehension problem, they did not cite the inconsistencies. Instead, they explained their difficulty with comments such as: 'The words were longer' or 'I didn't like that part as well'. As Garner points out, poor comprehension monitoring might not be a cause of poor comprehension – it might result from it: 'lack of attention to glaring gaps or blatant inconsistencies might occur because of a history of print's making only minimal sense to a reader' (1980, p61).

Further evidence that poor comprehenders concentrate on problems at the level of individual words, rather than in the text as a whole, comes from another study by Garner (1981). She investigated the monitoring skills of fifth- and sixth-grade poor comprehenders by asking them to rate two sorts of passage: one containing inconsistencies, and one containing polysyllabic words they did not know the meaning of (e.g. *expeditiously*, *multifarious*). The poor comprehenders did not differentiate between consistent and inconsistent passages, but tended to rate the passages with difficult words as less comprehensible than those with inconsistencies.

Garner and Kraus (1981–82) showed that almost all of a group of seventh-grade good comprehenders detected inconsistencies in a text, but none of the poor comprehenders did. They also gave the children a questionnaire about reading and found that, although none of the poor comprehenders had decoding problems, few mentioned understanding or extracting meaning and the majority mentioned the importance of word decoding in reading. This response was never made by the good comprehenders. Baker (1984a) has also shown that poorer readers identify fewer problems with texts than do better ones, and use fewer criteria for deciding that texts are incomprehensible. Even in an editing task, where children were actively encouraged to criticise texts containing gross inconsistencies, Garner and Taylor (1982) found that 80% of the poor comprehenders never mentioned the meaning disparity, even if the experimenter explicitly pointed out the inconsistent sentences.

An obvious way for readers to remedy comprehension difficulties would be to look back to the relevant part of the text. However, Garner and Reis (1981) found that only the oldest (eighth-grade) successful readers consistently used this strategy in a study they conducted on 'middle school' children. They concluded (in keeping with the other studies discussed above) that only the oldest good readers recognised their comprehension failures, and only they did anything to try to remedy their difficulties. However, encouragingly, Garner (1982) showed that even poor comprehenders could benefit from being given very direct training in using text lookbacks to help with comprehension problems.

The above studies have illustrated the extensive work on the relation between comprehension monitoring and comprehension ability. However, although there has been much work on the relation of *metalinguistic* skills to general reading ability, there has been little on good and poor comprehenders specifically. Forrest-Pressley and Waller (1984) took third- and sixth-grade children varying in comprehension skill (measured by the Gates–MacGinitie comprehension test) and administered tests of the ability to verbalise, and to make use of knowledge about language, attention, and memory. They then used regression analyses to discover the most important predictors of reading ability. For the younger group, performance on language tasks (recognition and production of letters, words, and sentences) accounted for 41% of the variance, while the second most important factor was the ability to verbalise knowledge of the above linguistic terms, accounting for just over 7% of the variance. Language performance was also most important in the sixth graders, although verbalisation was not predictive of reading skill in that group. This finding suggests that linguistic awareness is important in reading comprehension, but unfortunately for our purposes, the relations found between comprehension and metalinguistic skills may also reflect variations in decoding skill, which was highly correlated with comprehension skill (correlations of .60 to .80).

Another aspect of metalinguistic skill that may be important in reading comprehension is the ability to violate structural regularities, or to play with language. There are many examples of nonliteral language use, such as sarcasm, metaphor, irony, lying and joking, and marked developmental changes in the way that children use such nonliteral forms (Gardner and Winner, 1986; McDowell, 1979). Development in the use and understanding of jokes and riddles is particularly interesting for our purposes, as such language forms generally depend on having an awareness of ambiguity, and hence, we would argue, of words as objects distinct from their referents, that is, metalinguistic awareness. We know of no studies relating riddle comprehension to comprehension skill, but describe our own research on this topic in Chapter 6.

Summary

In this chapter, we have considered both skilled adult reading, and the development of reading skills, and have looked at the roles of both lower-level word-recognition and syntactic processes and higher-level comprehension and monitoring processes. In both sections, we have stressed the importance of integration of information in text in the production of a coherent mental model, and the role that working memory might play in this task. In the case of children, we have suggested four main loci for comprehension problems: automaticity of word decoding and meaning access, semantic and syntactic analysis of sentences, text-level processes such as inference and integration, and metacognitive monitoring of understanding. In the chapters that follow, we will discuss our own work in each of these areas.

3 Processing words and sentences

Introduction

The main objective of the work in this chapter is to try to *rule out* some differences between our groups of skilled and less-skilled comprehenders. The studies in this chapter fall into two main parts. In the first we will discuss one of the major approaches to poor comprehension: that most problems are, in fact, occurring at the level of word recognition, not necessarily because recognition is inaccurate, but because it is not sufficiently fast and automatic. Our own results suggest that children can still experience comprehension difficulties in the absence of problems at this level. In the second part of the chapter, we will turn to children's ability to understand various syntactic constructions, and will present some work in which we looked for differences between the groups in their syntactic skills.

Word-decoding speed and automaticity

As we saw in Chapter 2, a popular explanation of children's problems with text comprehension is that, because immediate memory is strictly limited, slow and inefficient word decoding will take up some memory capacity that could otherwise be used for comprehension and, hence, comprehension will suffer. This sort of explanation of comprehension problems is likely to be particularly applicable in young children whose word-decoding skills have not become fully automatic.

Although difficulties at the word-decoding level are unlikely to account for differences between good and poor comprehenders who are matched on their ability to read words accurately, decoding may still not occur quickly and automatically enough to avoid comprehension problems. Indeed, some work by Perfetti and Hogaboam (1975a) has shown that there were differences between good and poor comprehenders in speed of decoding, even when the poor comprehenders were able to read, and knew the meanings of, all the words on which they were being tested. These results show that decoding speed is not solely a question of vocabulary knowledge, although the less-skilled comprehenders were particularly slow on words whose meanings they did not know.

However, some of our own work has shown that skilled and less-skilled comprehenders, when they are matched for word recognition accuracy and vocabulary knowledge, do *not* differ in decoding speed or automaticity. The first three experiments in this chapter summarise this work. The first two of these will be described only very briefly here, since they did not produce any differences between the groups. More detailed accounts of the experiments can be found in Oakhill (1981, Chapter 3).

Experiment 3.1: *Speed and accuracy in word decoding*

The first experiment was designed to explore whether there are differences in word-decoding speed between skilled and less-skilled comprehenders. As we pointed out in Chapter 1, there is evidence to suggest that, while recoding may not be *necessary* for retrieving the meaning of words, it can have other functions in reading, and ability to use phonological coding is related to reading skill in children (Barron, 1978; Coltheart et al., 1986; Snowling, 1980).

The experimental task was to sort pairs of words into two groups – one of rhyming and one of non-rhyming word pairs. Both visually similar rhymes (e.g. ride–hide) and visually dissimilar rhymes (e.g. side–cried) were used. In the case of the dissimilar rhymes, phonological recoding is obligatory to make the rhyming judgement. If skilled and less-skilled comprehenders differ primarily in their decoding speed, then they would be expected to differ more in the time taken to sort visually dissimilar rhymes than similar ones.

Twenty-eight children, divided into equal groups of good and poor comprehenders participated in the experiment. The groups were selected as we described in Chapter 1, and were 7–8 years old. We measured both accuracy and sorting speed. The results showed that there was no difference between the groups in either the speed or the accuracy with which they sorted either the rhyming or the non-rhyming word pairs.

This experiment, therefore, provided no evidence of differences between the skilled and less-skilled comprehenders in either speed or accuracy of word decoding.

Experiment 3.2: *Speed and accuracy of semantic access*

In the previous experiment, we examined only decoding: the tasks did not require access to word *meanings*. Although decoding to sound may play a role in reading (e.g. semantic information may be accessed via a phonologically indexed lexical entry), it is neither necessary nor sufficient for reading comprehension to occur. The role of semantic access in reading is more obvious, but as with decoding, it may be more or less efficient, and the reader who can recover the meaning of a word quickly and easily may well be better at understanding text. An experiment by Perfetti, Hogaboam and Bell (cited by Perfetti and Lesgold, 1979) investigated the facility with which good and poor comprehenders access word meanings. They found that good comprehenders were no faster than poor ones at either word- or picture-matching tasks, both of which they argued call for only a low level of semantic processing. However, they did find that good comprehenders were faster at a categorisation task, in which the subjects had to *make use of* the information accessed to decide whether a word or picture belonged to a given category. McFarland and Rhodes (1978) have also shown that good readers are more efficient at encoding semantic information. We therefore tested our skilled and less-skilled comprehenders on a categorisation task, which required a decision about whether a visually presented word was a member of a given category, as well as on a more straightforward semantic access task: deciding whether or not a word matched an object in a picture. If the groups of readers differ in the speed at which they are able to retrieve the meaning of single words, they would be expected to differ on both tasks. If, however, the less-skilled comprehenders are slower *only* when they are required to make fuller use of the semantic information retrieved, they should be slower than skilled comprehenders in completing the categorisation, but not the matching, task. We used the same subjects as in Experiment 3.1, so they had already been shown not to differ in card-sorting and phonological decoding times.

For the semantic categorisation task a pool of words was produced, to include words that belonged to four categories familiar to children of this age: 'animals', 'parts of the body', 'things you can eat' and 'clothes'. One category (clothes) was used in a practice set containing six clothes and six non-clothes words. For the experimental trials, we used ten words from each of the other three categories, and thirty from a list of words of similar length, which did not fit into any of the categories, so that each set had ten category and ten non-category words. The words included were only those that could be read without error by a group of children of the same age and reading ability. Each of the words was printed individually on a card.

For the word/picture matching task, some simple line drawings were presented to six children of the same age, not participating in the experiment, and we only used pictures whose names the children agreed on. For the non-matching conditions, words and pictures were paired randomly (with the proviso that they did not match). The pairs of words and pictures were then mounted on blank cards to provide three packs of cards, with ten matching and ten non-matching pairs in each pack, and a practice set.

The children were told to sort the pack of cards into (for example) 'names of animals and things that are not animals', or to sort the pack into 'a pile with pictures and words that match and a pile of those that do not match'. There were three trials for each task, and a practice trial before each type of task. The time taken to sort each pack was recorded and errors were noted. The sorting times were averaged over the three trials for each task.

There were no reliable differences between the groups, either on the matching task (mean = 1.57 sec./card for skilled and 1.53. sec/card for less-skilled children) or on the categorisation task (mean = 1.28 sec./card, mean = 1.26 sec./card for the skilled and less-skilled children respectively).

The error rate was very low, and too few errors were produced to warrant a statistical analysis. The error rate of the less-skilled comprehenders on the categorisation task was 1.2% and on the matching task 0.5%, and that of the skilled group was 0.4% in each case.

Contrary to previous findings (Prawat and Kerasotes, 1978; Perfetti, Hogaboam and Bell, cited by Perfetti and Lesgold, 1979), less-skilled comprehenders do not seem to be slower at accessing the meanings of single printed words, even when the task requires the use of word meanings.

Experiment 3.3: *Automaticity of meaning access*

The results of Experiments 3.1 and 3.2 indicate that factors other than the speed of decoding a word and retrieving its meaning are important in the development of reading comprehension. However, the tasks called for conscious access to the meanings of words, and may not reflect differences in the more automatic recognition that probably takes place in normal reading. Hence, Experiment 3.3 was designed to assess the extent to which accessing the meaning of single printed words is automatic in the two skill groups. The importance of automaticity, in addition to accuracy, in word recognition has been pointed out by LaBerge and Samuels (1974). The distinction is far from trivial: when asked to name words, readers may be able to produce a phonological representation of the visual stimulus, but the relative automaticity with which they are able to do so may influence the amount of semantic processing that can occur for the word, because of the competition between processes in short-term memory (STM). Moreover, Kolers (1970) has argued that skilled readers do not operate at the word level but perceive meanings more directly, even to the point of partially disregarding the text. Less-skilled readers may differ from skilled ones in that they have not yet attained such direct and automatic access.

Although Experiment 3.1 did not provide any evidence for decoding differences between the groups, the tests did not provide a pure measure of phonological decoding, since the materials were meaningful words and, hence, a phonological representation could have been derived by routes other than grapheme-to-phoneme mapping. Pronounceable non-words would provide a better measure of the children's ability to make grapheme–phoneme conversions, and such materials were used in the next study.

Experiment 3.3 measured decoding speed not only for words but also for non-words. The use of non-words may tap differences in decoding skill between the groups which were not apparent in the previous two experiments because of the visual familiarity of the words: such differences may become apparent when the only possible route to pronouncing a word is by using grapheme–phoneme conversion. The use of non-words also removes the influence of word *meanings* on decoding.

In this experiment we used Golinkoff and Rosinski's (1976) picture/word interference paradigm to examine decoding ability for words and non-words (CVC trigrams, such as *pog*, *tiv*). One implication of Kolers's hypothesis – that, in skilled readers, printed words can be mapped directly onto concepts in semantic memory – is that it should be difficult to *ignore* the meanings of words. Golinkoff and Rosinski's paradigm depends on the fact that picture naming is subject to a semantic interference effect, i.e. the time to name a picture is longer when a conflicting word is superimposed on it (see, for example, Rosinski, Golinkoff and Kukish, 1975). Thus, the difference in time taken to name pictures when compatible or conflicting words are superimposed on them gives a measure of the interference produced by conflicting words and, thereby, the extent to which their meaning is automatically accessed. In Golinkoff and Rosinski's task, the children had to name a set of pictures as quickly as possible. The pictures were either presented on their own, or in one of three other conditions in which words or nonsense words were superimposed on them. In one condition, the words matched the pictures (e.g. *pig* printed on a picture of a pig), in the second condition, they conflicted (e.g. *pig* printed on a picture of a cat), and in the third condition non-words, such as *pog* were superimposed. If the meaning of a word is accessed automatically, it should interfere with naming a picture with a different name and, if such an interference effect is semantic, it should be larger when conflicting words are superimposed on the pictures than when non-words are superimposed. The children's task was always to name the pictures, and ignore the words.

There was also a trigram control condition (e.g. a picture of a dog, with the non-word *tiv* superimposed). If real words cause greater interference than trigrams, then we can infer that the interference has a semantic component. There were two further control tasks, which measured the speed at which the words and non-words (trigrams) could be decoded in isolation, and a picture-naming task to ensure that subjects were able to name all the pictures accurately.

Golinkoff and Rosinski (1976) used the paradigm to examine the relation between children's decoding ability, semantic processing of single words, and skill in reading comprehension. They found that poor comprehenders were slower than good ones at decoding non-words, but, although the less-skilled readers took longer to decode real words than the skilled readers, the difference

Figure 3.1. Examples of the materials used in Experiment 3.3

was not significant. In addition, although the good comprehenders were able to complete the picture-naming task more quickly than the poor ones, they did not show a larger semantic interference effect than the poor group – both groups were slowed to a similar extent when the words and pictures were in conflict. While these results suggest that less-skilled comprehenders have some difficulty with decoding, but not with single-word semantic access, the measure of reading comprehension that was used in their study is one that confounds word recognition and comprehension abilities. The poor comprehenders' slow word decoding indicates that they were poorer at word recognition and not just comprehension (see Chapter 1 for a more detailed discussion of these problems of subject selection). Thus, our experiment is, essentially, a replication of Golinkoff and Rosinski's, but using different and more stringent criteria for subject selection.

Golinkoff and Rosinski suggest two alternative relations between decoding skills and semantic processing. The first is that the meaning of a word is accessed by recoding the word to a phonological form, and that difficulty with such recoding will lead to difficulty with access. However, in the light of more recent studies (e.g. Barron and Baron, 1977), which show that even young children can go from print to meaning without the need for a mediating phonological code, it seems unlikely that children need to rely on phonological recoding in order to access a word's meaning (though, of course, they may need to do so in order to decode visually unfamiliar words). Their second, more tenable, suggestion is that children who can decode readily may, nevertheless, fail to access the meanings of words unless they are specifically required to do so, perhaps simply because they have been led to believe that the purpose of reading *is* decoding to sound, and not meaning access.

If automaticity of decoding differentiates good and poor comprehenders, then the skilled children should be more affected by the semantic interference condition in the picture-naming task, compared with their performance when word and picture are congruent or when the interference does not have a semantic component (trigram condition). The two groups would be expected to show similar abilities in the initial decoding tasks, since they were matched on decoding ability.

Method The materials used were essentially the same as those used by Golinkoff and Rosinski (1976), but are described briefly below. Further details can be found in Oakhill (1981: Experiment 3).

Decoding tasks. Twenty common nouns were used in the word-decoding test. For the trigram decoding, twenty pronounceable CVC trigrams were used. The sets of words and trigrams were typed separately on two test sheets. To ensure that subjects could readily identify the pictures being used, they were asked to name the twenty objects and animals, which were depicted on a separate sheet in simple line drawings.

Interference tasks. In the interference tasks a word or trigram was superimposed on each line drawing: in the semantic interference condition the drawings and the words did not match, in the trigram condition a trigram was assigned to each drawing, and in the congruent condition the word and drawing matched.

In both the semantic interference and trigram conditions, the words/trigrams were randomly paired with the pictures, with the restriction that words and

Table 3.1. *Mean reading times (seconds) per item, as a function of stimulus type (word/trigram) and comprehension level*

	Stimulus type	
	Word	Trigram
Less-skilled	0·85	3·00
Skilled	0·81	1·99

pictures did not match in the interference condition. Examples of the materials used are shown in Figure 3.1. Thirty children participated in the experiment: fifteen in each skill group. All of the subjects did both the decoding tasks and interference tasks, on separate days. When they did the decoding tests, we timed the subjects as they read aloud the words or trigrams on the test sheet as rapidly as they could without making mistakes. In an initial picture-naming test, the children were asked to name the set of pictures as rapidly as possible, and their times were recorded for the whole sheet.

At least one day later, the children were given the interference tasks. They were required to name the pictures as quickly as possible, ignoring the words. We recorded their naming time for the whole sheet of pictures in each condition, and noted any errors.

Results We analysed the times for the picture-naming and word and trigram decoding tasks separately from the interference tasks. Too few errors were made in the interference task to enable us to analyse them.

Picture-naming task. Poor comprehenders took longer than good comprehenders to complete the picture-naming task (mean = 1.80, 1.27 seconds per item, respectively). This difference was significant, $t(28) = 3.43$, $p < 0.01$ (two-tailed).

Decoding tasks. Table 3.1 presents the mean time taken to read words and trigrams aloud. The results of the analysis of decoding times indicated a significant main effect of semantic content: trigrams took longer to name than words, $F(1,28) = 47.96$, $p < .001$. The skilled comprehenders were not significantly faster overall, and the interaction between stimulus type and comprehension level did not reach significance, $F(1,28) = 4.02$, $p < .10$. However, as can be seen from Table 3.1, the skilled comprehenders were considerably faster than the less-skilled ones to name the trigrams (1.9 vs 3.0 seconds/item), but not the words (the groups took 0.81 and 0.85 seconds/word, respectively).

Interference tasks. The mean picture-naming times for the three conditions are presented in Table 3.2. The results of an analysis of variance showed that good comprehenders were faster at picture naming in all conditions, $F(1,28) = 7.29$, $p < .025$, and that decoding speed depended on the type of word superimposed, $F(2,56) = 103.11$, $p < .001$, but this variable did not interact with comprehension level. An F test for simple effects showed that the difference between the types of superimposed word was significant, both for the less-skilled group, $F(2,28) = 39.96$, $p < .001$, and for the skilled one, $F(2,28) = 87.7$, $p < .001$. Newman–Keuls tests showed that the congruent word condition was significantly different from the semantic interference and trigram conditions for both comprehension groups ($p < .05$), and that there was no significant difference between semantic interference and trigram conditions for either comprehension group. There was, therefore, a general interference effect for both comprehension groups but no *additional* effect for semantic interference.

Discussion We found an overall difference between the comprehension-skill groups in the speed with which they could name pictures (regardless of interference condition). This difference was also evident in Golinkoff and Rosinski's (1976) results, although they do not discuss any possible explanations for this specific difference. In the present experiment the less-skilled comprehenders were not only slower to name pictures in the congruent word condition (mean difference = 4 seconds/sheet), but were also slower (mean difference = 10.1 seconds/sheet) in the initial picture-naming task, where the pictures were presented without any words superimposed.

The experiment did not address the question of *when* the differences in picture naming arise: the less-skilled group may not be slower at *recognising* pictures but may be slower at producing a response. However, this seems an unlikely explanation of their problem since they were no slower at producing word names. Moreover, there is evidence (Guenther, Klatzky and Putnam, 1980) that pictures and words differ not only in the nature of the perceptual information extracted from them, but also in the conceptual information they activate in semantic memory. Guenther et al. found that pictures afford faster and more automatic access to meanings than to names, but that for words the reverse is true. Thus, there is no reason why the ability to name words and to access their semantic representations should necessarily correlate with the ability to name pictures. Although visual features play a part in the identification of both pictures and words, the abilities involved in the identification and integration of the visual characteristics of a picture may differ between the groups of readers, even when they do not differ in ability to name words, or to access the meanings of familiar words (as shown in Experiment 3.2).

In the interference tasks, both groups were slower at naming pictures with conflicting words than pictures with congruent words. The failure to find any difference between the semantic interference and trigram conditions indicates

Table 3.2. *Mean naming times (seconds) per picture, as a function of type of words superimposed and comprehension level*

	Congruent words	Interference conditions	
		Trigram	Semantic
Less-skilled	0·85	1·80	2·03
Skilled	0·65	1·54	1·61

that the difference between the three conditions was not due to semantic interference but, rather, due to facilitation when the words and pictures matched. Since the skilled comprehenders were no more affected by the semantic interference condition in the picture-naming task than the less-skilled group were, the automaticity of semantic access is apparently *not* a factor that contributes to the less-skilled comprehenders' problem.

There was also some evidence that skilled comprehenders are faster at naming trigrams, which could indicate that they tend to use a phonological code in word recognition, whereas poor comprehenders may rely on a more holistic, visual route, retrieving phonological information from word meanings. If this were the case, poor comprehenders would be expected to take longer in a trigram-naming task, as they would need to utilise a less-familiar strategy to decode the stimuli. However, this seems an unlikely explanation as one would expect that such different strategies would also affect *word* naming speed. In Experiment 3.1, the groups were not found to differ in the speed at which they could decode words, although the words might have been so familiar that all children could recognise them by a whole-word strategy, without decoding to sound. In addition, it should be noted that in another experiment we found no evidence for differences in trigram naming between good and poor comprehenders (see Oakhill, 1981: Experiment 4).

In conclusion, it would appear that semantic access for single, high-frequency words is *not* impaired in less-skilled comprehenders. However, the less-skilled group do experience some difficulty in decoding non-words and in naming pictures.

Discussion of Experiments 3.1 – 3.3

In the first three experiments, we explored the idea that reading-comprehension problems might arise because of slow and/or non-automatic processing. The idea that speed and automaticity are important aspects of processing efficiency was introduced earlier: in a limited capacity system, rapid and automatic word decoding and semantic access will leave more capacity available for storage. The hypothesis that skilled readers may be better because their processing is more efficient was not supported. Our subjects did not differ in speed or automaticity in tasks requiring the decoding and semantic access of single words, at least within the range of measures used. A further experiment, which measured naming times for both high- and low-frequency words, also failed to show any differences between the skill groups (see Oakhill, 1981: Experiment 4). Thus, it appears that the speed and automaticity with which single words are decoded is not associated with poor comprehension when differences between the groups in vocabulary and skill at word-recognition are eliminated. Although the experiments reported here have not explored other factors that may differentiate between the groups at the single-word level, it seems that comprehension differences cannot readily be captured by looking *only* at single words. Indeed, it would be surprising if they could, considering the manner in which the groups were selected.

One highly reliable and unexpected finding from this first series of experiments was the difference between the groups in speed of picture naming. This result may reflect differences in knowledge about the semantic attributes of a stimulus. While such differences in semantic memory were not apparent in the word categorisation and semantic retrieval tasks, these tasks could be performed on the basis of relatively low-level semantic information. The possibility that the two groups differ in the richness of their semantic representations of single words warranted further investigation, and Experiment 4.3, in the next chapter, investigated the groups' abilities to assign particular meanings to single words, according to the context in which they occur.

Syntactic skills

As we mentioned in Chapter 2, both syntactic and semantic skills showed a marked development during the primary school years, and differences in such abilities may be related to comprehension differences. The idea that poor comprehenders have difficulty in using the syntactic constraints in text has been explored extensively by Cromer and his colleagues (Cromer, 1970; Steiner, Wiener and Cromer, 1971; Oakan, Wiener and Cromer, 1971) and by Weinstein and Rabinovitch (1971). We have already discussed these studies in some detail in Chapter 2.

An experiment that explored differences between good and poor comprehenders' use of both syntactic and semantic cues in text was conducted by Isakson and Miller (1976). They found that poor comprehenders who have adequate decoding skills are less sensitive to both syntactic and semantic cues in text. Their subjects read aloud sentences of three different sorts. Some were meaningful, for example:

The old farmer planted the bean seeds in the rich, brown soil.

Others were semantically anomalous, but still contained a syntactically appropriate transitive verb, for example:

The old farmer paid the bean seeds in the rich, brown soil.

and the third type were both syntactically and semantically anomalous, because the transitive verb in the original was replaced by an intransitive one, for example:

The old farmer went the bean seeds in the rich, brown soil.

Isakson and Miller reasoned that, if children are extracting the meaning of a sentence as they are reading, then they should experience some difficulty when they encounter the anomalous verbs, and might actually change the text to make it comprehensible. Children who read word by word should be no more likely to make errors on anomalous words than elsewhere. The results showed that, whereas the reading errors of good comprehenders increased when the sentences contained anomalies – they made more errors on the semantic plus syntactic violations than either of the other two types – the errors of the poor comprehenders were similar for all types of sentence. The authors concluded that, instead of using syntactic and semantic cues in the text to help their understanding, poor comprehenders treat each word separately. We decided to replicate this experiment because, although Isakson and Miller claim that the vocabulary skills of their subjects were equivalent, they do not report any statistical tests, and the figures that they report show that the poor group's vocabulary scores were lower than those of the good group. In addition, the results of their study show that the poor comprehenders made significantly more errors overall, further evidence for the possibility that these children were poor decoders, and not just poor comprehenders.

Experiment 3.4: *Semantic and syntactic awareness*

We adopted the method used by Isakson and Miller to assess differences between the groups in their sensitivity to semantic and syntactic violations. We devised four sentences of each of the three types: normal, semantically anomalous and both semantically and syntactically anomalous. There were three different sets of materials, so that each sentence content appeared in each type of sentence. We used simple vocabulary to minimise decoding difficulties.

We tested twenty-three skilled and twenty-six less-skilled comprehenders on the sentences. Within each group, equal numbers of children were assigned to the three sets of materials as far as was possible. They read aloud the twelve sentences, which were presented in a random order. The children were told to read the sentences as well as they could and, if they could not guess a word, to go on to the next one, as no help would be given.

Results Following Isakson and Miller, we looked at the numbers of reading errors for each sentence type. Isakson and Miller had four dependent measures: reading errors on the two words before and after the verb, errors on the one word before and the one word after the verb, errors on the verb itself, and total errors in the sentence. We felt it would be instructive to assess reading errors occurring before the verb separately from those after the verb, because some readers may not anticipate the error if they do not look ahead in the sentence, and would only make errors on anomalous sentences after reading the verb. Also, we noted that errors occurred more frequently in the phrases surrounding the verb than elsewhere in the sentence. Rather than arbitrarily restricting errors to one or two positions from the verb, we therefore examined errors made in the three-word noun-phrase before the verb (e.g. *the old farmer*) and in the noun phrase after the verb (e.g. *the bean seeds*). For the post-verb errors, it was notable that in the anomalous conditions, some subjects made errors in the following preposition that made the sentence slightly less anomalous. For example, a sentence in the semantic and syntactic anomaly condition was: *a little boy put a big picture of his new brown dog*, and some subjects read *of* as *on*. In computing errors after the verb, we therefore included errors on the preposition, as well as errors on the three-word noun phrase after the verb. Our other two measures were similar to those used by Isakson and Miller: errors at the verb position and total errors in the sentence. Our definition of errors also followed the previous study: the errors included repetitions, substitutions, omissions, and for all measures except errors on the verb (for which the category is not appropriate), insertions of words. The data were analysed by analysis of variance, with skill group between subjects and error type within subjects.

All four analyses showed a broadly similar pattern of results. More errors were made on the verb position (mean error rates from 13% to 29%) than on any of the other measures (mean error rates ranging from 4% to 8.5%) and only the analysis of errors on the verb is reported in detail here. There was a main effect of sentence type, $F(2, 94) = 9.77$, $p < .0001$. Newman– Keuls tests (with p set at .05) showed that errors on the sentences with semantically and syntactically anomalous verbs were significantly greater than errors on either of the other two types of sentence, as shown in Table 3.3. There was no main effect of group, $F < 1$ and no interaction of skill group with error type, $F < 1$. Analyses of the other dependent variables showed a similar picture, except that both types of anomalous sentence produced significantly more errors than the normal sentences, and error rates on the two types of anomalous sentences were not significantly different from each other. None of the analyses showed any hint of an interaction between skill group and sentence type, all $Fs < 1$. There was one other notable result: the analysis of errors after the verb showed a main effect of group, $F(1, 94) = 3.95$, $p < .05$, and the other analyses showed non-

Table 3.3. *Mean percentages of errors at verb position as a function of sentence type and comprehension skill*

Sentence type:	Normal	Semantic violation	Semantic + syntactic violation
Less-skilled	10·6	15·4	29·8
Skilled	16·3	23·9	28·3
Mean	13·5	19·6	29·0

significant trends for the same effect. In each case, the results were in the same direction: skilled children tended to make more errors than less-skilled ones (mean errors after the verb = 5.5% for less-skilled, and 8.2% for skilled children). This result is in the opposite direction from that observed by Isakson and Miller: their analysis showed a highly significant effect of group indicating that their poor comprehenders made substantially *more* errors than their good comprehenders. This result supports the suggestion that their poor comprehenders, unlike ours, were rather poor at decoding.

Discussion This experiment provided no evidence that the skilled and less-skilled comprehenders are differentially sensitive to the semantic and syntactic cues in a text. Both groups, like the good comprehenders tested by Isakson and Miller, made more errors on the verbs as the sentences became increasingly anomalous, the combination of syntactic and semantic violations producing more errors than the other two conditions. Our own findings suggest that an awareness of semantic and syntactic constraints is present in less-skilled comprehenders when they have adequate vocabulary and word-recognition skills. In the next experiment, however, we tested this possibility further by assessing more directly the children's ability to understand and remember complex syntactic constructions.

Experiment 3.5: *Effects of syntactic complexity on sentence understanding and recall*

Although Mann et al. (1980) found that good and poor comprehenders' immediate recall was affected to a similar extent by variations in syntactic structure, all of the structures that they used were relatively simple. Indeed, Mann et al. suggest that good and poor readers may differ in their ability to recall more complex constructions such as centre-embedded sentences, and these were the focus of our next experiment on sentence understanding. Reid (1972) showed that 7-year-olds often misunderstood embedded clauses, such as: *The girl standing beside the lady had a blue dress.* Their responses to the question: *Who had a blue dress*? were correct in only 41% of cases. There are two distinct factors that may be influencing comprehension of such sentences: children may simply not understand the syntactic structure, or they may be unable to cope with the high processing load imposed by an embedded clause. In order for a relative clause to be interpreted, the head noun phrase must be retained in working memory until it can be assigned its place in the clause. One explanation of relative clause difficulty is that the grammatical function of the noun phrase within the relative clause can only be decided when the 'gap' is found (Wanner and Maratsos, 1978). This explanation predicts that object-relative clauses are more difficult to understand than subject-relatives because the distance between the head noun phrase and the gap is greater in object relatives (see example below). Gazdar (1981) proposed that 'gaps' are needed only in object- relative clauses, although the difference in memory load between subject- relative and object-relative clauses is upheld in his analysis. Wanner and Maratsos demonstrated that, when subjects were reading sentences containing relative clauses, transient processing load increased in the region between the relative complementizer and the gap. They also found a peak in processing load immediately following the gap. At that point, presumably, the missing constituent is retrieved from working memory, assigned to the gap, and its grammatical function in the relative clause computed.

The present study manipulated three factors which might contribute to difficulty in understanding sentences:

1. The overall memory load was varied by using sentences of either two or three clauses.
2. Syntactic complexity was manipulated by using either embedded or conjoined clauses.
3. The subject noun phrase of the first clause was either the subject or the object of the second clause (these two conditions are referred to as s-s and s-o respectively).

The third variable is of particular interest in embedded clauses because it also introduces varying levels of memory load. In object relative clauses (s-o) such as:

The cats (that the dogs chased ...)

the 'gap' theory would hold that the constituent 'cats' must be held until the gap following 'chased', whereas in subject relative clauses such as:

The cats (that chased the dogs ...)
'cats' will be assigned to the gap after 'that'.

By using different types of relative clause, and by varying the length of the sentence, we were able to assess whether any differences between the groups were related to their ability to understand embedded sentences generally, or were related to the processing load imposed by such sentences. If the former explanation were true, then the groups would be expected to differ more on the embedded than on the unembedded sentences overall and, if the latter, they would be expected to differ only on the longer and more complex sentences.

Two dependent variables were used in this experiment: recall of the sentences, and ability to answer a question about each sentence. The questions were used not only to test the children's comprehension of the syntactic structure, but also to ensure that they were reading for meaning. The materials were presented both visually and auditorially to the same subjects, in separate test sessions, in order to see whether any differences obtained were specific to reading.

Sixteen sentences were constructed, with eight different versions of each, all with the same basic semantic content (each subject saw or heard only one version), produced by crossing the three factors outlined above (complexity, length and subject- or object-relative). In order to ensure that differences in performance were not confounded with differences in sentence meaning, the non-embedded sentences were the coordinate structure counterparts of the relative sentences. The following illustrate the eight sentence types:

Two-clause

Conjoined
The foxes hunt rabbits, and the foxes follow the wolf (s-s).
The foxes hunt rabbits, and the wolf follows the foxes (s-o).
Embedded
The foxes that follow the wolf hunt rabbits (s-s).
The foxes that the wolf follows hunt rabbits (s-o).

Three-clause

Conjoined
The foxes hunt rabbits and follow the wolf, and the wolf lives in the forest (s-s).
The foxes hunt rabbits, and the wolf follows the foxes and lives in the forest (s-o).
Embedded
The foxes that follow the wolf, which lives in the forest, hunt rabbits (s-s).
The foxes that the wolf, which lives in the forest, follows hunt rabbits (s-o).

We ensured that all the words were within the children's vocabulary. The subject of the first clause and the object of the second clause were interchangeable, so that the same lexical items could be used in all sentence versions. In all the embedded sentences, the relative pronoun *that* was used at the beginning of the second embedded clause and *who* or *which* at the beginning of the third.

Although each of the three-clause non-embedded sentences also contained one gap, due to the ellipsis of a noun phrase, the processing load imposed by this ellipsis was similar for both s-s and s-o sentences, and was much smaller than the load imposed by either type of embedded sentence.

After each sentence, the children were asked a question. The questions concerned the subject of the verb in the first clause, and were of the same form for all sentence types. For example, the question for the last example above was: *Who hunts rabbits?*.

Design and Procedure Twenty-eight subjects participated in the experiment: fourteen in each skill group. Each subject received two exemplars of each sentence type. So that the lexical content was not confounded with sentence type, we rotated the pairs of lexical contents over the different types of sentences, giving eight sets of materials altogether, and equal numbers of subjects were assigned to each set as far as was possible.

The sentences were either read aloud to the subjects, or were typed on cards for them to read. All subjects did both the spoken and read versions. The modality in which sentences were presented was counterbalanced across subjects within groups: subjects either read the sentences aloud, or had them read to them by the experimenter, in separate test sessions. The sentences were presented to each subject in a different random order.

The subjects were tested individually. After the task was explained, the subjects were told to repeat back the sentences *exactly* as they had heard or read them, or to say anything they could remember even if they could not recall the exact words. They were also told that their responses would be tape-recorded.

Each test session was preceded by eight practice trials, including two very simple, one-clause sentences (all the children were able to repeat these with 100% accuracy). The children then read, or were read, each sentence twice. Directly following the second reading the subjects attempted to recall the sentence, and their responses were tape-recorded. The experimenter then asked them the question about the sentence. One week later, the children were tested in the other modality, using a different set of sixteen sentences.

Results The recall protocols were scored according to a strict criterion (exact wording recalled) and a lenient criterion (gist meaning recalled).

The results for the strict recall criterion showed that two- clause sentences were recalled more often (35.1%) than three-clause ones (6.7%), $F(1,26) = 55.81$, $p < .001$; non-embedded sentences were recalled more often (27.2%) than embedded (14.5%), $F(1,26) = 23.78$, $p < .001$, and s-s sentences (22.8%) were recalled more often than s-o sentences (18.9%), $F(1,26) = 4.68$, $p < .05$. There were no other main effects or interactions – in particular, the difference in recall between the skilled (26.1%) and less-skilled comprehenders (15.6%) was not significant.

When the scoring procedure was relaxed to include all sentences where the gist was correctly recalled, the results were very similar to those for verbatim scoring: all the main effects except presentation modality were significant, and there were no interactions between the variables. However, the skilled comprehenders' recall was better overall (54.2%) than that of the less-skilled group (33.3%), $F(1,26) = 14.49$, $p < .001$.

Analyses by materials[1] were not feasible for these data because, as we mentioned above, the size of the groups precluded exact counterbalancing of the sets of materials over subjects. However, we computed the verbatim recall scores for each set of materials, and these showed that the different lexical contents produced similar patterns of results.

The question-answering data are shown in Figure 3.2. Skilled comprehenders answered more questions correctly (76.8%) than less-skilled comprehenders (69.2%), $F(1,26) = 4.53$, $p < .05$, and there was a small but significant four-way interaction between comprehension level, modality, type of clause and number of clauses, $F(1,26) = 5.00$, $p < .05$. This interaction appears to be due to the skilled readers' exceptionally low error rate on the two-clause, s-o sentences in the auditory mode, but there is no obvious way to explain this complex pattern of results. Overall, both groups answered more questions correctly with auditory (76.6%) than with visual presentation (69.4%), $F(1,26) = 8.73$, $p < .01$. More questions were answered correctly for non-embedded sentences (87.7%) than embedded sentences (58.2%), $F(1,26) = 73.11$, $p < .001$; and more questions were answered correctly for sentences with s-s clauses (76.3%) than for those with s-o clauses (69.6%), $F(1,26) = 9.67$, $p < .005$. Embedded clauses produced fewer errors in the auditory than in the visual modality, resulting in a two-way interaction between presentation modality and level of embedding, $F(1,26) = 16.07$, $p < .001$. This interaction arose because performance on embedded clauses was generally better when they were read aloud.

Discussion This experiment suggests that skilled and less-skilled comprehenders do not differ in their verbatim memory for meaningful sentences. However, this finding does not mean that the groups *understood* the sentences equally well. Indeed, the skilled comprehenders were able to recall the gist of more sentences, perhaps because they made more active attempts to understand the sentences rather than simply to remember them. Their method of comprehension may have led them to derive more elaborate representations, which provided information about the sentence meanings, even when the exact wording had been forgotten. This interesting hypothesis, to which we will return in the next chapter, is supported by the skilled comprehenders' ability to answer more questions correctly – in order to answer the questions, it was often necessary to make referential links within the sentences.

The results provided no evidence, either from the recall or the question-answering data, that the groups differ in their ability to understand these particular syntactic constructions. Neither were the groups differentially affected by the processing load imposed by the sentences. The recall scores did not reveal

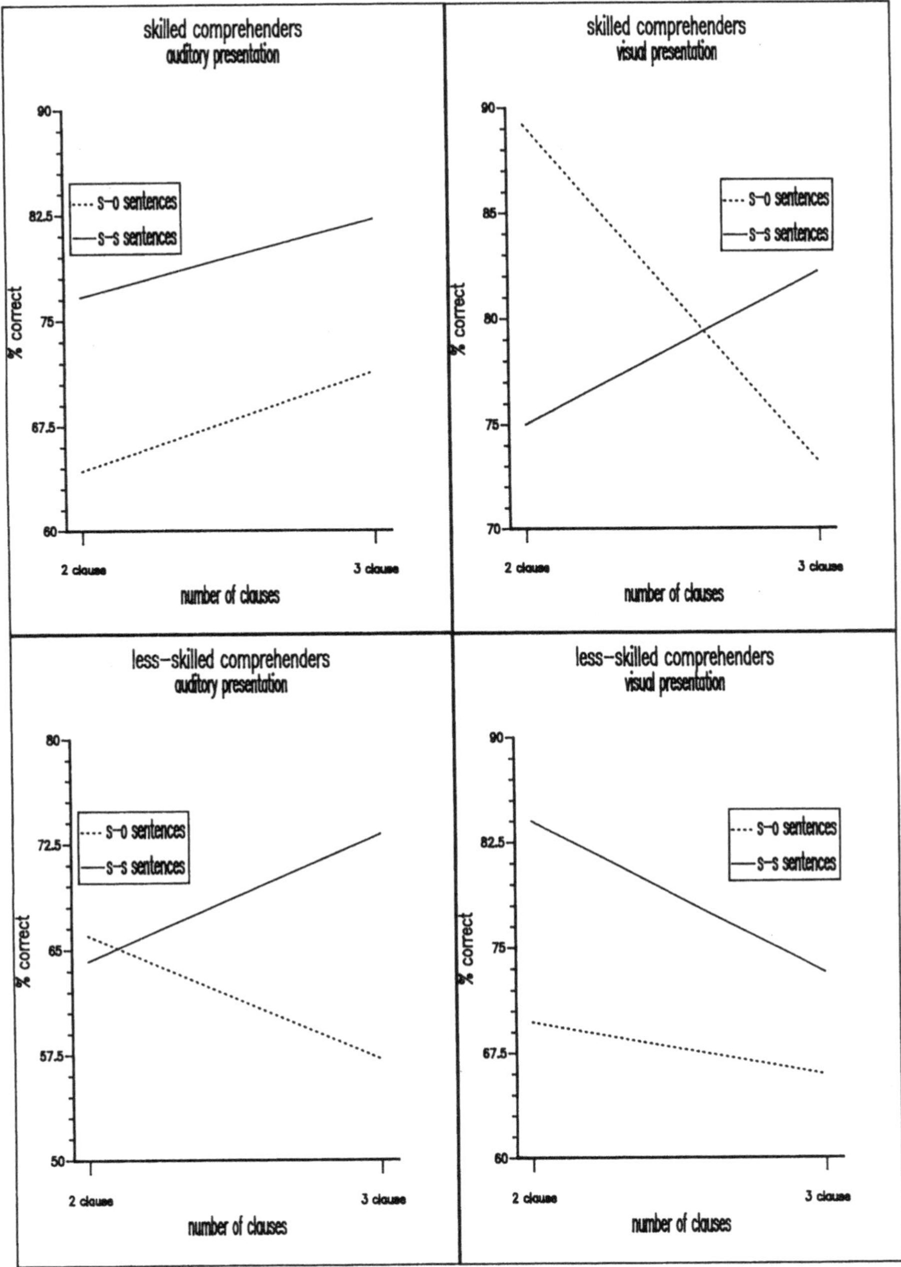

Figure 3.2. Mean percentages of questions correct, as a function of comprehension skill, modality of presentation, number of clauses and clause type (s-s or s-o)

any differential consequences of presentation modality between the groups. Indeed, there was no overall effect of presentation modality on recall. However, the ability of both groups to answer questions correctly was enhanced in the auditory modality for embedded sentences, probably because of the additional prosodic cues to an embedding provided by speech. Non-embedded sentences, which are easier in general, did not show this modality advantage.

Although the varying loads on working memory, introduced by varying the syntax, failed to affect the groups differentially, the repetition task provided a somewhat unsatisfactory measure of the effects of processing load during *comprehension*, because the subjects did not necessarily have to understand the sentences in order to repeat them back. Indeed, the gist recall and question-answering data suggest that fewer less-skilled than skilled comprehenders fully understood the sentences, and so the varying processing loads may not have had the chance to exert their effects on comprehension. We will return to the issue of the relation between memory and comprehension skill in Chapter 5.

Before leaving the question of syntactic skills, we decided to test our skilled and less-skilled comprehenders' ability to understand a wider variety of syntactic constructions by administering a standard test of sentence understanding.

The Test for Reception of Grammar (TROG)

In this test (developed by Bishop, 1983), the children are read sentences and, for each sentence are asked to select one of four pictures that 'goes with' what the experimenter says. There are twenty blocks of items in the test as a whole: the first few items assess whether the child can identify individual words and simple word combinations where understanding of function words, word order and inflectional endings is not critical (for example, *the boy is running*, where the alternative pictures show a boy sitting, a cow running, and a cat sitting). The rest of the items test a variety of different types of construction, which are presented in increasing order of difficulty, with four equivalent exemplars of each sentence type in each block. For example, the most difficult block tests comprehension of embedded sentences such as *The cat the cow chases is black*. The incorrect pictures in this case all feature cats and cows (one black and one white in each case), but two show a cat chasing a cow, and one shows a cow chasing a white cat. The child has to choose the correct picture for all four sentences in order to pass a block. Testing continues until the child fails five consecutive blocks.

We tested seventeen less-skilled and seventeen skilled comprehenders on the TROG, following the procedure prescribed by Bishop. All but three children (two less-skilled and one skilled) were able to attempt all the items (i.e. they did not fail five consecutive items), but no child was able to pass all the blocks of

Table 3.4. *Performance on the TROG*

Block	Total blocks failed		Mean errors/subject*	
	Less-skilled	Skilled	Less-skilled	Skilled
A–F†	3	1	0·18	0·06
G (sing/plural pronoun)	4	1	0·29	0·06
H (reversible active)	0	0	0	0
I (masc/fem pronoun)	3	1	0·24	0·06
J (sing/plural noun)	5	2	0·41	0·12
K (comparative)	1	3	0·12	0·18
L (reversible passive)	5	4	0·41	0·47
M (in and on)	2	3	0·12	0·24
N (postmod. subject)	9	6	0·88	0·41
O (x but not y)	7	7	0·53	0·59
P (above and below)	7	3	0·53	0·13 (16)
Q (not only but also)	5	3	0·44 (16)	0·19 (16)
R (relative clause)	11	10	0·94 (16)	0·69 (16)
S (neither x nor y)	8	4	0·73 (15)	0·25 (16)
T (embedded sentence)	16	17	2·73 (15)	2·63 (16)

* These means only include subjects who attempted the block. The numbers of subjects attempting a particular block, if less than the total in a group (17), are shown in parentheses.
† These blocks are combined for exposition purposes because so few errors were made.

items. Performance was particularly poor on blocks 18 (relative clauses) and 20 (embedded clauses), which 21/34 and 33/34 children failed respectively.

The errors on the TROG can be classified in two ways: either the number of blocks failed, or the numbers of items failed within any one block or over the test as a whole. We have looked at both these measures, and have also correlated them with the children's reading comprehension scores. The numbers of blocks failed and errors are shown in Table 3.4.

Blocks failed and total errors. The mean number of blocks failed was slightly higher for the less-skilled than for the skilled comprehenders (5.06 blocks vs. 3.82 blocks), but the difference was not significant ($t = 1.38$, $df = 32$). However, the difference in the total number of errors for those subjects who attempted all blocks (sixteen skilled and fifteen less-skilled comprehenders) was marginally significant, $t\ (29) = 1.68$, $p < .1$, one-tailed (mean errors less-skilled = 7.67, skilled = 5.69). However, as we shall see below, these tendencies towards differences between the groups were largely attributable to differences on a small number of blocks.

Number of blocks failed showed a moderate, but non-significant, correlation with Neale Comprehension score ($r = -.32$) and the correlation with Neale Accuracy score was not significant ($r = .19$). Total number of errors showed a

Table 3.5. *Mean errors on TROG combined categories*

Blocks	Total blocks failed		Mean errors/subject*	
	Less-skilled	Skilled	Less-skilled	Skilled
N, T (embedded clauses)	25	23	3·5 (15)	3·0 (16)
R, N, T (relative clauses)	36	33	4·5 (15)	3·7 (16)
Q, S (not only/also, neither/nor)	13	7	1·1 (15)	0·4 (16)
M, P (prepositions)	9	6	0·7 (16)	0·3 (16)
G, I, J (pronouns)	12	4	0·9	0·2

* These means only include the subjects who attempted all relevant blocks. The numbers of subjects, if less than 17, are shown in parentheses.

significant correlation with Neale Comprehension score ($r = -.47$, $p < .02$) but not with Neale Accuracy ($r = -.20$).

We also classified the errors on blocks D-L as either 'grammatical' or 'lexical' errors, following Bishop's scoring procedure. However, almost all of the errors were grammatical (the less-skilled made a total of four, and the skilled a total of two lexical errors).

Errors on specific blocks. We assessed the numbers of errors made by subjects on each of the twenty blocks, for all the subjects who attempted a particular block. There were no significant differences for any block except P (above/below), on which the less-skilled comprehenders made more errors (mean = .53) than the skilled comprehenders (mean = .13).

Errors on groups of blocks. Because some of the blocks fell naturally into groups of similar sentence constructions, we combined them in some further analyses. The blocks we selected to combine were:

N and T (centre-embedded clauses)
R,N and T (relative clauses)
Q and S (not only but also, neither/nor)
M and P (prepositions)
G,I and J (singular/plural nouns and pronouns, masc/fem pronouns)

The total numbers of failures on these items, and the mean errors for those subjects attempting these items are shown in Table 3.5. The only significant difference to emerge was on the noun/pronoun category (blocks G, I and J). The less-skilled comprehenders performed more poorly as measured by errors

($t = 2.06$, $df = 32$, $p < .025$, one-tailed) and blocks failed ($t = 1.91$, $df = 32$, $p < .05$, one-tailed). The only correlation between errors on these combined categories and Neale Comprehension scores was, again for the noun/pronoun blocks ($r = -.45$, $p < .02$).

Discussion In general, these results provide very little support for the idea that the less-skilled comprehenders have a *general* comprehension deficit at the level of sentences. We were quite surprised to find that there was little or no difference between the groups on even the most complex embedded sentence structures. The marginally significant differences between the groups can best be explained in terms of differences on specific types of sentences. In particular, the groups differed in understanding of singular/plural nouns and pronouns generally, and there was some evidence that they had trouble with one sort of preposition (above/below). The question of how the groups differ in understanding of pronouns, and other sorts of anaphor, is addressed in much more detail in our experiments in Chapter 4.

General discussion

In the first part of this chapter, we examined the hypothesis that good and poor comprehenders differ in the speed and automaticity with which they are able to recognise single words. Our data do not provide any evidence that the skilled and less-skilled readers we have used in our experiments differ in this respect. The less-skilled comprehenders recognise words quickly and automatically, and have no difficulty in recovering word meanings. The only difference between the groups to emerge from this series of experiments was in picture naming: the less-skilled comprehenders were consistently slower to name simple drawings of common objects.

In the second series of experiments, we explored differences between the groups in their syntactic skills. Again, there was very little evidence for differences between the groups, even in their understanding of complex embedded constructions. However, the less-skilled comprehenders did show deficient understanding in specific areas: their ability to understand sentences containing singular/plural nouns and pronouns, and certain prepositions in particular was impaired.

4 Inferences and the integration of text

Introduction

In the previous chapter, we found little evidence that skilled and less-skilled comprehenders differ in ability in the lower-level skills of word decoding and syntactic analysis. In the present chapter, we will explore higher-level comprehension skills: the ability to connect the ideas from different parts of a text, and to make inferences.

In order to understand stories adequately, readers must be able to draw appropriate inferences spontaneously when they hear or read a story, so that an integrated representation or *mental model* of the text as a whole can be built (see Chapter 2). Such processing makes demands on working memory, an issue that will be discussed in the next chapter. In this chapter, we will describe a series of experiments that explore differences between the groups in their ability to make inferences and to integrate separate pieces of information in a text. We will then relate the results of these experiments to the idea that successful comprehension depends on the construction of an integrated *mental model* of the text.

In the first three experiments, we test the hypothesis that skilled and less-skilled comprehenders differ in the extent to which they make use of inferential and constructive processing in order to understand and remember text. The experiments also consider some factors that may contribute to differences in the children's inferential ability. The second set of three experiments explores differences between the groups in their ability to understand *anaphoric* links in text – pronouns and other types of cohesive ties.

Constructive inferences

As we discussed in Chapter 2, in order to understand a text fully, it is necessary to establish the connections between the different parts, and to link them up appropriately. This integrative processing is one form of inference that is necessary for text comprehension. Bransford and his colleagues (e.g. Bransford, Barclay and Franks, 1972) stressed that comprehension is a constructive and integrative process, and numerous studies using adult subjects have shown that they make inferences and integrate information from separate sentences in a text, rapidly forgetting the exact wording of the original sentences once they have extracted the meaning. The effects of these constructive processes can be detected in subjects' memory for text.

One method of investigating whether such constructive processing has occurred is by using a recognition memory test. Paris and his colleagues (see, e.g. Paris and Carter, 1973; Paris, 1975) have carried out many studies to investigate children's inferential processing, based on the work of Bransford and his co-workers. For instance, Paris and Carter (1973) argued that if children construct integrated representations of texts then, in a recognition test of the sort described above, they should falsely 'recognise' sentences that are consistent with the meaning of those texts, but which do not actually occur in them. The children in their study were read short passages such as:

The bird is inside the cage.
The cage is under the table.
The bird is yellow.

and then had to say whether they had heard each of a series of sentences, some of which had been presented, and some of which were true inferences (e.g. the bird is under the table). Both 7- and 10-year-olds consistently accepted true inferences as sentences they had actually heard. In fact, they were just as likely to say that they had heard such sentences as ones that had been presented in the original passages. This finding suggests that children of both ages integrated the information from different sentences of the passages and what they had stored was a meaning-based representation, rather than specific words or sentences. It is also possible, of course, that the children accepted the inference items not because of the processing they did *at the time of comprehension* but because the inference items were more confusing *at the time of the test.*

We made use of this recognition memory procedure to assess whether skilled and less-skilled comprehenders differ in the extent to which they use constructive processing during text comprehension. Unfortunately, there were some problems with the materials in Paris and Carter's study. In their recognition test the original sentences and the true inferences contained only words from the original passages. The other items (false inferences), to which the correct answer was 'no', contained *new* words. For example, in the above passage, one of these sentences was *The bird is on top of the table*. The inclusion of the new words *on top of* meant that it was possible for the children to reject this sentence on the basis of the new words alone. In our own experiments, we constructed our test sentences using *only* words from the original passage, to avoid this possible confound.

Table 4.1. *Mean percentages of recognition errors for the three sentence types in each skill group (memory instructions)*

	Original sentence	Valid inference	Invalid inference
Less-skilled	40·38	50·00	29·88
Skilled	29·38	64·38	19·25

Experiment 4.1: *Constructive integration*

In our experiment, as in Paris and Carter's, the children listened to a series of short (three-sentence) stories. Following the presentation of the set of stories, they received a recognition test, which comprised original sentences and two types of foil: valid inference foils, containing information that could be inferred from the original story, and invalid inference foils, containing information that could not be inferred from the original story, or that was actually inconsistent with it. For example, in the case of the passage:

The mouse ate the food.
The food was bread.
The mouse looked for some cheese.

the valid inference foil was *The mouse ate the bread*, and the invalid inference foil, *The food was some cheese*. It was predicted that, if skilled comprehenders differ from their less-skilled counterparts because they are more likely to build integrated representations of texts, then they would be expected to make a higher proportion of errors in recognising the valid inference foils, whilst making similar numbers of recognition errors on the original sentences and invalid inference foils.

Method Thirteen skilled and thirteen less-skilled comprehenders participated in the experiment. Eight 'stories', each three sentences long, were written using a suitably simple vocabulary. There were four recognition sentences for each story – two original sentences, and two foils, as described above. The original sentences included in the recognition test were drawn equally often from the first, second and third positions in the original stories. A full list of materials can be found in Oakhill (1982).

Each subject received the same eight stories and items for recognition. The stories were presented in a different random order for each subject. The four recognition sentences for a particular story were presented together, but the order of these sets of sentences, and the items within them, was randomised. The children were tested individually, and the stories and recognition items were read aloud to them. They were told that they should try to remember the stories, and that they would later be questioned on them.

Results One subject was excluded from the analyses, because she did not make a single 'yes' response. In order to maintain the matching between groups, the youngest female subject was dropped from the other (less-skilled) group. The results with these two subjects excluded are shown in Table 4.1. An analysis of variance of the responses to the inference foils showed that more errors were made on the valid than on the invalid items: $minF'(1,48) = 25.83$, $p < .001$. There was no main effect of comprehension skill (both Fs < 1, but there was an interaction between type of foil and comprehension skill: $F_1(1,24) = 7.78$, $p < .025$, $F_2(1,14) = 7.34$, $p < .025$. As predicted, skilled comprehenders made more errors than less-skilled comprehenders on the valid inference items, but fewer on the invalid foils. The less-skilled group also made slightly more errors on the original sentences, but the difference between groups was not significant, either by subjects, $t(24) = 1.27$, or by materials, $t(14) = 1.65$.

Discussion These results support the idea that skilled comprehenders are better able to integrate information from different parts of a text, and are more likely to represent the text as an integrated whole. However, one problem in interpreting these results is that the children knew that their memory would be tested. There is evidence that children of the age tested can modify their study behaviour to take account of different instructions (Appel, Cooper, McCarrell, Sims-Knight, Yussen and Flavell, 1972). However, this skill is only beginning to emerge at about 7 years, and may be better developed in skilled than in less-skilled comprehenders of this age. In addition, Kail (1979) points out that the period between 6 and 9 years is a transitional one as far as use of strategies is concerned. He showed that, although some children were able to use memorisation strategies, and use them well, others of the same age used them inconsistently or ineffectively. In the light of these findings, we were concerned that the differences between skilled and less-skilled comprehenders that we found in the previous experiment may have arisen because the groups differed in their ability to use appropriate memorisation strategies when they were expecting a memory test, rather than reflecting any fundamental difference in their propensity to integrate the ideas in the text. If the good comprehenders had chosen to derive integrated representations of the stories to aid their memory, such a strategy could have led to exactly the pattern of false recognition errors observed.

We therefore designed a further experiment to assess this alternative explanation of the results. The experiment was, essentially, a replication of the earlier one but, to avoid evoking deliberate memorisation strategies, the children were not told that they should try to remember the stories, nor that

Table 4.2. *Mean percentages of recognition errors for the three sentence types in each skill group (listening instructions)*

	Original sentence	Valid inference	Invalid inference
Less-skilled	25·96	53·36	30·77
Skilled	19·95	63·46	21·15

their memory would be tested, but simply that they should *listen* to a series of stories. We found a pattern of results which exactly paralleled those we had obtained before, showing that the results of Experiment 4.1 were not simply an artefact of the skilled group's greater use of particular strategies for memorisation. The data are shown in Table 4.2 for comparison.

Again, the results from this experiment support our earlier conclusion that the less-skilled comprehenders do not have any straightforward memory deficit. It seems, rather, that the skilled comprehenders are more actively involved in the construction of meaning from text, although a retrieval explanation is not ruled out by our data. However, additional support for *processing* differences between the groups was provided by an experiment that we discussed in the last chapter (Experiment 3.5). This experiment showed the skilled and less-skilled comprehenders' memory to be similar when a verbatim criterion was used to assess recall of sentences. However, when the scoring criterion was relaxed to include gist recall, the skilled comprehenders' performance was significantly better than that of the less-skilled group. The higher level of gist recall by the skilled group suggests that they were making a more active attempt to understand the sentences, rather than simply trying to retain the wording.

Implicit inferences and instantiation

We have discussed the importance of inferences for connecting up the ideas that are explicit in a text. But texts also leave many ideas implicit, and inferences are crucial to filling in the missing information using appropriate general knowledge. However, only a tiny proportion of all the possible inferences can, or need to be, made from a text, and those that are made need to be guided by the reader's model of the text so far, which can be used to indicate where there are gaps to be filled by inferential processing. The previous experiment looked at only one type of inference. In the next two, we will look at inferential processing more generally.

Studies of adults have shown that they use general knowledge to fill in information that is only implicit in a text (e.g. Bartlett, 1932; Dooling and

Lachman, 1971; Bransford and Johnson, 1972). There is also evidence that even quite young children can infer presuppositions, consequences, and affective states of characters in short stories when they are explicitly required to do so (Paris, 1975; Paris and Upton, 1976; Stein, 1979). However, the finding that children are *able* to make such inferences does not necessarily mean that they *will* draw them, particularly during reading, where attention may be focused on other aspects of the task. There is considerable evidence that children do not spontaneously engage in inferential elaboration (e.g. Brown, 1975; Anderson and Shifrin, 1980). Moreover, previous comparisons of good and poor readers (e.g., Waller, 1976; Prawat and Kerasotes, 1978; and Experiment 4.1, above) have investigated inferential skills when all the premise information is explicit in the text. The aim of the two studies that follow was to see whether the groups differ in their ability to make 'implicit' inferences that incorporate relevant general knowledge in the understanding of text. Explicit inferences are derived directly from the information that is presented: they are deliberate deductions. Implicit inferences make sense of a situation in terms of relevant general knowledge (i.e. all the premise information is not presented in the text).

One reason why less-skilled comprehenders are poorer at comprehension might be that, even though they have the relevant knowledge, they do not make inferences spontaneously to incorporate that knowledge. From the results of the *Neale* comprehension test, it was not clear whether the groups differed primarily because they could not remember the texts or because they possessed different amounts of knowledge, which was reflected in their ability to answer the more inferentially based questions. The precise relation between ability to make inferences and memory for text is not clear. Paris and Upton (1976) suggest that a positive relation exists between inferential ability and recall because inferential processing provides further access cues to the memory representation of the material (Tulving and Bower, 1974). By contrast, Omanson, Warren and Trabasso (1978) showed that increasing the number of inferences made does not necessarily increase recall. However, it is clear that inferences cannot be made unless the relevant material on which the inference is based has been remembered. Although in the previous experiment on constructive processing we showed that the less-skilled comprehenders did not differ from the skilled comprehenders in their ability to remember the original sentences from the passages, the less-skilled group were slightly worse. In any case, the test was one of recognition, where some answers will be correct by guessing alone, and this task was probably not a very good indication of the less-skilled comprehenders' unprompted recall of relevant information from a text they have just read. Accordingly, Experiment 4.2 was intended as an exploratory study of the relations between comprehension skill, general knowledge and inferential ability, using more natural and longer texts than those employed in the preceding experiment. We compared the groups' ability to recall information that was actually present in a story (literal information) with their ability to recall information that depended on an inference (inferential). There were also two types of recall condition: the children either had to answer questions from memory, or the text was available for them to refer to. These two conditions were included to investigate whether any difficulties are caused through poor memory for the material on which the inference was based, or by the lack of the relevant general knowledge necessary for understanding. The condition where the text was available was included to see whether any differences in inferential ability obtain between the comprehension skill groups even when they can refer to the premise information directly.

If the skilled comprehenders possess the knowledge and ability necessary to make inferences from text, they would be expected to perform better on the inferential questions. Moreover, as we discussed at the beginning of this chapter, the use of inferential processing probably leads to an improved mental model of the text, which in turn aids memory in general. Therefore, if skilled comprehenders utilise elaborative and inferential strategies more frequently when reading text, they would be expected to perform better on both inferential *and* literal questions when answering from memory.

Experiment 4.2: Understanding and memory for literal and inferential information

Method Four passages, each consisting of eight or nine sentences (100–120 words) were adapted from those used by Paris and Upton (1976).[1] An example passage is as follows:

John's Big Test

John had got up early to learn his spellings. He was very tired and decided to take a break. When he opened his eyes again the first thing he noticed was the clock on the chair. It was an hour later and nearly time for school. He picked up his two books, and put them in a bag. He started pedalling to school as fast as he could. However, John ran over some broken bottles and had to walk the rest of the way. By the time he had crossed the bridge and arrived at class, the test was over.

For each passage, four questions asked for literal information and four asked for inferential information not explicitly stated in the passage. The questions for the example story are presented below. The first four questions are literal and the second four, inferential.

1. What was John trying to learn?
2. Where was the clock?
3. How many books did John pick up?
4. What did John have to cross on his way to school?

Table 4.3. *Percentages of errors in question answering for each question type, presentation condition and comprehension skill group*

	Question type			
	Unseen		Seen	
	Literal	Inferential	Literal	Inferential
Skilled	10.9	15·6	1·0	9·9
Less-skilled	29·2	45·8	3·6	35·4
Overall	20·1	30·7	2·3	22·7

5. How did John travel to school?
6. What did John do when he decided to take a break?
7. Why did John have to walk some of the way to school?
8. How do you know that John was late for school?

The full set of stories and questions can be found in Oakhill (1984).

There were twelve skilled and twelve less-skilled comprehenders, who were tested individually. Each subject saw the four passages in turn, and answered all the questions about a particular passage before going on to the next one. The order of questions for each passage was randomised separately for each subject. The presentation of questions with the passage available always followed the condition where subjects were asked to respond from memory. After completing the memory test, the children were given back the passage, and the questions were repeated.

The subjects were told that they should try to remember what the story was about and that they would be asked some questions about it. Each subject read the passage aloud once and was then asked the eight questions about it. We then gave back the story and asked the questions again. The children were told to look up the answers in the passage to check them or find the answer if they had previously been unable to remember it.

Results The percentage error rates (including omissions) are shown in Table 4.3.

The data were analysed by analysis of variance, with comprehension ability between subjects and presentation condition (seen/unseen) and question type (literal/inferential) within subjects. There was a main effect of each of the factors: skilled comprehenders made fewer errors than less-skilled comprehenders, min $F'(1,51) = 12.85$, $p < .001$; fewer errors were made when the passage was available, min $F'(1,42) = 33.72$, $p < .001$; and fewer errors were made on literal than inferential questions, min $F'(1,46) = 9.42$, $p < .005$. The three two-way interactions were also significant: comprehension ability interacted with whether the passage was present or absent, min $F'(1,42) = 5.23$, $p < .05$; type of question (literal/inferential) interacted with whether the passage was present or absent, min $F'(1,52) = 7.14$, $p < .025$; and type of question also interacted with comprehension skill, $F_1(1,22) = 11.97$, $p < .005$; $F_2(1,30) = 3.98$, $.05 < p < .1$. However, these two-way interactions were qualified by a three-way interaction between comprehension level, question type, and presentation condition: when the passage could not be seen, skilled comprehenders were better than less-skilled ones at answering both types of question but, when the passage was available, their superior performance only obtained for the inferential questions, $F_1\ (1,22) = 5.21$, $p < .05$; $F_2\ (1,30) = 4.12$, $.05 < p < .1$. This interpretation of the three-way interaction was borne out by analyses for each condition separately. These analyses showed that question type and comprehension skill interacted in the condition where the passage was available: $F(1,22) = 26.19$, $p < .001$ but not in the condition where it was not available: $F(1,22) = 2.85$, $p > .1$.

Discussion This experiment demonstrated that skilled and less-skilled comprehenders differ in their ability to answer both sorts of questions (literal and inferential) when the text is not available to refer to. However, unlike standard comprehension tests, our study gives us some more information about the differences between the groups in question-answering ability. As we argued in the introduction to this experiment, it is not clear from standard comprehension tests whether those children who have difficulty do so because they are unable to *recall* the relevant parts of the text, or because, when questions are inferentially based, they are not able to make the necessary *inferences* to relate the questions to the text and to general knowledge. In the present study, we compared the children's ability to answer questions that tap both sorts of ability, and compared performance when the children had to answer from memory with performance when they had the text available to refer to. Our results showed that the difference between the groups was much larger for inferential than for literal questions, and this difference in performance between the groups on the inferential questions was apparent even when the text was available for the children to look at. In this condition, there was no difference between the groups in ability to answer the literal questions. This pattern of results cannot be explained on the assumption that the less-skilled comprehenders have a general memory deficit, since their poorer performance on the inferential questions persisted even when the text was available. The results are consistent with the idea that skilled comprehenders are more likely to use relevant general knowledge to make sense of information that is only implicit in a text, and that this inferential processing helps not only their understanding of, but also their memory for the text. In addition to the extra processing involved as a corollary of the inference-making, the representation of the text in memory may be more complete and consistent if inferences are made.

There are three main reasons why the less-skilled comprehenders may fail to make implicit inferences: they may lack requisite knowledge to make the inferences; they may not realise that inferential processing of this sort is appropriate; they may have the requisite knowledge, but be unable to access it and integrate it with information in the text because of processing limitations. The first explanation, that the less-skilled comprehenders lack the appropriate knowledge to make the sorts of inferences required seems very unlikely. However, other work of ours suggests that the other two explanations may both be true to some extent. The possibility that less-skilled comprehenders do not understand that reading involves bringing *appropriate* knowledge and experience to bear on a text is supported by some incidental data from an experiment on the understanding of anaphoric expressions, which we will be discussing later in this chapter (see Experiment 4.6). In that experiment, some of the children's responses indicated that, although they understood that it was appropriate to use one's general knowledge to understand a text, they did not realise how the application of that knowledge should be constrained by the information present in the text. They often seemed to make arbitrary responses to questions, and then went on to justify their responses in an *ad hoc* manner. The skill of understanding how to apply one's existing knowledge to text understanding is one aspect of *metacognitive* ability, which will be discussed more fully in Chapter 6. It is certainly not the case that the less-skilled comprehenders are *unable* to make inferences. The less-skilled comprehenders' problem seems to be one of degree, rather than an absolute inability: both this and the previous experiment show that they *can* make inferences, so it is reasonable to suppose that they would be able to make greater use of inferential processing if they were alerted to its value. Indeed, as we shall see in the chapter on remedial procedures, a straightforward training procedure, in which the children are encouraged to make predictions about the events in a story, and to make inferences, can have dramatic effects on the comprehension ability of the less-skilled comprehenders. Such training may improve comprehension because it makes the children realise the legitimacy of making inferences, and of using information not explicit in the text.

The other possibility that we mentioned – that the less-skilled comprehenders have difficulty in making inferences because of processing limitations – will be discussed further in the next chapter. However, these two putative explanations of comprehension failure are not mutually exclusive: it may be precisely *because* of their better working memory that skilled comprehenders are able to retrieve and use appropriate knowledge when making inferences. Training less-skilled comprehenders in inferencing procedures may make the process more automatic, thus reducing the working memory demands though, of course, the children will not be able to make more efficient use of working memory unless they realise the legitimacy of appropriate inferences. We will return to the issue of working memory later.

In the next experiment, the question of whether or not the less-skilled comprehenders possess the relevant knowledge to make particular sorts of inferences is addressed further.

Experiment 4.3: *Instantiation of nouns*

During the *Neale* comprehension test we noticed that some children tended to recall particular meanings for some words (e.g. 'bedroom window' for 'my window'; 'roller skates' for 'skates') indicating that they had elaborated on the original text to some extent. As we have already discussed, during the normal course of text understanding, readers need to make use of context and world knowledge to restrict the meaning and reference of words. This process has been termed *instantiation* by Anderson (e.g. Anderson and Ortony, 1975; Anderson, Pichert, Goetz, Schallert, Stevens and Trollip, 1976). Anderson argues that people give a word a much more specific interpretation in context than in isolation, i.e. they instantiate a particular sense for the word as a function of the context in which it occurs.[2] The work by Anderson and his colleagues has investigated adults' instantiations of nouns, and other work (Garnham, 1979) has shown that similar effects can be obtained for verbs. For example, Anderson et al. (1976) presented their (adult) subjects with sentences such as:

The fish attacked the swimmer

and showed that the specific term *shark*, though not actually presented to the subjects, was a substantially better cue to retrieving the sentence than the noun actually presented, *fish*. Experiments by Paris and Lindauer (1976) and by Anderson, Stevens, Shifrin and Osborn (1977) have demonstrated that young children can also make instantiations, although they do not always do so spontaneously.

We know of only one experiment that has attempted to relate instantiation to skill at reading comprehension. Merrill, Sperber and McCauley (1981) showed that less-able readers are less likely than skilled ones to select the contextually most appropriate interpretation of a word. In their experiment, fifth-grade children read a series of sentences in which certain attributes of a key word were emphasised. For example, in *The boy sat near the fire*, some attributes of fire, such as *warmth*, come to mind more readily than others, such as *smoke*. After reading each sentence, the children had to name the colour of the ink in which a target word (e.g. *smoke* or *warmth*) was printed. It is well known that the meaning of a word, and how salient that meaning is, can increase the time to name the colour of the ink in which it is printed. In the case of the good comprehenders, the words that were related to the attribute emphasised by the context (warm) interfered with colour naming, but words related to unemphasised attributes (smoke) did not. Poor comprehenders showed interference effects for both types of words. In addition to sentence contexts, Merrill et al. also used word contexts. In this case, all subjects showed equal increases in interference when the target word followed a semantically related word (e.g. *cat-fur* or *cat-claw*) compared with the condition where it followed an unrelated word (e.g. *man-fur*). Merrill et al. argue that these results indicate differences in the way in which good and poor comprehenders encode sentences. Whereas the good comprehenders derive a contextually appropriate encoding, the poor comprehenders have a more general, but presumably less useful, representation of the sentence – more of the target word's attributes are available to them.

The present experiment was designed to investigate whether the ability to make single-word instantiations differentiates between skilled and less-skilled comprehenders. We also tested whether the subjects possessed the knowledge on which the instantiations were based, even if they were not able to infer appropriate instances spontaneously.

The paradigm used in the present study is one of cued recall, similar to that used by Anderson et al. (1977) with adults. The sentences were presented auditorially so that the presentation time could be controlled. It was predicted that less-skilled comprehenders would not be so likely to draw inferences of instantiation and, therefore, they would be less likely to be able to recall the original sentences when given specific instances as cues (i.e. *shark* as a cue to the sentence *the fish attacked the swimmer*) than the skilled group would.

The previous experiments on inferential processing provided no information about *when* inferences occur, or whether the locus is the same for both comprehension-skill groups. It may be the case that children in neither group make inferences spontaneously during comprehension, and that the skilled children are simply better at retrieving premise information and making inferences at the time of testing. In the present study, response times to the cue words were measured to assess the locus of the inferential processing. If an inference is made during the initial comprehension process, then it should take no longer to retrieve the sentence given a specific or a general cue. If, however, specific cues operate in an *ex post facto* manner, the successful retrieval of sentences, given such cues, should take longer than when words presented in the original sentences are used as cues.

Method Twenty simple declarative sentences, all containing general nouns, were written using a suitable vocabulary. In order to test whether the contexts would bring to mind the particular instances predicted, the sentences were tested on an independent group of thirteen children of the same age and ability range as the experimental subjects. These children were asked to judge the most likely specific meaning of the relevant nouns. For instance, a child might be read the sentence 'The animal chased the mouse' and asked 'What sort of animal do you think it was?'. The sixteen sentences producing the most consistent responses in this test (at least 77% of subjects giving the same response) were chosen for use in the experiment.

In order that a subject did not receive an original and an instantiated cue for the same sentence, the cue words were divided into two lists. Each list contained ten original and ten instantiated cues: half the subjects in each comprehension-skill group received one cue list and half the other, so that each subject received either an original *or* an instantiated cue for a particular sentence. The order of presentation of both sentences and cues was randomised independently for each subject.

Twelve skilled and twelve less-skilled comprehenders participated in the experiment. The children were told that the experimenter was interested in how well children remember things, and that they would be read some sentences which they were to think about and try to remember, and about which they would later be questioned. Each sentence was read aloud to the subject, who then repeated it to ensure that they had heard the sentence correctly and that they maintained their concentration. Following presentation of the entire list of sentences, recall instructions were read to the children: they were told that they would be read some 'clue' words to help them remember the sentences they had been read, and that after they heard each 'clue' they should recall as much of the sentence it reminded them of as they could, saying any words they could recall even if they could not remember the whole sentence. We presented the sixteen cue words, and recorded the responses for later transcription and scoring. We prompted the subjects if an answer was not forthcoming in the five seconds following the presentation of each cue word. A trial was terminated if the child produced no response within twenty seconds, and was scored as an error.

Results We transcribed and scored the sentences using a gist recall criterion: semantically equivalent paraphrases were permitted. The percentages of correct responses for each cue type are shown in Table 4.4.

An analysis of variance showed a main effect of comprehension level: skilled comprehenders recalled more sentences than less- skilled ones, min $F'\ (1,48) = 7.20$, $p < .025$, and a main effect of type of recall cue: more sentences were recalled with specific than with general cue words, $F_1(1,22) = 4.30$, $p < .05$, though this effect did not reach significance in the analysis by items: $F_2\ (1,30) = 2.41$, $p > .05$. The specific cues improved the recall of the skilled readers much more than that of the less-skilled readers, resulting in an interaction between cue type and comprehension level, $F_1\ (1,22) = 6.97$, $p < .025$ $F_2\ (1,30)$

Table 4.4. *The percentage of sentences recalled as a function of comprehension level and type of recall cue*

	Cue type		
	General noun	Specific noun	Mean
Less-skilled	38·5	35·4	36·95
Skilled	45·8	71·9	58·85
Mean	42·15	53·65	

Table 4.5. *Mean correct response times (seconds) to cue words for each cue type and skill group*

	Cue type	
	General noun	Specific noun
Less-skilled	2·23	2·77
Skilled	2·50	2·49

= 3.90, $.05 < p < .1$. Indeed, the specific cues had, if anything, a negative effect on the performance of the less-skilled readers, whereas Newman–Keuls tests showed that they produced a reliable improvement in the performance of the skilled readers ($p < .05$).

The response times, from the presentation of the cue word until the subject started to speak, were measured for correct trials from an audiotape. Only times up to five seconds (i.e. up until the first prompt) were included in the analysis. The mean response times are shown in Table 4.5. An analysis of variance on these data revealed no effect of comprehension level or of cue type. However, the interaction between comprehension level and cue type was marginally significant by subjects, $F_1(1,19) = 3.15$, $p < .09$ ($F_2(1,15) = 1.23$). An F test for simple effects showed that the less-skilled comprehenders took significantly longer to respond to specific than to general cues, $F(1,18) = 8.76$, $p < .02$, whereas the same comparison for skilled comprehenders was not significant.

The subjects were also asked to choose between two probable specific meanings for the nouns in the sentences they had heard. For instance, they were re-read the sentence 'The fruit was full of juice', and asked 'Do you think the fruit was a banana or an orange?' Both groups gave a very high proportion of predicted responses on this task (the percentages of non-predicted responses were 2.1% and 0.5% for the less-skilled and skilled groups respectively).

Discussion First, it is important to note that the materials in this experiment, like those in Experiment 4.1 in this chapter, were *read to* the children. It would appear that the less-skilled comprehenders' difficulties are not specific to reading, but are a more general language comprehension problem. The results of the forced-choice test at the end of the experiment show that all of the children had the requisite knowledge that would have enabled them to make appropriate instantiations. However, the results of the cued recall task indicate that the groups differ in the extent to which they spontaneously instantiate particular meanings when they are presented with short sentences. Differences in recall between the groups were only apparent when specific cues were presented, indicating that skilled comprehenders are more likely to make such instantiations than are the less-skilled group, thereby enabling them to recall more of the original sentences when given such cues. However, it should be noted that this pattern of results did not hold over all the sentences. In a few cases, *both* groups found it easy to recall a sentence given a specific cue. Some examples of such sentences are as follows (the specific cues are shown in parentheses):

The insect stung the boy (bee).
The boots kept his feet dry (Wellingtons).
The game was lost by one goal (football match).

This finding indicates that the less-skilled comprehenders are also able to make instantiations, but perhaps do so only when the context is very familiar, or when the range of instantiations is particularly limited. A further finding was that, when given the specific cues (which never occurred in the original sentences), subjects from both groups often recalled the sentence, not in its original form, but with the specific noun cue substituted for the original (general) noun. However, whereas 59% of the less-skilled comprehenders' correct responses in this (specific cue) condition included the specific nouns, only 39% of the skilled comprehenders' correct responses did. This finding indicates that the skilled comprehenders also retained the original surface wording of the sentences more often than did the less-skilled group, and suggests that, even though they seemed to have encoded a particular meaning for the general nouns, the skilled comprehenders would perhaps be better able to revise their encoding if they found that they had made an inappropriate instantiation.

There was no difference in recall (either accuracy or speed) between the groups when they were given the general nouns as cues, which provides yet more evidence that the less-skilled comprehenders do not simply have an inferior memory. It was predicted that the decrement in recall from general to specific cues would be greater for the less-skilled than for the skilled comprehenders. In fact, only the less-skilled comprehenders showed a slight but non-significant decrement: the skilled group actually performed significantly *better* with specific than with general cues. These differences indicate that the groups differ in the extent to which they make use of context and specific knowledge in the interpretation of text. The skilled comprehenders were more likely to derive a fuller representation of the events and entities described in the sentences, including specific instances of the general nouns, and such processing enabled them to recall the sentences more readily when presented with the specific noun cues.

The interpretation of this experiment has focused on elaboration processes *during* comprehension. It might be argued that the process of instantiation is retrospective, and that the implied meanings are generated only when the cues are presented. However, the response-time data do provide some tentative evidence that the skilled comprehenders were instantiating specific meanings at the time of initial comprehension, whereas the less-skilled group, who took longer to respond when presented with specific cue words, were using them to retrieve the sentences by some other process, such as a string of word associations.

The question arises as to exactly how the ability to instantiate particular meanings for general nouns might be related to comprehension skill. One possibility is that the more detailed a model of a piece of text that the reader has, the easier it will be to incorporate new incoming information. Instantiations and other elaborations of text could act as aids to guide which of the infinite number of possible inferences should be made during comprehension.

Discussion of Experiments 4.1–4.3

These three experiments show that the groups differ in their ability to make various types of inference from texts: those that connect up the ideas in a text, those from general knowledge, and inferences about likely meanings of particular words in context. The experiments also showed that the less-skilled comprehenders' difficulty in making inferences did not arise simply because they could not recall the texts – in Experiment 4.2, where the texts were present for the children to refer back to, the less-skilled comprehenders were still poorer at answering questions that required an inference. In the next chapter, we will consider whether these problems with inference making are related to the childrens' working memory skills.

A further finding from Experiments 4.1 and 4.3 – that some young readers still have comprehension problems for auditorially presented materials – showed that their problem is not specific to reading.

Understanding anaphoric devices

In the last three experiments, we have considered the important role of inferences in integrating text. An important factor in guiding text integration is the use of *anaphoric* links, such as pronouns and verb-phrase ellipsis. Although the resolution of anaphoric expressions is only one factor in text integration, such expressions are very common in texts, and successful comprehension often depends on their proper interpretation. As the results of the TROG test (described in Chapter 3) showed, the less-skilled comprehenders had some difficulty in understanding sentences containing pronouns. The next three experiments were designed to investigate more thoroughly whether children's comprehension is related to their ability to understand pronouns and other sorts of anaphor.

Experiment 4.4: *Effects of gender cue and memory load on pronoun resolution*

The ability to resolve pronouns depends on a number of factors, even when the pronoun is referentially determinate. The reader has to search for potential antecedents, and assess the acceptability of any that are found. The distance between a pronoun and its antecedent has been shown to affect comprehension time in adults (Cirilo, 1981; Clark and Sengul, 1979). Another factor that has been shown to affect how easily both children and adults understand pronouns is whether or not there is a gender cue to their antecedent (Wykes, 1981; Garnham and Oakhill, 1985). When a pronoun has more than one possible antecedent in a sentence, successful resolution may demand inferences based on semantic and world knowledge. Given the less-skilled comprehenders' difficulty in making inferences, we were interested to see whether the need to make an inference to resolve a pronoun (i.e. when no gender cue information is available) would selectively affect the performance of that group. The necessity for such inferences is clear in examples such as the following:

Sam sold his car to Max because he needed the money.
Sam sold his car to Max because he needed it.

Although the sentences are superficially very similar, the pronoun *he* is more likely to refer to Sam in the first, and Max in the second. In the absence of disambiguating syntactic information, such as gender cues, the reader must use general knowledge about buying and selling, and the motives involved, in order to resolve the anaphor (see Ehrlich, 1980). In this experiment, we varied both, whether or not there was a gender cue to the pronoun's antecedent, and whether or not the two clauses of the sentence could be seen simultaneously. If the less-skilled comprehenders experience problems in making appropriate inferences to resolve the pronouns, then they should have particular difficulty when no gender cues are available and when the clauses have to be viewed separately.

Method We wrote thirty-two two-clause sentences, using suitable vocabulary. All of the sentences consisted of a main clause containing two referents: either

Table 4.6. *Mean percentages of errors in choice of pronoun antecedents as a function of memory-load, gender cue and skill group*

	Sentence type			
	No memory load		Memory load	
	Gender cue	No cue	Gender cue	No cue
Less-skilled	13.50	27·08	20·83	37·50
Skilled	2·13	15·63	6·25	23·96

two of the same sex (no cue condition), or of different sexes (gender cue condition), followed by a subordinate clause beginning *because*. The subordinate clauses always provided a reason for the event in the main clause. For example:

Peter lent his coat to Sue
because she was cold.

Memory load was manipulated by either allowing the children to see the whole sentence, or by only allowing them to view the two clauses separately. Half of the sentences in each memory condition contained gender cues.

In the no-cue conditions, the 'correct' antecedent was confirmed by asking adults for their judgements of the more likely antecedent. The correct antecedent was equally often the first or second noun phrase in the main clause, and this factor was counterbalanced within gender cue conditions and memory conditions. Each sentence was followed by a forced-choice question (e.g. *Who was very cold, Peter or Sue?*).

Four sets of materials were prepared, so that each sentence occurred in each condition (with/without cue, with/without memory load). There were twelve children within each skill group, and equal numbers were assigned to each of the sets of sentences. The children were tested individually. They were asked to read each sentence aloud, and then the question was read to them. In the memory-load condition, the separate clauses were covered as the subject read them. In the no-load condition, the whole sentence was available until the subject provided an answer to the question. The subjects received the two memory conditions on different days, and order of memory conditions was counterbalanced within skill group.

Results The percentages of errors made are shown in Table 4.6. The data were analysed by analysis of variance with one between-subjects' factor (comprehension skill) and two within factors: memory load and gender cue. All the main effects in the analysis of variance were significant. Skilled comprehenders made fewer errors than less-skilled comprehenders, minF' $(1,64) = 6.15$, $p < .05$. The no memory load condition resulted in fewer errors than the memory load condition, $F_1(1,22) = 7.06$, $p < .025$, $F_2(1,62) = 6.15$, $p < .025$; and fewer errors were made when a gender cue to the pronoun's antecedent was provided, minF'$(1,78) = 22.14$, $p < .001$. There were no significant interactions between the factors.

Discussion Although the less-skilled comprehenders' performance (like that of the good comprehenders) was affected by the gender cue and memory variables, their error rate even in the simplest condition (gender cue and the sentence available to refer back to) was fairly high (13.5%) given that there were only two possibilities. It seems inconceivable that even poor comprehenders of this age do not understand that, for instance, the pronoun *he* should have a male antecedent. A more likely explanation is that the less-skilled comprehenders failed to attend properly to the pronouns and, even when they could refer back to the sentence to answer the question, they sometimes chose not to do so, relying instead on their (presumably inaccurate) representation of it. In the next experiment, therefore, we altered the task, so that the children were induced to attend more carefully to the sentences, before being asked questions about them.

Experiment 4.5: *Effects of inferential complexity on pronoun resolution*

In this experiment, the sentences used were very similar to those in Experiment 4.4, but we asked the subjects to provide an appropriate pronoun to fill a gap in the second clause of the sentence. All of the sentences contained a male and a female antecedent, so that the subjects had to think about their choice of pronoun. The childrens' first task was to fill in an appropriate pronoun (*he* or *she*) in the space in the sentence, for example:

Sally gave her shoes to Ben
as a present
because... needed them.

The second task was to judge whether a statement that followed the sentence was true or not, for example *Sally needed the shoes*. In this experiment, we also varied the complexity of the inference required to decide on an appropriate pronoun. In the example above, it is easy to work out that the person who needed the shoes is likely to be the recipient of them, rather than the donor. In other sentences (which were very similar to those used in Experiment 4, above), more complex inferential processing was required. For example:

Steven gave his umbrella to Penny
in the park
because... wanted to keep dry.

In this case, the reader has to work out that someone who wants to keep dry might want an umbrella, as well as that the person wanting the umbrella was the recipient of it. Half of the sentences in the experiment required a 'simple', and half a 'complex', inference. We expected that the sentences requiring complex inferences would prove more difficult overall, but that the less-skilled comprehenders, since we have already shown that they have deficient inference skills, would find the sentences requiring complex inferences particularly difficult.

Method There were twenty-four sentences, half with simple and half with complex completions. The gender and position of the correct antecedent were counterbalanced within the inference factor. Half of the sentences for verification were true, and half false.

Fourteen skilled and fourteen less-skilled comprehenders were tested individually. Each child was presented with four practice trials using similar materials, and was given feedback, before the experiment proper. It was explained that a word (always *he* or *she*) was missing from each sentence, as shown by the dots, and that the child's task was to try to fill in the missing word. They were then to read the second sentence, and decide whether it was true or false, depending on whether it fitted with what the first sentence said. The sentences were presented in a different random order for each subject. The subjects read the sentences aloud to the experimenter and any errors were corrected promptly, but choices of pronouns were not corrected.

Results The mean percentages of errors in the gap-filling task are shown in Table 4.7. The data were analysed by analysis of variance with groups and sentence type as factors. There was a main effect of comprehension skill, $\min F'(1,34) = 4.81$, $p < .05$: the less-skilled comprehenders made more errors overall. There was also a main effect of sentence type, $F_1\ (1,26) = 1.85$, $p < .01$, $F_2 = 5.57$, $p < .05$: the complex inference sentences were harder overall. The interaction between the factors was not significant (both Fs < 2.0), but planned comparisons showed that the difference in the groups' performance on the complex sentences was highly significant, $F(1,26) = 12.10$, $p < .002$, whereas the corresponding difference for the simple sentences did not reach significance, $F(1,26) = 4.00$, $p = .06$.

The mean percentages of errors on the sentence judgement task are shown in Table 4.8. Analyses of variance on these data showed a main effect of comprehension skill, $\min F'(1,35) = 8.71$, $p < .01$, but no main effect of sentence type. Although the interaction between sentence type and skill level was only marginally significant, $F_1(1,26) = 3.64$, $F_2(1,11) = 3.95$ (both ps < 0.1), planned

Table 4.7. *Mean percentages of errors as a function of sentence complexity and comprehension skill (gap-filling task)*

	Sentence type	
	Simple	Complex
Less-skilled	23·17	32·75
Skilled	11·92	16·67

Table 4.8. *Mean percentages of errors as a function of sentence complexity and comprehension skill (true/false judgements task)*

	Sentence type	
	Simple	Complex
Less-skilled	25.58	33.33
Skilled	14·92	13·70

comparisons again showed that the difference between the groups was highly significant in the case of the complex sentences, $F(1,26) = 16.00$, $p < .0005$, but only marginally significant for the simple sentences, $F(1,26) = 3.61$, $p = .07$.

Discussion These data again show the less-skilled comprehenders to be generally worse than the skilled group at understanding the function of pronouns, but provide some evidence that their performance is related to the level of inferential processing required to work out the more appropriate pronoun. Taken together, the results of these two experiments show that the less-skilled comprehenders have considerable difficulty in resolving and supplying appropriate pronouns.

However, both experiments could be criticised for using very short and unnatural texts to investigate children's understanding of pronouns. Because the differences between the groups were so striking, we decided to look at their understanding of anaphoric expressions more generally, using more naturalistic materials.

Experiment 4.6: *Anaphor resolution in a narrative text*

The two experiments described above have shown that there are limitations on less-skilled comprehenders' ability to resolve pronouns. However, there are many other ways of marking text cohesion other than the use of pronouns. The importance of various types of anaphoric expressions in establishing text cohesion is summed up by Halliday and Hasan (1976, p.4) as follows:

> Cohesion occurs where the *interpretation* of some element in the discourse is dependent on that of another. The one *presupposes* the other, in the sense that it cannot be effectively decoded except by recourse to it. When this happens, a relation of cohesion is set up, and the two elements, the presupposing and the presupposed, are thereby at least potentially integrated into a text.

Halliday and Hasan provide a taxonomy of types of cohesive ties that appear in text, and we used this taxonomy to sample a wider range of cohesive ties than the studies above. *Reference* includes links such as personal pronouns, which we have already studied in some detail, and demonstratives, such as *this* and *that*. Like other cohesive ties, references can be used to point back to a previous item in text. For example, in the sentences

(a) Mary Jane Wilson went for a walk. She found 10p on the ground.

she stands for Mary Jane Wilson. The pronoun could be replaced by *Mary Jane Wilson* and the sentence would still mean exactly the same as it did before. *Substitutions* and *ellipses* are rather similar to each other. In both cases, a noun phrase, verb phrase or clause is replaced. This replacement can be marked by the substitution with a word such as *one* and forms of the verb *do*, such as *do so*, *has done*.

Examples of substitutions are:

(b) John has an ice cream and I want one too.
(b') Has the plane landed? Yes it has done.

where *one* replaces *an ice cream* and *has done* replaces *has landed*. In other cases a gap (*ellipsis*) can be left:

(c) Has the plane landed? Yes it has.

Lexical ties are rather more diverse and subtle in nature. They involve semantic links that run through a text. These can include word reiterations and the use of synonyms, but the links can also be more nebulous associations of meaning. For example, in:

(d) Mary was in her garden. The flowers smelt lovely.

the words *garden* and *flowers* are connected by being related to the same general topic, and we understand the flowers to be the ones in Mary's garden.

Halliday and Hasan describe another type of cohesion, *conjunction*, that we did not include in the investigation described next, but that we discuss in the work on story reproductions reported in Chapter 7. Conjunctions are words like *and*, *but*, *so* and *then*, that indicate the relation between separate propositions in the text.

We know that text comprehension is guided by anaphors (Hirst and Brill, 1980), but our studies of pronouns suggest that less-skilled children are rather poor at resolving anaphors. If their performance in our experimental tasks is an indication of how they normally read, the results suggest that they could fail to resolve around 25% of such anaphors.

Many studies of anaphor resolution, including our own, test children by asking a question about the text, for example, *Who found 10p on the ground*? (see sentence (a) above). But use of this method for natural texts, as opposed to the carefully constructed sentences we used in the pronoun studies, is open to the criticism that correct answers can sometimes be obtained without really understanding the anaphors. For example, there might only be one plausible referent (as in the above example, where only one person is mentioned), or clues might be given from other parts of the text (for example, if sentence (a) was followed by *Mary smiled and put the money in her pocket*). Moberly (1979) devised a rather more difficult task: after reading a story, children were given a fresh copy of it with certain anaphors underlined, and had to insert after each one the words in the text that each anaphor 'pointed back to'. Thus, they were required to identify which words in the text an anaphor replaced, or referred to. Despite extensive practice on this task, fourth- and sixth-grade children were correct for only an average of 62% and 72% of anaphors respectively.

A further problem in resolving anaphors may arise if, as we have suggested, less-skilled children process information less efficiently during reading than do skilled ones. Anaphors refer to other words elsewhere in the text, but these words may be at some distance from the anaphor. The less-skilled children, particularly if they are not building an integrated representation of the text as they read, may be unable to retrieve the preceding text containing the referent, and so have difficulty in resolving the anaphor. For example, if a long description of Mary's walk intervened between the two sentences in (a), the reader may forget the name of the person who was taking a walk, and be unable to give the referent of *she*.

As we mentioned earlier, there has been some research showing that anaphors are harder to resolve as distance increases, particularly for people whose working memory is relatively inefficient: Light and Capps (1986) found that the greater the person's working memory span (on the Daneman and Carpenter test described in Chapter 2), the greater the distance across which they could link pronouns with their antecedents. We expected that less-skilled comprehenders would be at a particular disadvantage as the distance between anaphors and antecedents increased.

Method We wrote a 700-word story, attempting to adopt a relatively naturalistic style, and selected from it six examples of each of the four types of anaphor described above: reference, substitution, ellipsis and lexical ties. Within each of these types, there were two examples at each distance. The anaphor was either *immediate* - the antecedent was in the sentence immediately preceding the anaphor, or *mediated* - more than one sentence distant, but with

Table 4.9. *Materials from Experiment 4.6*

Bill and Alice Go Fishing

Bill was proud of his new fishing rod and reel. His mother had given it to him for his birthday. On Saturday morning, Bill was going on a fishing trip with his Uncle, the Captain. As he [IR′: Bill] carried his rod to the bus stop, he met Mrs Tripp from next door.

'Are you going fishing?' she asked.

Bill smiled at her. He liked her because she often made a little cake just for him when she [MR′: Mrs Tripp] was baking. 'Yes, I am,' [RE: going fishing] he replied.

'Who gave you your new fishing rod?', she asked.

'Mum did,' [IS: gave me the fishing rod] said Bill. 'It is for sea fishing. That is where I am going now. [RR′: Saturday morning] I've got another smaller one. [MS: fishing rod] but I've lent it to my friend Alice, because she wants to catch fish too.'

'Well I hope you both do!' [IS: catch fish] said Mrs Tripp. 'Remember to bring some home for Tiger.' Tiger was Mrs Tripp's cat. He looked at Bill sleepily from the window and yawned. 'I hope you have a lovely time!' said Mrs Tripp.

Just then the bus came and Bill quickly picked up his bag. He paid the driver and sat on the front seat upstairs, so that he could look out for Alice. That was his favourite place. 'I hope I do [RS: have a lovely time] too,' thought Bill to himself. Alice got on at the stop outside her house, and sat next to Bill. 'I've brought some sandwiches,' said Bill. 'I hope you have remembered yours.' [IR′: sandwiches]

'Of course I have,' [IE: remembered my sandwiches] said Alice. She looked out of the window. 'It's very windy today. I think the sea will be rough.'

Soon the bus drew in at the Marina. The Captain was busy loading up his fishing boat. He fixed the motor [IL: of the boat] in place and put his bag under the seat. They ran down towards him. Soon, everything was ready. 'Who wants to sit here?' asked the Captain.

'I do!' shouted both the children at once.

'Well I suppose you [RR′: Bill and Alice] both can, [ME: sit here] if there's room,' said the Captain.

Soon they were out on the open sea. The waves [IL: of the sea] were high and the wind was blowing hard. 'I told you so,' [RS: that it would be rough] Alice said to Bill. Bill held the edge of his seat with his cold, wet fingers. His tummy felt as if it was going up and down and from side to side at the same time. He had been throwing his fishing line towards the beach. But now, it lay at his feet. The Captain was trying to light his pipe. Bill watched the smoke drift past. Each time, the wind blew out the tiny flame. [ML: of the pipe] He tried [ME: to light his pipe] once more. Then he threw the empty box away.

Bill said, 'Isn't it time to go home yet?' His face was pale green.

'I hope not,' [MS: it's not time to go home yet] replied Alice. Alice had caught three fish. Poor Bill hadn't got any. [IE: fish] He looked gloomily at the grey water. He didn't feel like eating his sandwiches. He crumbled pieces of bread and threw them overboard. Seagulls flew down to scoop them up. Suddenly, a big white gull swooped over the boat and dived into the water. A moment later, it cme out, holding a silver shape in its beak. 'Did you see that?' called the Captain. Then, something even more surprising happened. The gull flew over the boat and the fish dropped from its beak. It landed right at Bill's feet. 'I reckon that's [MR′: the fish] in return for the sandwiches,' said the Captain, laughing. Bill wrapped the fish up and put it in his bag.

Table 4.9. *Cont.*

Bill felt much happier as the boat turned in to the shore. It had been a long day and they were very tired. He wished he had kept some food for himself. Bill and Alice fell asleep on the bus home. At last, Bill was walking wearily up the garden path. There at the kitchen table sat Mrs Tripp. 'I remembered!' [RE: to bring some fish for Tiger] called Bill, putting his bag down on the step. [ML: of the house] Tiger jumped down from the sill [RL: of the window] and rubbed his head against Bill's legs.

'I'm glad you caught some fish with your new present,' [RL: fishing rod] said Mum.

'Well I didn't really,' thought Bill to himself, 'but perhaps I'll tell Mum what really happened another time.'

Examples of questions:
Meaning question: What does 'he' stand for here?

Text question: Who carried his rod to the bus stop?

Notes:
Underlined words show anaphors tested.

Material in brackets shows anaphor category and antecedent.

Key: I = immediate, M = mediated, R = remote. R′ = reference, E = ellipsis, S = substitution, L = lexical.

an intervening mention of the item, or *remote* - more than two sentences distant, with no direct mediating reference. There were two types of task for each anaphor: saying which words the anaphor 'stood for', or 'pointed back to' (Meaning question), and answering a question about the anaphor (Text question). Table 4.9 shows the entire story, with anaphors of each type indicated, and an example of each type of question.

After all sixteen children in each skill group had been given practice with examples of each anaphor type, each child was tested individually. The experimenter read the story aloud, aiming to produce as relaxed and natural a situation as possible. Then she read through a new copy of the story, with the target anaphors underlined in red, and the text visible to the child. As each marked anaphor was encountered, the child was asked the Meaning question. If a wrong answer was given, the Text question was also asked, to check whether the child had at least formed an appropriate mental model of the text, even if they did not have an explicit awareness of how links are made in text. If children correctly answered the Meaning question, though, the Text question was not presented, because this would imply that the first answer was wrong. In such cases, we considered that the Text question would have been answered correctly.

Results We classified answers to each of the two questions as correct if the relevant piece of text, or the gist of it, was given. We analysed the results for the two question types separately because the tasks were not independent, for the reasons described above. For each question type, we performed an analysis with skill group between subjects and distance and anaphor type within subjects, as well as separate analyses for each type of anaphor, with skill group and distance as factors. We do not report analyses by materials, because there were only two items in each cell.

The performance of the groups on the two types of question (pooled over anaphor type) is shown in Table 4.10. In an analysis of performance on the Meaning question, the less-skilled comprehenders performed more poorly than skilled comprehenders overall, $F(1, 30) = 26.63$, $p < .0001$. This difference was also apparent in the separate analyses for each type of anaphor, as shown in Table 4.11: all Fs $(1, 30) > 5.5$, all ps $< .025$.

Performance on the Text questions (also shown in Table 4.10) was almost perfect for the skilled children (90% correct), whereas the less-skilled ones were poorer overall on these questions (72% correct). The difference between groups was significant in the overall analysis, $F(1, 30) = 20.94$, $p < .0001$ and for all four types of anaphor analysed separately, all Fs $(1, 30) > 5$, all ps $< .05$ (see Table 4.12). This result suggests that the poor comprehenders were worse at scanning the text for an answer, and is consistent with the results of our previous experiment where we showed differences between the groups in ability to answer questions even when the text was present (Experiment 4.2, above).

The children's performance also varied according to the distance between an anaphor and its antecedent, as shown in Table 4.10. Anaphors that were further from their antecedents were in general harder to resolve, in both of the tasks, and these differences were significant in the overall analysis of the data, Fs $(2, 60) = 30.32$, $p < .0001$ and 30.08, $p < .0001$ for Meaning and Text questions respectively. Separate analyses of the Meaning questions for the different types of anaphor also showed a main effect of distance in all cases, all Fs $(2,69) > 16.00$, all ps $< .0001$. However, there was only one instance of an interaction between skill group and distance, in the case of the ellipses: $F(2,60) = 5.33$, $p < .01$. Planned comparisons showed that the poor comprehenders were considerably worse than the skilled ones in the remote condition ($p < .05$). In the case of the Text questions, there were fewer effects of distance, as performance was better overall, but there were still significant main effects for the ellipses and substitutions (both Fs $(2.60) > 11.00$, both ps $< .0001$), though no interactions with skill group (all Fs < 1.7).

There is, therefore, little support for our idea that less-skilled children are particularly hampered in establishing links between parts of a text as the load on memory is increased. Although the less-skilled children were poorer overall at understanding the anaphors, the effects of distance, where present, were usually apparent for both groups.

To investigate further their understanding of anaphors, we looked at the

Table 4.10. *Mean percentages correct at each distance for the two question types and two skill groups*

	Distance			
	Immediate	Mediated	Remote	Mean
Meaning question				
Less-skilled	65·6	46·9	38·6	50·4
Skilled	81·3	68·7	61·0	70·3
Text question				
Less-skilled	83·6	75·8	57·0	72·1
Skilled	97·7	92·2	80·5	90·1

Table 4.11. *Mean percentages correct for each anaphor type at each distance for the two skill groups (Meaning questions)*

	Distance		
Anaphor type and skill group	Immediate	Mediated	Remote
Reference			
Less-skilled	65·6	40·6	21·9
Skilled	90·6	65·6	25.0
Difference	25·0	25·0	3·1
Ellipsis			
Less-skilled	90·6	50·0	43·8
Skilled	93·8	65·6	87·5
Difference	3·2	15·6	43·7*
Substitution			
Less-skilled	81·3	81·3	20·1
Skilled	96·9	96·9	43·8
Difference	15·6	15·6	23·7
Lexical			
Less-skilled	25·0	15·6	68·8
Skilled	43·8	46·9	87·5
Difference	18·8	31·3	18·7

Note: * = planned comparison significant at $p < 0{\cdot}05$.

Table 4.12. *Mean percent correct for each anaphor type at each distance for the two skill groups (Text questions)*

Anaphor type and skill group	Distance: Immediate	Mediated	Remote
Reference			
Less-skilled	71·9	68·8	53·1
Skilled	96.9	93.8	93.8
Difference	25·0	25·0	40·7
Ellipsis			
Less-skilled	93·8	62·5	62·5
Skilled	100·0	84·4	87·5
Difference	6·2	21·9	25·0
Substitution			
Less-skilled	84·4	87·5	40·6
Skilled	96·9	100·0	50·0
Difference	12·5	12·5	9·4
Lexical			
Less-skilled	84·4	84·4	71·9
Skilled	96·9	90·6	90·6
Difference	12·5	6·2	18·7

incorrect responses that children gave, as opposed to correct or 'don't know' responses. Twenty per cent of the less-skilled comprehenders' error responses were wrong choices of anaphors (as opposed to 'don't knows'), compared with only 9% of the skilled comprehenders' answers. The less-skilled children showed two types of mistake demonstrating apparent misunderstandings of how to interpret cohesive ties, which we will describe in turn.

Part of the story went as follows: *Bill was proud of his new fishing rod and reel. His mother had given it to him for his birthday. On Saturday morning, Bill was going on a fishing trip with his Uncle, the Captain. As he carried his rod to the bus stop, he met Mrs Tripp from next door.* The children were required to say who the first *he* in the final sentence referred to. So far in the story, four people have been mentioned, two male (Bill and his Uncle, the Captain), and two female (Bill's mother and Mrs Tripp). The female characters can be ruled out (although one poor comprehender did give a female as the answer), and several features of the context suggest that Bill is the answer: he is the main character, mentioned in the title, he has just been given a fishing rod, he was going on a trip. If the reader has built up a model of the story so far, it will be easy to find the correct answer. Even so, four poor comprehenders said that *he* referred to Bill's uncle, the most immediately preceding plausible response.

So it looks as though less-skilled children may sometimes look for the nearest plausible response, whereas skilled children are more likely to use a mental model of the text.

The less-skilled children also made another sort of mistake: they sometimes referred outside the text to find a response. Four less-skilled children answered the above question with *John*, the name of a character who appeared in the training sentences, although they then corrected themselves. A further example of this tendency occurred in response to the sentence, *That is where I am going now*, where *now* refers to the time of the story, Saturday morning. Nine less-skilled comprehenders gave incorrect responses for the Meaning question on this item, compared to only two skilled comprehenders. While these wrong responses were usually plausible, in that children named a day of the week, they picked a different day from the one mentioned in the story. The way they did this suggested that they just 'picked a day, any day': they often did not scan the text, and some gave 'pseudo-explanations' for their answers. For instance, one child said that *now* was the day of the interview. She had made the mistake of referring to the real world, rather than the world of the text, and compounded these two worlds in her explanation that the characters would have had time to go fishing 'today' (real-world time) because, like her, they started school late on that day. This error is particularly striking, in that this child could have scanned the text for the single instance of the name of a day, and thus answered correctly but, rather than looking back to the text, she used her own knowledge inappropriately. It also indicates that the less-skilled comprehenders sometimes realise that it is appropriate to use general knowledge to help understand a text, but that they may not realise what aspects of their knowledge are appropriate or the constraints on its use.

Such errors suggest that some children, even at the age of 7, still have difficulty in coordinating information in the 'two worlds', the real world and the text world. Although it is often appropriate to assign real-world knowledge to the text world (e.g. Bill is a boy, he has two arms and two legs, he goes to school), there are some attributes of the real world that cannot necessarily be applied to the text world, including personal knowledge, such as starting school late on a particular day. This sort of error is similar to the sorts of errors sometimes encountered in semi-literate adults: they do not separate the formal properties of language from its meaning (e.g. Luria, 1976).

Given these results, it is not surprising that some children show poor comprehension. Often, an incorrect assignment of an anaphor can change the whole sense of a story. In our story, a crucial anaphor, *that*, referred to a fish given to the main character in return for some bread, which satisfies one of the boy's main goals of providing some fish for the neighbour's cat. Fourteen of the sixteen skilled comprehenders showed that they understood the meaning of this anaphor, but only eight of the less-skilled comprehenders did so. Informal questioning at the end of the story suggested that many of the latter group had missed the main point of the story, which depended on successful resolution of this particular anaphor.

The level of performance was higher in our study than in previous work, probably because we interviewed children individually. The order of difficulty for the different anaphor types was not consistent with the order found by Moberly, nor were her findings consistent with previous research. We suspect that this is because of uncontrolled differences in other factors affecting the ease of anaphor resolution: how redundant the text is, whether or not the referent is the focus of the text, the number of plausible alternative referents for each anaphor, to name the most obvious sources. There is probably more than one way to resolve an anaphor, and further work is needed to investigate more closely the processes involved in resolution.

Discussion of Experiments 4.4–4.6

If the levels of performance observed in these three experiments on anaphor resolution are representative of differences between the groups when they are reading extended text, and if less-skilled comprehenders fail to keep track of the anaphoric links in a text in the way that these results would suggest, then this failure may constitute part of their difficulty with comprehension. This failure to understand anaphoric links could have pervasive and serious effects on comprehension, hindering their ability to build up the coreferential links in a text.

It seems likely that the less-skilled group's comprehension could be improved, at least to some extent, by directing their attention to the importance of pronouns, and training them to consider how pronouns should be interpreted in relation to the rest of the text. This could be done either by asking explicit questions about the antecedents of referring expressions as children are reading, to encourage them to attend to them, or by adapting the type of lexical inference training which we discuss in Chapter 8 – the experimenter could point out anaphoric expressions and discuss their meanings with the children. Dommes, Gersten and Carnine (1984) found that children given explicit training in identifying pronouns' antecedents showed better post-training performance on such tasks than those given no treatment or those who were given practice in paraphrasing the texts. Exactly how effective training will be may depend on the difficulty of the pronoun resolution: it remains to be determined whether less-skilled comprehenders are simply unable to make the inferences necessary for understanding more complex anaphoric references (see Experiment 4.5, above), or are just overloaded when the difficulty of the resolution task is compounded by the additional inferential processing. It seems unlikely that children of 7–8 lack the necessary semantic and world knowledge for making the sorts of inferences required in our experiments. However, the results of the last experiment indicate that the less-skilled comprehenders may sometimes apply their knowledge in inappropriate and sometimes bizarre ways.

We have explored more generally how the presence or absence of cohesive links affects children's memory for a text, but this work is more closely related to our experiments on story re-telling and is, therefore, described in Chapter 7.

General discussion

In the first part of this chapter, we provided evidence to show that, whilst less-skilled comprehenders are good at recalling information from text verbatim, they are poor at recalling the gist meaning. In these experiments the skilled comprehenders were more likely to use relevant general knowledge to make sense of information implied in a text, and such inferential and constructive processing helped not only their understanding but also their memory for the text. We suggest that these inferential processes are an important part of the construction of an integrated model of what the text is about. The data also showed that, even when the less-skilled comprehenders are able to make inferences, they do not necessarily do so during comprehension.

In the second part, we explored differences between the groups in their ability to understand pronouns and other sorts of anaphoric link. The experiments showed that there were marked differences between the groups in their ability to understand a range of anaphoric expressions.

We considered briefly that one plausible explanation for the differences observed between the groups in these experiments is that they differ in the strategies they use to monitor their understanding during story reading. Younger children often fail to produce appropriate strategies for remembering (Flavell, 1970). Perhaps a similar sort of deficiency is evident when less-skilled comprehenders read or are read stories. They may not spontaneously attempt to interrelate information in the stories, draw potential inferences, or elaborate relations, to the same degree as skilled comprehenders because they do not understand the relevance of such processes to comprehension. This is a question to which we will return in Chapter 6, when we consider differences between the groups in their use of comprehension monitoring during text comprehension.

The ability to make inferences might be related to working memory capacity – if more capacity is available during the process of understanding a sentence, then that extra capacity will be available for the integration of the information in the sentence with relevant knowledge and experience. We will look at the evidence for a relation between comprehension skill and working memory capacity in the next chapter.

5 Allocating resources during reading

Introduction

In Chapter 3, we provided evidence from several different perspectives showing that less-skilled comprehenders do not show deficiencies in decoding or basic syntactic skills that might account for their poor text understanding. The experiments in Chapter 4 showed that less-skilled comprehenders' recall was close to the literal form of the text, and they showed less evidence of integrating information and making inferences than good comprehenders did. The findings suggest that these deficits were unlikely to be due simply to limited storage capacity in memory – less-skilled comprehenders were as good in their verbatim recall as the other group – or to a lack of general knowledge required for inferences, as the study of instantiation (Experiment 5.3) showed. We suggested that the group differences observed might be better explained in terms of working memory: the capacity to store and process information concurrently. In this chapter, we investigate this idea using two approaches: assessments of working memory efficiency, and studies of reading time for text, to investigate the on-line allocation of processing resources.

Working memory

Correlational studies have shown that children who have reading problems are generally poorer on tasks that require the repetition of sequentially presented auditory or visual stimuli (for a full account see Torgesen, 1978–9). However, none of these studies has addressed the question of whether children with a *specific comprehension problem* (as opposed to some more global reading problem) have a deficient short-term memory. Indeed, when we administered the WISC memory-span subtests to groups of good and poor comprehenders, there was no difference in forward or backward digit span between the two groups. Scores for backward span (mean = 3.8 trials correct) were identical, and those on the forward span test were not reliably different (the means were

4.8 and 4.3 trials correct for the skilled and less-skilled comprehenders respectively, $t(28) = 1.22$).

As we discussed in Chapter 2, there is evidence that successful comprehension depends on having an efficient *working memory*. Working memory is conceived of as a limited-capacity memory system. It comprises a *central executive* which is the locus of conscious control, plus a number of slave systems, each dedicated to processing information in a particular form. The most widely studied of these is the 'articulatory loop', a putative system capable of storing a small amount of articulatory information. There are a number of sources of evidence to support the existence of such a system. First, memory span correlates closely with reading speed both in adults (Baddeley, Thomson and Buchanan, 1975) and in children (Hulme, Thomson, Muir and Lawrence, 1984). Second, the finding that adults recall words with short articulation times (e.g. wicket) more easily than those with longer articulation times (e.g. typhoon) (see Baddeley et al., 1975) also suggests that the processes underlying immediate memory involve an articulatory component.

The ability to use the articulatory loop may play a particularly important role in reading. To enter the articulatory loop, or its associated phonological store, printed words must be recoded to a phonological form. The most plausible reason for the importance of phonological recoding in comprehension, and one that was first proposed by Huey (1908/1968), is that it provides a more durable medium than visual coding for storing the early parts of a sentence so that these can be combined with what comes later. A number of studies have shown that good and poor readers differ on memory span tasks, and that these differences can be accounted for primarily in terms of differences in the efficiency of phonological recoding in working memory, which are independent of general intellectual ability (see Stanovich, 1986; Wagner and Torgesen, 1987). For instance, Mann, Liberman and Shankweiler (1980) showed that, although good readers were better overall at recalling word lists and sentences, they were more disrupted than poor readers when the words to be recalled had similar sounds. Mann et al. took this as evidence that poor readers fail to make use of phonetic coding in short-term memory. However, this explanation seems unlikely, since the materials were presented to the children auditorially, so it is unclear how else they could have been encoded. A more plausible explanation would be that the good readers make more use of rehearsal than the poor readers, and that this is where the confusions arise.

Experiment 5.1: *Use of phonological recoding in short-term retention*

In the present experiment, we explored the possibility that skilled and less-skilled comprehenders differed in use of the articulatory loop. In order to assess the ability of the children to engage in phonological recoding and rehearsal

Table 5.1. *Mean recall scores for each presentation modality and word length in each skill group (max = 4)*

Modality:	Spoken words				Pictures			
Number of syllables:	1	2	3	Mean	1	2	3	Mean
Less-skilled	2·85	1·60	1·67	2·07	2·58	1·88	1·56	2·10
Skilled	2·63	1·98	1·73	1·86	2·00	1·77	1·31	1·82

strategies, we employed the technique reported by Hitch and Halliday (1983). Those authors presented children of three ages (6, 8 and 10 years) with short lists comprised of either one-, two- or three-syllable spoken words. The children in all three age groups recalled more short than long words, suggesting that the amount that could be recalled was related to the capacity of the articulatory loop. In a second condition, Hitch and Halliday presented the children with a series of pictures corresponding to the words in the lists. Only the 8- and 10-year-olds were sensitive to name length in this condition, indicating that they, but not the younger children, recoded the pictures to a phonological form and used verbal rehearsal to remember them. Hitch and Halliday's study suggests that children develop the ability to use recoding and rehearsal at some point between 6 and 8 years. In this experiment we investigated the performance of skilled and less-skilled comprehenders on a slightly modified version of Hitch and Halliday's task.

Method We tested fourteen children in each group, using lists of four words or pictures whose names were one, two or three syllables in length (e.g. spoon–leaf–swan–crown, hammer–mushroom–giraffe–monkey). We made sure that the children knew the names of all the pictures, which were drawn from a corpus of pictorial material (Snodgrass and Vanderwaert, 1980). The pictures were high in naming agreement (the extent to which adults spontaneously label the picture with the intended name), and the average frequency of the words was the same at all lengths (they were matched using the average of Grade 3 and 4 frequencies from Carroll, Davies and Richman, 1971).

All subjects received both the picture and the word conditions. Half of the children in each skill group received the words first, and half the pictures. Each test comprised four trials at each syllable length, making twelve trials in all for each modality. The items were presented either from a tape (words) or by means of a slide projector (pictures) at the rate of one item every two seconds.

Before each different sort of trial (word vs. pictures), the subjects were given a practice session, with feedback. The practice items were presented in the same modality, but using different materials from those used in the experiment proper, and the children were reminded to recall the words or pictures in the same order as they were presented. Half of the children saw the word trials first and half the picture trials first.

Results and discussion Items were scored as correct if they were recalled in the correct serial position. The mean numbers of correct items are shown in Table 5.1. As we expected, an analysis of variance showed a significant main effect of name length: $F(2,44) = 23.65$, $p < .0001$. This effect arises because the lists consisting of one-syllable names were much easier to recall than the others. However, there was no significant difference between the groups, and no effects or interactions involving modality.

The results of this experiment do not support the idea that poor comprehenders have a deficient short-term memory, nor that they use different strategies for encoding and maintaining lists of words or pictures. Both groups were affected by syllable length in their recall of items presented pictorially, showing that they recoded pictures verbally and used rehearsal to aid memory, as did the 8-year-olds in the study by Hitch and Halliday. In support of other of our findings (see Chapter 3) this once again suggests that the poor comprehenders do not have any *general* deficit in short-term memory capacity.[1]

The assessments of memory that we have made so far – here and in Chapter 3 – were primarily measures of capacity: they did not tax the individual's ability to store *and* process information simultaneously. However, reading involves the concurrent decoding, storage and semantic processing of text. Articulatory coding and rehearsal is a fairly basic method of processing information, and is only a precursor to more in-depth processing and storage needed for text understanding. The difference between memory tests that require largely storage, and those that involve a greater degree of processing, has been stressed by Daneman and Carpenter (1980; 1983). They have developed a test of working-memory capacity, the *reading-span* test. In their test, subjects are required to read and understand sentences (processing requirement) while simultaneously remembering the final word in each (storage requirement). Daneman and Carpenter showed that, in adults at least, performance on this test correlated more highly with various measures of reading comprehension than did more general tests of memory capacity. Good and poor comprehenders may therefore differ in working memory, even though they perform similarly on measures of memory capacity.

Experiment 5.2: Differences in working memory

The obvious way of testing for working-memory differences between the groups is to use Daneman and Carpenter's reading-span test. However, there is a problem in interpreting the results from experiments using this test. As Baddeley, Logie, Nimmo-Smith and Brereton (1985) have pointed out, Daneman and Carpenter's findings are open to different interpretations: it could be that the span test taps a very general processing capacity, as Daneman and Carpenter suggest, or that it merely shares a verbal comprehension component with the measures of comprehension with which it correlates. The processing requirement of the test, reading out sentences while storing the final word in each, has an obvious linguistic component. The good comprehenders might have an advantage on such a test purely *because* of their superior verbal comprehension. As we wanted to find out whether the two groups differ in general, rather than specifically verbal working memory, we adapted the span test by using numerical, rather than verbal, materials.

Baddeley et al. found a much weaker correlation with reading comprehension in adults when a counting span, rather than a verbal working-memory span, test was used. In order to go beyond the trivial explanation that all the reading span results have shown is that sentence comprehension correlates with paragraph comprehension, Daneman and Tardif (1987) compared correlations of various measures of verbal ability with performance on a verbal-working-memory span test and two non-verbal measures: one that tapped mathematical, and the other spatial, processes. From their results, Daneman and Tardif argue against the notion of a single central processor and posit, instead, at least two systems only one of which – the verbal-symbolic processor – has any direct involvement in reading. Furthermore, they argue that the processing component of the tasks is the important aspect in predicting individual differences – the predictive power of their tasks was not affected by whether or not they had an additional storage component.

Method Forty-two children in each skill group were given our memory-span test, which used lists of three-digit numbers (with no repetition of digits within a number). The children were presented with lists of three-digit numbers, with either two, three or four numbers in each list. So, for example, a two-group list might be 742 – 139. The subjects received eight experimental trials at each level of difficulty (= length of list), after receiving two practice trials at the same level. The blocks of trials were presented in order of increasing difficulty (i.e. starting with two groups of digits per list). The subjects were shown only one group of digits at a time, which they viewed through a cardboard 'window', and had to read the digits aloud. This decoding of written digits to a spoken form was the main processing requirement (not a trivial task for the average 7-year-old child).

Table 5.2. *Mean number of final digits recalled for each number of digit groups (strict recall criterion) in each skill group*

Number of groups:	2 (max = 16)	3 (max = 24)	4 (max = 32)
Less-skilled	14·29	11·76	11·12
Skilled	14·55	15·62	14·98
Difference	0·26	3·86	3·86

As soon as the child had read the final digit in a group, the experimenter moved the window on to the next group or, at the end of a list, on to blank space. After reading all the numbers in a list, the whole list was hidden and the child had to recall the final digit of each of the numbers. For example, in the series of two three-digit numbers, given above, the children read out the first set of digits (as single figures: 'seven-four-two', rather than 'seven hundred and forty-two'). This set was then covered while they read the second set. This in turn was covered, and the children recalled the final digits in order (i.e. 2-9). The load on working memory was increased by presenting more groups of numbers. Examples of lists of each length, and the required response, are:

835–402 (Answer: 5–2); 528–134–489 (Answer: 8–4–9); 069–801–027–902 (Answer: 9–1–7–2).

We ensured that none of the correct responses contained phonologically confusable items (e.g. 5–9) or easily memorable sequences (e.g. 1–2–3), or included a zero, as children sometimes vacillated between the labels 'zero' and 'nought'. We also prevented the children from using external memory aids such as counting on their fingers or audible rehearsal.

Results We scored the children's responses using both a strict criterion for recall (number of final digits recalled in the correct order) and a lenient criterion (number of final digits regardless of position). The patterns of results from these two methods of scoring were very similar, and from now on we will only consider the data from the strict method. The data are shown in Table 5.2.

The scores in the easiest version of the task – recalling the final items from two groups of three digits – were uniformly high. Although the extremely good performance in this condition shows that both groups understood the task requirements, their performance was at ceiling and we therefore excluded the data in this condition from the statistical analyses. An analysis of variance was performed on the numbers of final digits correct for the three- and four-group lists. The analysis showed a main effect of comprehension ability: $F\ (1,82) =$

29.66, $p < .0001$. The main effect of list length was not significant and neither was the interaction between the two factors (both $Fs < 1$). These data show that the less-skilled comprehenders understood the task requirements, but performed comparatively less well than the skilled group in the conditions that imposed greater loads on working memory.

There was a highly significant correlation between working-memory score and comprehension ability: $r(82) = 0.51$, $p < .0001$. This correlation is well within the range of .46 to .59 reported by Daneman and Carpenter between their reading-span task and a general comprehension measure. The correlation we obtained is higher than that between counting span (a non-verbal measure, similar to ours) and reading comprehension in adults ($r = .279$) reported by Baddeley et al. (1985). Our results suggest that, in children at least, reading comprehension is related to a verbal-symbolic processor, as Daneman and Tardif suggest, rather than to a specifically language-based system. Thus, although our previous results have shown that the two groups did not differ on tasks requiring the short-term storage of word and picture lists, they do differ on a task that requires concurrent storage and processing, which is probably closer to the requirements of comprehending written material.

Discussion of Experiments 5.1–5.2

The experiments reported in the first part of this chapter were designed to investigate the hypothesis that limitations in STM contribute to comprehension failure. Such limitations could come about in two main ways: the capacity of some individuals may be smaller, or else available capacity may not be used efficiently. In a limited capacity storage system, if too many processes are occurring simultaneously, then the system may become overloaded, resulting in the loss of information from memory.

The first hypothesis – that the span of STM is limited – was investigated by testing skilled and less-skilled readers' retention of digits. The groups were not found to differ on a standard digit-span test, indicating that there were no general differences between them in STM capacity. A further experiment explored recall of word and picture lists, and investigated possible differences between the groups in their use of phonological recoding and rehearsal in STM.

Taken together, the results of these experiments suggest that the poor comprehenders do not have a general deficit in short-term memory capacity, and do not differ in the basic memorisation strategies that they utilise. However, they do not necessarily have adequate capacity of the sort required for understanding text. The results of our non-verbal working-memory test showed that poor comprehenders make less efficient use of working memory than do skilled comprehenders. This deficit is not, however, a general problem of verbal memory: we have shown that the less-skilled comprehenders are as good as skilled ones at recalling lists of unconnected words, and at using articulatory coding. It would seem that problems only arise when substantial storage and processing demands are made concurrently. It is possible that poor comprehenders fail to adopt appropriate strategies when extra processing demands are imposed, and that their normal strategies break down. (We will be discussing the use of strategies further in Chapter 6.) The difficulties of poor comprehenders may, at least in part, be related to their poorer use of working memory. This would account for their performance in the experiments described in Chapter 4: less-skilled children do not integrate information in text, and make fewer inferences during reading, skills that require use of both the storage and processing components of working memory. Their relative lack of inferential processing is more marked in cases where inferences are complex, or when greater memory loads are imposed (e.g. see Experiments 4.5, 4.6).

We have not specified precisely which aspects of comprehension are dependent on working memory. There is some research on older subjects that addresses this issue. Dixon, LeFevre and Twilley (1988) studied the relation between the standard reading-span test and various measures of reading skill in undergraduates. They found that the span test predicted performance on a standardised comprehension test, but not on a test of inferential ability requiring the use of world knowledge in making plausible inferences. They argued that the comprehension tests with which reading span has been found to correlate require memory for only superficial features of the text. Their inference task, on the other hand, required the construction of a deeper, referential representation (e.g. a mental model), and the processing efficiency needed for this was not measured by the reading span test. We would argue that performance on the comprehension test we used, the Neale Analysis, does rely on the construction of a mental model of the text, as only a few of the answers can be derived directly from a superficial representation of the text.

Investigating locus of processing using reading time

We have suggested several ways in which working memory limitations may have detrimental effects on text integration and inference. However, we cannot tell from the results exactly where the difference between groups lies. For example, in the constructive inference experiment (4.1) the skilled children may have produced more false recognitions either because they integrated the sentences as they read, or because they made inferences when they heard the foil sentences. Thus, less-skilled comprehenders may differ from skilled comprehenders not in their ability to draw inferences, but in *when* they do so. Data from the experiment on instantiation (Experiment 4.3) provide some support for the idea that skilled children, but not less-skilled ones, draw inferences *during* the process of comprehension. Less-skilled comprehenders may simply leave it too late, and may have forgotten some of the original premises by the time an inference is required. Their ability to recover from such difficulties may be further hampered by their poorer working memories, in that they may be less able than skilled children to think back to the original text and make inferences from it.

To make a further assessment of this hypothesis of differences in locus of processing, we needed to look at processing during reading. The most direct method of doing this is to measure reading times for different segments of text. We therefore investigated differences between the groups in reading strategies using on-line measures of reading.

We developed a portable microprocessor system to present our materials and to store, sort and analyse the data. In the two experiments we report below, children were presented with short stories clause-by-clause on a visual display unit. They read each display silently, pressing a response key to produce the next display, and using separate response keys to answer yes/no questions about what they had read. The procedure was self-paced, in that the child could pause between each story or task, and press a key in response to the prompt 'Next one' as soon as they were ready to continue.

We should note here that such methods have rarely been used with children of this age, although they are common in research with adult readers. We found the procedure very labour-intensive and time-consuming, as children had to become familiar with the equipment. We also had to make sure that children did not show slow reading times for particular sentences simply because they encountered a word they could not decode. Our first method of overcoming this potential problem was to have the children read aloud, so that the experimenter could provide any words at which they hesitated. However, a central aim of using the reading-time equipment was to provide a relatively unobtrusive index of processing efficiency. Reading aloud can produce oral dysfluency that works against this aim, therefore we performed the studies reported here using silent reading. Before each experiment, children practised using the equipment, reading a short story and answering questions using the response keys, and read a list of the more difficult words used in the experiment. We hoped thereby to avoid the problem of children becoming 'stuck' on a word, although the experimenter was at hand to help if required.

The reading-time method enabled us to measure the time spent examining particular segments of text, and in answering questions about the text displayed. In this way, we could investigate the relative time to read text and to answer a question. Children who draw inferences as the text is presented will spend relatively longer reading those parts of a text that require an inference to be understood, and less time answering a related question, than children who do not draw the inference until the question appears.

Experiment 5.3: *Reading time and pronoun resolution*

We have shown previously that the two groups differ in their ability to resolve anaphors in text (Experiments 4.4–4.6). As a preliminary investigation, we therefore decided to look more closely at the locus of children's processing of anaphors. In this experiment, we studied resolution of pronouns which were either syntactically ambiguous (no gender cue) or unambiguous (gender cue present). The position of the antecedent was counterbalanced so that, within each cue condition, it occurred equally often as subject or object of the first clause. This gave four different types of sentences, as shown in these examples:

No gender cue, object-referring:

Betty showed Karen how to do the sums because she was bad at number.

No gender cue, subject-referring:

Betty showed Karen how to do the sums because she was good at number.

Gender cue, object-referring:

Bob showed Karen how to do the sums because she was bad at number.

Gender cue, subject-referring:

Betty showed Kevin how to do the sums because she was good at number.

After each sentence, children answered a question requiring pronoun resolution, e.g.

Who was good at number?
Betty Kevin

They responded by pressing the response key that was on the same side of the response box as the position of the name on the screen.

Method Twelve children in each skill group took part in this study. There were four practice items and forty experimental ones, evenly divided between the four conditions, and in one of four randomly ordered lists in which each material appeared in each of the four conditions across lists. We measured the time taken to read the entire sentence, and the time to respond to the question.

Results The results were analysed using analyses of variance, with group between subjects and antecedent position and presence of gender cue within subjects, with the additional factor of line (sentence or question) for the sentence-reading and question-response times. In common with our other studies of reading time, we adopted the procedure of replacing times for wrong responses by each subject's mean time for the particular experimental condition or, if there were not enough data for within-subjects' replacement, by the mean times for other subjects in a particular condition.[2] We also performed analyses of data including the times for incorrect responses, but do not report these unless the pattern of results differed from the analysis of correct responses.

Responses to questions. The skilled children performed slightly better than the less-skilled ones, with mean percentages correct of 74 and 71 respectively, but the difference was not significant, $F_1 < 1$ $F_2 (1, 9) = 2.66$, $p < .14$. There was also a main effect for presence of gender cue, $F_1 (1, 22) = 9.43$, $p < .01$, $F_2 (1, 9) = 5.6$, $p < .05$. As anticipated, there were more correct answers for sentences with gender cues (76%) than without (69%). Both groups showed a bias to pick the object, as shown by the main effect of antecedent position, $minF' (1, 33) = 13.31$, $p < .01$. This could simply reflect a tendency to press the key on the dominant side, as the 'object' response was always the right-hand key. However, this explanation does not account for the significant interaction between antecedent position and cue, $F_1 (1, 22) = 9.14$, $p < .01$, $F_2 (1, 9) = 6.24$, $p < .05$. Inspection of this interaction showed that the object-bias was particularly marked in the more difficult condition, when gender cues were absent. The mean numbers of correct responses in each condition are shown in Table 5.3.

Reading times. The skilled children tended to take slightly longer to read the sentences and answer questions than the less-skilled ones (6.50s vs 6.16s for both lines combined), but the main effect of group was significant only by materials and not by subjects, $F_1 < 1$, $F_2 (1, 39) = 10.86$, $p < .002$. There was also a main effect of line, $min F' (29) = 150.34$, $p < .0001$, which just reflects differences in line length that we did not attempt to control. The interaction of line and group was significant by materials but not by subjects, $F_1 (1, 22) = 2.0$, $p < .17$, $F_2 (1, 39) = 14.08$, $p < .001$. As Table 5.4 shows, both groups spent about the same amount of time on the questions, but the skilled children took longer to read the sentences containing the pronouns, although the latter difference was significant by Tukey's HSD test for materials only, at $p < .05$. The pattern of results is consistent with the idea that skilled children resolve the pronoun on reading the sentence and so have an advantage when answering the question. This interpretation is supported by the fact that the skilled children showed a significant positive correlation between sentence reading time and number of correct answers to questions, $r (11) = .59$, $p < .05$, whereas less-skilled children showed no such relation, $r (11) = -0.04$, n.s.

The results of this preliminary study were not clear-cut, and the data for individual children were very variable. However, there was some indication that the groups might differ in their reading strategies. For skilled children, the longer they took to read the sentences, the more likely they were to answer a question about the sentences correctly. Poor comprehenders showed no such relation. We mentioned in Chapter 1 Carver's (1987) argument that differences between good and poor readers could be accounted for by differences in study

Table 5.3. *Mean number of correct responses to pronoun questions as a function of antecedent position and presence of gender cue (max = 10)*

	Antecedent position		
	Subject	Object	Difference
Gender cue	7·08	8·21	1·13
No gender cue	5·66	8·12	2·46*

* = $p < 0{\cdot}05$ (Tukey's HSD).

Table 5.4. *Mean time (seconds) to read the clauses containing pronouns and to answer the questions in each skill group*

	Clause	Question
Less-skilled	8·36	3·98
Skilled	9·21	3·80
Difference	0·85*	−0·18

* = $p < 0{\cdot}05$ by materials only (Tukey's HSD).

time. In this experiment, poor comprehenders certainly spent less time on the clauses containing a pronoun than the good ones did. Carver would argue that giving children more study time would improve their comprehension. However, this seems unlikely in the case of our poor comprehenders for two reasons. Firstly, they showed no relation between reading time and response accuracy, so they were no more likely to answer correctly when they spent a relatively long time reading a clause. Secondly, poor comprehenders do not seem to benefit from the opportunity of studying a text. In Experiment 4.2, the children were permitted to study the text to find answers to questions, but did not do any better on inferential questions than when they answered such questions from memory. Similarly, Experiment 4.4 showed that poor comprehenders made more errors in pronoun resolution than skilled children even when they could inspect the clause containing the pronoun. Thus, the problem seems to lie not in the study time available, but in how to use that time. The good comprehenders may have been more aware of the need to resolve pronouns as they were reading than the poor comprehenders were. We investigate the issue of comprehension awareness in more detail in the next chapter.

Experiment 5.4: *Reading time and conditional statements*

The previous experiment provided some evidence for the existence of differences between the two skill groups in reading strategies. However, the strategy differences did not lead to significant differences between the groups in their performance on the questions. One possible reason for this pattern of results is that the texts we used may have been so short that they were easy to memorise verbatim, and the differing strategies had no effect on the outcome. We therefore decided to assess the effect of strategy differences on comprehension using longer texts, and by investigating directly the effect of a memory load on performance. We also took the opportunity to assess children's comprehension skills using inferences other than anaphoric reference. We used a type of deductive inference, conditional reasoning of the form 'If A, then B. B, therefore A'. We embedded such inferences in short descriptions, and varied demands on working memory by inserting filler sentences between the first and second propositions.

Children read short stories containing descriptions of the form:

1 If A occurs, then B will occur.
2 A occurs.
3 C (a probable consequence of B) occurs.
4 Why did C occur?

For example, one of the stories was as follows:

Paul had fifty pence to spend at the fair.
1 If Paul didn't buy a hot dog, he could ride on the big wheel.
2 Paul didn't buy a hot dog.
3 Later, Paul was very happy.
4 Why was Paul very happy?

The correct answer to the question (4) requires the reader to integrate the conditional statement (1) with the assertion of the antecedent (2), that Paul didn't buy a hot dog, and to infer the consequence, that Paul must have spent his money on a ride. The occurrence of the consequence explains the further consequence (3) that Paul was happy. In half the stories, a filler sentence was inserted between the conditional (1) and the assertion of the antecedent (2), to increase the processing load, e.g.

1a He liked going to the fair very much.

We expected that poor comprehenders would find the questions harder to answer than good comprehenders, because they required inferential processing, and that performance would decrease for less-skilled children in particular, when a filler intervened between antecedent and consequent.

Method Sixteen children in each skill group read two practice and sixteen experimental stories. Half of the stories contained filler sentences (the memory load) and half had no such load. We used two different lists of materials, such that each story appeared without a filler in one list, and with a filler in the other. In each list, half the materials included fillers, and the stories were randomly ordered. Children were randomly assigned to lists, with the proviso that equal numbers in each skill group were given each list. We measured the time taken to read the antecedent (2) and the further consequence (3), as well as checking whether children had made the required inference to the question (4).

Results We analysed the results by analysis of variance, with skill group and list (list 1 or list 2) between subjects and memory load (absent or present) within subjects, with the additional factor of line (antecedent or consequent) for the analysis of reading times.

Responses to questions. Coding the responses to the questions was straightforward, as the children either gave unambiguously correct responses (e.g. for the example given above, 'because he went on the big wheel'), or incorrectly negated the antecedents (e.g. 'because he had a hot dog') or gave 'don't know' responses. As we anticipated, the poor comprehenders gave fewer correct answers than the good comprehenders did, with average percentages correct of 73% and 83% respectively. The main effect of group yielded F_1 (1, 28) = 4.73, $p < .05$, F_2 (1, 15) = 7.38, $p < .05$. However, memory load did not affect the number of correct responses, nor did it interact with group, all Fs < 1. There were no other significant effects, except an uninterpretable interaction between list and memory load.

Reading times. We analysed reading times using the same method as the question responses, with the additional factor of line type (antecedent or consequent). We replaced times for which wrong responses were given with mean scores within subjects.

All analyses showed highly significant main effects for line type, and we do not report these further, as they could merely reflect differences in line length, which we did not attempt to control. Because there was an indication of a three-way interaction between line type, memory load and skill group, F_1 (1, 30) = 1.8, $p < .19$, F_2 (1, 15) = 7.57, $p < .01$, we analysed the data separately for each skill group. Again, we omit mention of the significant effects of line type.

The analysis for the skilled group showed no main effect of memory load, both Fs < 1, but an interaction of line and load that was significant by materials, though not by subjects, F_1 (1, 15) = 2.88, $p < .11$, F_2 (1, 15) = 8.06, $p < .01$. In contrast, the less-skilled children showed no significant effects other than for line type. The mean times for each group are shown in Table 5.5. The poor comprehenders showed no differences in response time between the two memory load conditions for either the antecedent or the consequent. The good comprehenders, on the other hand, tended to spend less time on the antecedent

Table 5.5. *Mean time (seconds) to read the antecedent and consequent sentences with and without a memory load in each skill group*

	Less-skilled			Skilled		
	No load	Load	Diff.	No load	Load	Diff.
Antecedent	5·15	5·18	−0·03	5·69	5·30	0·39
Consequent	4·01	4·00	0·01	3·98	4·27	−0·29
Difference	1·14	1·18	−0·04	1·71	1·03	0·68*

* = $p < 0{\cdot}05$ by materials only (Tukey's HSD).

when there was a memory load than when there was no load, and more time on the consequent when there was a load than when there was not. This higher-order comparison was significant by materials, but not by subjects, as shown in Table 5.5. Although such a pattern was not anticipated, the results may be interpreted in the following way: in the 'no load' condition, the assertion of the antecedent immediately follows the conditional statement. This may act as a cue to draw the deductive inference that the second clause of the consequent is true. Skilled children therefore may have picked up this cue, and made the inference as they read the antecedent. When a filler sentence intervened between conditional and antecedent, they deferred drawing the inference until the further consequence in (3). The less-skilled children showed similar reading times within each line for the two load conditions, and so did not seem to be responsive to such cues, as their lower scores on responses to questions also suggests.

Discussion of Experiments 5.3–5.4

The results of these reading-time studies provide limited support for our idea that less-skilled comprehenders do not make inferences until they are asked a direct question requiring them to do so. In Experiment 5.3, this delayed-processing strategy had no effect on correct responses, but this may have been because the texts were very short, and inferences could easily have been drawn retrospectively. In the experiment just described, in which we used longer texts, the skilled children gave more correct answers, and we suggested that this was because they made inferences as they were reading.

The less-skilled children seem to engage in less inferential processing during reading, and this affects the representation of the text that they later have available to answer questions. However, the results were not conclusive, and none of the experiments showed a direct effect of reading strategy on comprehension, as measured by response accuracy. One possible reason for the lack of clear results is that, despite extensive practice, and our use of familiar vocabulary, the children produced reading times with wide individual variation. This variation may have obscured differences between the groups and between conditions. Thus, although this method did produce some interesting results, we feel that further refinements are needed to make reading-time techniques useful for this age group, and we did not pursue this line of research further. However, in the next chapter, we report a study in which we found group differences in inspection times when varying fairly gross aspects of textual cohesion, in comparison to the more subtle factors varied in the experiments of this chapter.

General discussion

In this chapter, we went beyond the account given in Chapter 3, that less-skilled children show no general memory deficit that would explain their poor text comprehension. We suggested instead that less-skilled comprehenders have a poorer *working memory*: that is, they are less able to remember and process information concurrently. It is this form of memory that appears to be particularly important in reading and in constructing a mental model of a text.

In the present chapter, we also investigated differences in locus of processing, and found evidence that was consistent with our suggestion that skilled children construct mental models as they read or listen. We also introduced another way of describing working memory inefficiency: in terms of strategies. Thus, in the reading-time studies, if the presence of a pronoun is not taken as a cue to draw an inference about its referent, then in longer texts, it may be impossible to retrieve the relevant information later, when it is needed. Work in adults suggests that they build up mental models of text *as they read*, and this concurrent construction will maximise the efficiency of working memory. The finding that reading time in less-skilled children was not related to their ability to resolve pronouns is consistent with our earlier finding, that allowing poor comprehenders to study a text did not improve their comprehension (Experiment 4.2). It seems that these children would not know how to make use of extra reading time. Even if made aware of their comprehension failure, it is unclear whether they would be able to use extra study time to resolve a comprehension problem.

The findings of our previous experiments on inference and integration could be expressed in terms of the concurrent construction of a mental model of a text while reading or listening. For example, in our study of constructive inference (Experiment 4.1), regardless of whether they were instructed to memorise or to understand text, the skilled children seemed to integrate ideas and construct a coherent mental model, whereas the less-skilled comprehenders tended to generate a representation closer to the verbatim text. Spontaneous use of integration requires that some judgement, explicit or implicit, is made during reading, of what information is important, what inferences are warranted, and what sort of information might be expected later in a text. That is, reading is a highly strategic activity, and underlying expectations can guide the nature of the reader's processing activities. As the research in the previous chapter shows, even less-skilled comprehenders have expectations about pronominal references. In this 'concurrent processing' model, inferences drawn from the text may be represented, implicitly or explicitly, in a mental model, and are as accessible as the original information. New consistent information will therefore be judged 'original'. The next chapter looks more closely at the issue of strategies in comprehension, comparing the two groups' ability to make judgements, explicitly or implicitly, about which parts of a text are most important. We also look more generally at children's awareness of their own text comprehension.

6 Metacognition and reading

Introduction

In previous chapters, we have suggested that good comprehenders are more strategic readers, in the sense that they make relevant inferences when they can, and hence build up a detailed internal model of the text as they go along. The less-skilled children seem to use a less efficient strategy – they often appear to treat each phrase of text as an isolated unit, and tend not to integrate successive ideas. If they are required to perform some integration, for example by being asked a direct question requiring an inference, their pattern of reading times suggests that, unlike skilled children, they have not already made such inferences during reading. This may mean that they have to backtrack or retrieve large chunks of previous text, so that they can make required inferences, or that they just make incorrect inferences. Thus, the differences we found between the groups in the use of inference and integration may be accounted for in terms of poor working memory and inefficient on-line strategies.

Another important aspect of skilled comprehension is metacognitive awareness (e.g. see Garner, 1987). Metacognition is a general term referring to the ways in which people use their knowledge about mental processes to monitor and possibly to alter their performance. For example, if we believe that text recall is better if we remember the gist, rather than the verbatim form of the text, we will not try to memorise every word in the text. It may be that poor comprehenders show less metacognitive awareness than good comprehenders. This conclusion seems likely in view of the fact that metacognitive skills such as comprehension monitoring would make demands on working memory. Brown (1980) lists several metacognitive processes in which skilled readers engage: clarifying the purposes of reading, identifying important aspects of the message, allocating attention to relevant information, monitoring their comprehension of the message, reviewing and self-testing, taking corrective measures when needed, and recovering from disruptions and distraction. In this chapter, we look at some of these metacognitive skills: are children able to focus on the most important aspects of a text, to what extent do they monitor their text comprehension, are they able to reflect on language as an object of thought, and more generally, what is their understanding of the purpose of reading and comprehending text?

Understanding purposes in reading

Interviews on children's explicit knowledge about reading

Children's understanding of the importance of comprehension, and the causes of comprehension failure, changes at around the age of 8. For example, Sinclair (1980) found that kindergarten children suggested dealing with a listener's comprehension failures by improving surface characteristics of the message – talking more loudly, repeating the message or correcting speech errors – while 8-year-olds cited the role of semantic characteristics, such as ambiguity and unclear reference, in causing comprehension failure. The first study in this chapter explored knowledge about comprehension in the two skill groups.

We investigated knowledge about reading simply by interviewing fourteen children in each skill group, placing particular emphasis on their beliefs concerning comprehension. We asked children how much they liked reading, about characteristics of good and poor readers, and how poor readers can improve. Obviously, interview responses should be treated with some caution, as they tap children's articulated knowledge about reading, rather than being a direct measure of the knowledge that they put into practice.

First we asked what makes someone a good reader and made this question more concrete by asking each child to pick the best reader in their class. This question was deliberately ambiguous: children were free to describe the causes or the characteristics of a good reader. For most of the children in both groups, speed and accuracy were the hallmarks of a good reader: someone who reads quickly and 'knows' many words. Knowing words for these children seemed to mean the ability to decode words accurately. 'Not knowing words' was a particularly important indicator of poor reading for the less-skilled children: eleven of fourteen such children mentioned this factor spontaneously, compared to only four of the fourteen skilled children, and this difference was significant (chi square (1) = 5.16, $p < .05$).

The emphasis on decoding is not surprising, because most of these children had only recently begun to master such skills. It is at about this stage in their education (a year or two after beginning formal reading tuition) that children's definitions of reading begin to alter in emphasis in favour of comprehension. Johns (1984) reported a gradual change in conceptions of reading reported by first- to sixth-grade children: the younger ones tended to define reading in terms of word recognition or decoding whereas the older ones stressed meaning and understanding. Myers and Paris (1978) also provide evidence that younger and poorer readers believe that good reading means saying all the words correctly.

In our study, some children attributed a moral aspect to reading: poor readers were described as 'lazy', 'not attending', 'not trying their best': 'they chatter a lot and are very lazy and daydreaming'. Many of the schools we visited used reading schemes, in which children read a series of books that increase in difficulty, and can only progress onto the next book when they have mastered ones at the preceding level. The use of such schemes meant that most children were well aware of their position in relation to peers, and of their progress: 'Kevin started on Oxford 1 [the first book of a reading scheme] and now he's on Oxford 5' – 'Clare is good, because she's usually there [in the reading corner] when I change my book.'

The children's views were not necessarily a direct reflection of the teacher's approach. In one class, the teacher required correct answers to comprehension questions about a story before children could progress to the next book. One child in this class asserted that a good reader 'doesn't have to read every word'. If you don't understand, he argued, you can read an easier book or failing that, look at the pictures. But another child from the same class argued that if you knew all the words, you could go on to a higher book.

On the whole, the children's view of reading was optimistic: all except two children, one in each skill group, stated that poor readers could improve their reading, and most agreed that improvement comes through practice, or simply 'by getting older'. There was no evidence that poor comprehenders experienced reading as a difficult or unpleasant activity. When asked how much they liked reading, this group gave slightly higher ratings than the good comprehenders. Most children mentioned specific books that they enjoyed reading: some of these were books from a reading scheme but more were 'real' books. Poor comprehenders also rated themselves as slightly better readers than good comprehenders did. In their own terms of reading as decoding, they were good readers. Furthermore, their teachers often concurred with these judgements.

We also asked children to choose the better reader of two fictional children, one who reads words well but doesn't always understand, and another who understands stories but cannot read words very well. Most children in both groups picked the good decoder as the better reader. However, there was also evidence that the children were looking to a future in which comprehension would become more important: about half the children in each group said that they would prefer to be like the good comprehender, and that this child would get on better than the good decoder. One good comprehender saw the advantages of comprehension: 'Jane [good comprehender] will get on better because she understands. Mary [good decoder] will be a better reader than Jane, but Jane can understand lots of things. I'd rather understand.'

The interview data support our own intuitions that many of the poor comprehenders were not concerned about their comprehension failures, and viewed reading primarily in terms of decoding. As one child said, after picking the good comprehender as a better reader than the good decoder, 'but it's not really reading, though, is it?'. It is quite possible for children who want to do well and gain approval to become very skilled at reading words far beyond their comprehension. Progress is easily gauged and such a child is perceived by peers as successful. Furthermore, wrong decoding can be corrected immediately, whereas poor comprehension can only be assessed later. Comprehension is harder to measure and less universally acknowledged as important, in that the most visible educational resources are devoted to promoting decoding skills. Even the good comprehenders did not always mention good comprehension as an important feature of reading.

Tunmer and Bowey (1984) propose a metalinguistic account of how children may come to be good decoders but poor comprehenders. Children's initial task of learning correspondences between written symbols (graphemes) and their spoken sounds (phonemes) means attending to surface features of words and ignoring their sentential context. As soon as the correspondences are mastered, though, children need to be aware of the syntactic groupings of words, in order to understand the text. Children need this explicit awareness, in the early stages of reading at least, because they need to transfer their implicit knowledge of spoken language to written language. Some children, according to Tunmer and Bowey, fail to apply their implicit syntactic knowledge in this way, and so continue to read word-by-word. They cite evidence from Weaver (1979), among others, showing that instruction in grammatical structure (training in reordering jumbled words in a sentence) led to improved reading comprehension in comparison to children given no training. Weaver only used 'good' and 'average' readers, and further work is needed to show whether this link between grammatical awareness and reading comprehension applies to poor comprehenders.

It seems from the interviews that there is some difference between the groups on the first type of metacognitive skill mentioned by Brown (1980): understanding the purposes of reading. The next skill she mentions is identifying important aspects of the message. In both narrative and expository text, some aspects of the message are essential, and other aspects are less important details. In our memory for text, we tend to store features such as the basic plot, while details which do not contribute to the plot may be more easily forgotten. There are two general ways in which this differentiation between degrees of importance might be manifested: implicitly, in that important information is attended to and recalled better than trivial information, and explicitly, in the ability to specify which aspects of a text are most important. We look at both these aspects in the following experiments.

Experiment 6.1: *Recall of story information varying in importance*

Older readers are said to be better at remembering the propositional structure of a text and show more knowledge of story structure than younger readers

(Baker and Stein, 1981), although there is some dispute about the existence and size of any developmental differences (Stein, 1982). Brown and Smiley (1977) found that the ability to make explicit judgements about how important each unit of a text was to the text theme improved with age, although they note that performance depended partly on the complexity of the text. However, these authors also noted that subjects of all ages tested, from 8 to 18 years, were able to use importance information implicitly, in that they tended to recall information judged by adults as important better than information rated as less important. They also suggest that such effects could be found in even younger children. This differential recall according to importance level also depends on reading ability: the recall probability of a particular text unit by good seventh-grade readers was more clearly a function of that unit's structural importance than was the case in poor readers of the same grade (Smiley, Oakley, Worthen, Campione and Brown, 1977). However, even the poor readers in that study were able to make some discrimination in degree of importance: they recalled more material of the highest importance level than of the other three levels combined, although they did not distinguish among the lower levels of importance. These results were obtained for both reading and listening comprehension. Hess (1982) found that fourth- and sixth-grade less-skilled comprehenders recalled information differentially according to its thematic importance, although there was some indication that they did not do so to the extent that skilled children did. Given that our subjects were at the lower end of the age range used in the studies by Smiley and her colleagues and by Hess, we expected that the good comprehenders would show clear discrimination by importance level, whereas poor ones would be less likely to make such discriminations in their recall.

The influence of importance level on recall may have a diminishing influence over time for some less-skilled readers. Oakhill, Shaw and Folkard (1983) found that 11-year-old children who were classed as educationally subnormal (ESN) tended to recall important information better than less-important information when tested immediately, as did control groups matched with them for chronological age or for reading age. However, unlike the control groups, the ESN children were not affected by the importance level of information in the original story when their memory was tested one week later. Oakhill et al. suggest that these children did not make use of importance levels when consolidating their memory for text – that is, they did not attempt to build an integrated semantic representation of the story which reflected the differential importance of information. Our study of constructive integration (Experiment 4.1) showed that less-skilled comprehenders did not build integrated representations of short texts to the extent that skilled children did. The same might be true for their comprehension of relatively long stories. Thus, their recall of a story after a delay may be less affected by the level of importance of information in the story structure than skilled children's recall.

Method We conducted this experiment with two sets of children in separate terms, and have combined the data here, as both sets gave similar results. There were twenty-eight children in each skill group.

The materials comprised a simplified and shortened 700-word version of a story selected from a suitable collection of stories for 7-year-olds ('Titus in Trouble': Corrin and Corrin, 1982). The story was about a boy in Victorian London who finds some lost jewels. We prepared an initial pool of sixty-five questions about the story, with four possible responses for each question. Four adults read the story and then rated each question on a ten-point scale according to how important the information it tapped was to the story. These ratings were used to derive two sets of twenty-four questions, with six questions at each of four levels of importance. Mean ratings at each level were significantly different from those of every other level, with no overlap of importance scores between levels. The questions within each set appeared in the same temporal order as the events to which they referred appeared in the story.

The children heard the story in groups of three to six, knowing that they would be asked questions afterwards. Apart from this requirement, though, the experimenter, who was quite familiar to the children, did not present the story as a memory test: this procedure was intended to reproduce the sorts of conditions in which the children usually heard stories read to them. Immediately after the story, the experimenter gave out one of the two sets of typed multiple-choice questionnaires. The experimenter read out each question in turn, repeating it as often as necessary, and encouraged children to guess if they did not know the answer. The children recorded their responses by marking one of the four alternatives, as they had been shown in a short practice trial. One week later, at about the same time of day, the children completed a second, unexpected questionnaire containing the alternate set of questions. The order in which the two forms were presented was counterbalanced. Four children were absent for the second test, and these children completed the second questionnaire 1 to 5 days later than planned. This made no apparent difference to their overall performance.

Results The results were analysed by analysis of variance, with skill group and presentation order of the alternate question-forms between subjects, and time of testing (immediate or delayed) and importance level within subjects. There was a main effect of group, $minF'\ (1, 56) = 26.96$, $p < .0001$ showing that overall, the skilled children answered more questions correctly than the less-skilled ones, with mean percentages correct of 67.5 and 45.7 respectively. This result corroborates our earlier findings suggesting that the groups differ not purely in reading comprehension, but also in their aural comprehension skills. Furthermore, the conditions under which children heard the story in this study were similar to those they commonly encountered at school.

There was also a significant main effect of importance level, minF' $(3, 20) = 5.45$, $p < .05$. Newman–Keuls comparisons showed that scores on each level were significantly different from every other level at $p < .01$, except that the two middle levels did not differ from each other. Furthermore, there was a significant linear trend for scores to decrease with decreasing importance level, $F (1, 156) = 23.98$, $p < .001$. The scores for each level of importance on the two occasions of testing are shown separately for each skill group in Table 6.1.

Contrary to expectation, the two groups did not differ in their sensitivity to importance level: the interaction of group and importance level was not significant, $Fs < 1$. However, importance level did interact with time of test, $F_1 (3, 156) = 8.80$, $p < .0001$, $F_2 (3, 15) = 2.95$, $p < .07$. This interaction seemed to be due mainly to the fact that scores for the least important questions dropped particularly sharply after a week's delay (see lower part of Table 6.1). Thus, it appears that both groups of children tended to retain important information better than less important, and memory for the less important information was particularly poor after a week's delay. There were no other significant effects, except for an uninterpretable interaction of importance level with questionnaire form.

Discussion These results yielded no evidence that poor comprehenders fail to take advantage of differences in importance of information in text, suggesting that they have some knowledge, albeit implicit, of differences in importance level. We cannot, of course, rule out the possibility that this discrimination could be made on some fairly superficial basis, e.g. perhaps the incidents rated as more important were particularly salient, but not central to the story line. The issue of what makes particular information 'important' is not resolved here. Some authors (e.g. Kintsch and van Dijk, 1978) take the view that text recall is related to the 'height' of an idea in the hierarchical structure of a text, and that people represent the meaning of a text in the form of a structured list of propositions derived from the text using a set of rules. However, no rules have yet been formulated to derive such a list of propositions from a text. A different approach to text structure, the 'mental models' viewpoint, is to consider it not as an inherent attribute of text, but as a particular representation of text, dependent on an individual reader's knowledge of the world, that is not specific to story comprehension (e.g. see Garnham, 1987). Whichever account turns out to be correct, it seems that in this experiment, poor comprehenders structured their recall of text in a similar way to good comprehenders. Another possible explanation for better performance on more important items is that the questions addressing the information may have been easier than questions for less-important items. The latter possibility seems unlikely, though, as we had previously asked seven adults to rate the difficulty of the inference required in each question, and ratings were not significantly different for any of the levels

Table 6.1. *Mean scores for each importance level as a function of time of test and comprehension skill (max = 6)*

	Importance level (1 = highest)				
	1	2	3	4	Mean
Immediate					
Less-skilled	3·61	2·96	3·18	2·71	3·12
Skilled	4·89	4·32	4·39	4·00	4·40
Mean	4·25	3·64	3·79	3·36	3·76
Delayed					
Less-skilled	3·25	2·14	2·79	1·29	2·37
Skilled	4·64	3·89	4·00	2·29	3·71
Mean	3·95	3·02	3·39	1·79	3·04
Difference:					
Immediate–delayed	0·30	0·62	0·40	1·57*	

Note: * $p < 0{\cdot}01$ (Tukey's HSD test).

of importance. Also, even if importance levels were discriminated on a fairly superficial basis, it is still relevant to note that less-skilled children's recall reflected the adults' ratings of importance. This differential recall reflects the construction of an integrated representation of the events in the text.

Experiment 6.2: Explicit judgements of main ideas in stories[1]

Despite the finding that even young and poor readers tend to show discriminations in importance in their recall, previous research shows that their performance is not as good when they are asked to make explicit judgements about importance. Brown and Smiley (1977) found that, although third-graders recalled important information better than more trivial aspects of a story, they did not show any systematic pattern when asked to judge each unit in terms of how important it was to the text as a whole. Thus, they showed an implicit recognition of importance level, but no explicit awareness, unlike older children, who were capable of doing both. The authors suggest that the ability to identify important information could help children to improve their reading skills further: the children in their study showed better recall with age.

As well as containing information varying in level of importance, texts also often have a particular message or point to convey to the reader. The message might be quite explicit, as in fables which have a moral, or more implicit, as in stories that have an ironic 'twist' at the end. For example, in the story that we used in our study of anaphor resolution (Experiment 4.6), the main character is praised for catching a fish, even though he only did so because he felt sea-sick, and gave his sandwiches to a seagull, which rewarded him with the fish. Informal observation suggested that many poor comprehenders completely missed the point of this story, and thus failed to appreciate the referents of particular anaphors. We therefore investigated the abilities of children in the two skill groups to pick out the single most important point of a story, using two different media: verbal and pictorial.

Selecting the main point of a verbal story: Method Sixteen children in each skill group served as subjects. They listened to a story describing the adventures of a boy trying to earn his living in Victorian London. He is rather clumsy, and breaks a vase in a shop, which he has to pay for. As he has no money, he has to go out and earn some. After losing several jobs because of his clumsiness, the boy serendipitously finds some long-lost jewels when he accidentally drops a piece of furniture he is helping to move. The main twist in the story is that his initial problem is brought about by his clumsiness, but is also resolved by the same quality. Immediately after listening to the story, children answered a set of twenty-four questions (described more fully in Experiment 6.1) and then performed a rating task requiring them to pick out the main point. They heard a set of four statements about the story and were asked to pick the one that best described 'what the story was about, what the point of it was'. The statements fell into four categories, derived from those used by Yussen (1982), in a study of children's ratings of main points. One described the main point, one was the main event in the story, one described the story setting, and one represented an incorrect version of the main point. The four statements were as follows:

Titus's clumsiness brings him a reward (main point)
Titus comes across the family jewels (main event)
Titus's life in old London (setting)
Titus searches for treasure and finds it (incorrect main point)

Results The less-skilled comprehenders' ratings were almost evenly divided between the four statements, but ten of the sixteen skilled children made the correct choice. The skilled children's preference for the correct choice fell short of significance (binomial probability = .08). However, this group did make the correct choice, rather than any of the other three choices, significantly more often than the less-skilled children did, chi square (1) = 4.57, $p < .05$. Furthermore, the less-skilled children's performance did not approach significance, binomial $p = .37$. Thus, it seems that although both groups are able to discriminate between more and less important information in their recall, the skilled children are better at explicitly selecting the single most important point of a story. It could be argued that the less-skilled children just did not understand the task, considering that children had only a brief explanation of what was required, and were not given any practice. We sought to remedy this defect in the following study, in which children were given more explanation and practice in the rating task.

Selecting the main point of picture stories: Method Twelve children in each skill group, who were taking part in Experiment 7.1, served as subjects. Their main task in the experiment was to tell a story from a sequence of pictures. The sequences were taken from the Picture Arrangement Test (PAT) of the Wechsler Intelligence Scale for Children (WISC-R: Wechsler, 1974). These pictures had already been used successfully by Yussen (1982) in a study of main point ratings. The six sequences used were items 1, 2, 7, 8, 10 and 11, and short synopses of these stories are given in Chapter 7, where the main study is described (in Table 7.3). As in the previous study of ratings of verbal stories, four statements were devised for each story. For example, item 8 of the PAT shows a cowboy looking at a lasso in a shop window. He enters the shop and buys the lasso. He then uses it to tie up the shopkeeper and raid the till. The four statements about this story were as follows:

A cowboy tricks and robs the shopkeeper (main point)
A cowboy buys a lasso (main event)
A cowboy is in the shop (setting)
A kind shopkeeper gives the cowboy some money (incorrect main point)

Seven adults categorised the four points for each story into the four statement types with complete agreement.

After telling each story, subjects saw the four statements for that story, typed on separate cards, and were asked to say which was 'the most important thing about the story, the point of it'. They then placed the other cards in rank order of how well they described the story. The children had practice, with feedback, on this task, using the practice item of the PAT, to ensure that they understood what was required. On each occasion that they made a rating, children were reminded of what they had to do.

Results and discussion We first assessed whether children's performance was better than chance, to check whether they understood the task in principle. The skilled children showed better than chance performance on each of the six stories, with all binomial probabilities $< .01$. There were never fewer than seven of the twelve children in this group picking the correct choice on any of the six sequences. The less-skilled children fared less well: they picked the correct main point at a rate better than chance expectancy in only three of the six stories. For each of these, six or more of the children picked the correct main point (binomial $p < .01$). Thus, it seems that they were capable of understanding what was required. Interestingly, these three stories were the sequences that were the lowest three in the WISC sequences that we chose (the first, second and seventh of the twelve stories in the test), and therefore found to be easier to sequence than the other picture stories. Thus, although they seemed able to do the task, less-skilled children only succeeded for the less complex sequences. The complexity ratings on the PAT were derived empirically, but it is interesting for our purposes to make some speculation about why some of the stories were not appreciated by the poor comprehenders. The stories on which they did not succeed all involved deception or misunderstanding: the cowboy pretends to be a genuine customer (item 8 of the PAT), a boy, rather than planting a tree as he has been told, takes the worms unearthed during digging to go fishing (item 10), and a man interprets an accidental blow by a passer-by as intentional, and the passer-by interprets the man's retaliation as unprovoked (item 11). One of the simpler stories also involves a form of self-deception (painting a very flattering self-portrait), but this seems to involve an exaggeration, rather than a reverse of the truth, as in the other cases. The other two stories on which poor comprehenders performed well involve perhaps less complex twists: a boxer is at first losing, but fate is reversed and he wins, and two picnickers are surprised when they find out their food has been taken. Given that false belief is a complex concept emerging from around the age of four years (e.g. Wimmer and Perner, 1983; Perner, 1988), it may be that poor comprehenders lacked the conceptual skills required to appreciate the source of the misunderstandings in the stories. This is not to say that they cannot understand false beliefs in their simplest form; we are merely suggesting that they fail to recognise how false beliefs and misunderstandings contribute to the denouement of these sequences. The question of whether poor comprehenders can deal with multiple interpretations is further dealt with later in this chapter, when we investigate linguistic ambiguity and riddles.

In addition to comparing the results against chance, we also compared the overall performance of the two groups. For this purpose, we gave one point for recognition of the correct main point for each of the six stories. The scores were analysed by analysis of variance, with skill group between subjects. As expected, there was a main effect of skill group, $F(1, 16) = 14.77$, $p < .002$. Skilled children were more likely to pick the intended main point, with 79% of such choices, than less-skilled comprehenders, who did so only 46% of the time.

Given that the PAT is part of an intelligence test, it could be argued that the results show less-skilled children to be generally less intelligent than skilled ones. However, this seems unlikely, because Yussen (1982) found no significant relation between the PAT as used to test intelligence (sorting the pictures into the correct order) and the ability to judge the main point correctly.

Discussion of Interview Study and Experiments 6.1–6.2

The previous studies indicate not only some interesting differences between the two groups, but also show aspects in which their performance is similar. Both groups of children showed better recall of information that was more important in a story, and both showed a particular decline in recall of trivial information after a week's delay. The less-skilled children did show lower performance overall, supporting our contention that the difference between the groups in comprehension skills is not specific to reading, but is also apparent in a listening task.

The two groups did differ, however, in making judgements about the main point of a story. The central point of a story is what gives the individual events an overall coherence. Picking out this aspect requires two types of skill: making inferences in understanding what the story is about, and explicitly recognising the main point. Differential recall of information varying in importance does not require any explicit reflection on one's knowledge of the story, but merely depends on which ideas and events in the story are most accessible in memory. Poor comprehenders' lower performance in rating the point of the picture sequences suggests that they are less aware of the overall purpose of a story than the good comprehenders, who performed better than chance on even the most complex stories.

The interview data too show that, while both groups were concerned with the role of decoding in reading, poor comprehenders were particularly likely to mention this aspect. Apart from this difference, though, the two groups gave quite similar responses: there were no differences between the groups in assessments of how good they were at reading, and how much they enjoyed reading. Poor comprehenders' emphasis on local aspects of text (words), to the exclusion of more global features, was also reflected in our studies of importance ratings, in that these children could not reliably select the main point of a story. None of the above experiments required reading skill: rather, the studies assessed children's explicit knowledge about reading, their listening comprehension and their understanding of picture sequences.

Comprehension monitoring and comprehension repair

When we introduced our two typical good and poor comprehenders in Chapter 1, we noted that the good comprehender commented to herself about her understanding, saying that at one point, the story did not make sense. This monitoring of comprehension enabled her to re-read part of the text and to correct her misunderstanding. The poor comprehender showed no overt signs of miscomprehension, although her answers to the questions showed that she had failed to understand parts of the story. This contrast is a concrete example of the function of comprehension monitoring and repair in reading, and the importance of such skills has been increasingly recognised in research (e.g. Forrest-Pressley and Waller, 1984). Not only do skilled readers make efforts to understand what they are reading, they also check whether or not they have understood, and have various strategies available to redress any misunderstanding. Monitoring of progress is a necessary prerequisite to comprehension repair: unless you know that you have misunderstood, you will not make further efforts to clarify the text. The following two experiments investigate several aspects of monitoring and repair skills. The first experiment addresses the basic issue of whether children notice inconsistencies in text, and also whether increases in processing demands make comprehension monitoring more difficult. In the second study, textual inconsistencies were brought to children's attention explicitly, so that we could examine the ability to integrate apparent inconsistencies with information that would resolve the comprehension problem caused.

Experiment 6.3: *Detection of inconsistency in stories*

Work reviewed briefly in Chapter 2 showed that skilled readers are more likely to realise when they have not understood a text than less-skilled ones. Following Markman's (1979) demonstration that children often failed to recognise glaring inconsistencies in text, later work studied the conditions under which readers would detect anomalies. The results showed that even college students failed to report internal inconsistencies in text (Winograd and Johnston, 1982) but if conditions are favourable (e.g. subjects are given practice at criticising text, or are told what sorts of errors to look for), even 4–5-year-olds show evidence that they are aware of inconsistencies (Baker, 1984b; Tunmer, Nesdale and Pratt, 1983; Wimmer, 1979). Researchers since then have increasingly acknowledged the difficulty of studying monitoring by relying on subjects' reports. Readers, following Grice's (1975) maxim of consistency, tend to assume that text will make sense. They do not expect inconsistencies, and if these are encountered, may not comment on them, because they assume that the problem will be resolved later, or that there is a resolution, but it is not mentioned in the text and must be inferred. Subjects may also be reluctant to point out errors, particularly in an experimental setting.

One obvious way of testing whether readers do monitor comprehension routinely, even if they fail to point out inconsistencies for some reason, is to use a measure that does not require explicit recognition or judgement of inconsistency. For example, Revelle, Wellman and Karabenick (1985) used performance measures (verbal and non-verbal responses to ambiguous, unclear or impossible requests) to show that even 3-year-olds show rudimentary abilities to recognise and deal with comprehension difficulties. In studying comprehension monitoring during reading, on-line measures can be used. If readers resolve inconsistencies implicitly, then they should take longer to study inconsistent information than consistent information, even though they may not subsequently remark on the inconsistency, perhaps because they have already resolved it. A study by Harris, Kruithof, Meerum Terwogt and Visser (1981) used this method. Children of 8 and 11 years read four short stories in which grossly anomalous sentences had been inserted, taken from other stories. For example, the sentence 'He sees his hair getting shorter' appeared in an anomalous context, in a story entitled: 'At the dentist's', or a non-anomalous context, with the title 'At the hairdresser's'. Both age groups took longer to read such sentences in anomalous than non-anomalous contexts, but the older children were more able than the younger ones to detect the anomalous sentences, when they were asked, after reading the story, to pick out anything odd about the story. Similarly, Zabrucky and Ratner (1986) found that third and sixth graders read inconsistencies in stories more slowly than control information, although the older group was more likely to look back at the inconsistent information during reading, and to identify and explain the source of the inconsistencies.

There is also some evidence that anomaly detection is related to comprehension skill. August, Flavell and Clift (1984) gave fifth graders stories to read in some of which there was a page missing. The children were matched on non-verbal IQ, but differed in comprehension skill. Skilled children were more likely to detect stories with missing pages, to locate the omission, and to suggest what information could be added to repair the omission. August et al. argued that a subgroup of the less-skilled children, who showed slower reading times for inconsistent than for consistent text, were processing the text constructively, but that this processing did not lead to a conscious awareness of comprehension failure: some children made unwarranted inferences that made the stories more coherent. A second subgroup of the less-skilled children, however, may have had more basic problems in integrating text, since they did not show even minimal signs (e.g. slower reading times) of detecting a problem. Given that our less-skilled children are poorer at constructive processing than skilled children, it seemed likely that at least some of them would fall into this latter subgroup.

We investigated whether there were differences between the groups in implicit and explicit recognition of anomalies, using measures of reading time and direct questioning. Our reading-time measure was adapted from the study by Harris et al., in which children used a cardboard window that indicated which line of a page of text they were studying. This method is more naturalistic than our previous method of computer-presented materials, particularly for reading stories, as it enables the reader to look back to previous lines in the event of comprehension failure.

The anomalies used in this study concerned a violated precondition for a goal that was central to the story, or for a goal that was subsidiary to the main theme. The anomalies rested on a single word, and required the integration of

Table 6.2. *Example of an anomalous story for each goal type and distance*

Main goal – immediate Peter's birthday present Jane's friend Peter was having a party. Jane wanted to buy him a present, but there wasn't any money in the house at all. *Then Jane bought a cake for Peter. While Jane thought about what to wear, her mum wanted something to read, so she looked at a book in a shop. Jane had a lovely time at Peter's party.	Main goal – remote Peter's birthday present Jane's friend Peter was having a party. Jane wanted to buy him a present, but there wasn't any money in the house at all. Her mum looked at a book in a shop because she wanted something to read while Jane thought about what to do. *Then Jane bought a cake for Peter. Jane had a lovely time at Peter's party.
Subsidiary goal – immediate Peter's birthday present Jane's friend Peter was having a party. Jane wanted to buy him a present, but there wasn't any money in the house at all. *Her mum bought a book in a shop because she wanted something to read while Jane thought about what to do. Then Jane made a cake for Peter. Jane had a lovely time at Peter's party.	Subsidiary goal – remote Peter's birthday present Jane's friend Peter was having a party. Jane wanted to buy him a present, but there wasn't any money in the house at all. Then Jane made a cake for Peter. While Jane thought about what to wear, her mum wanted something to read *so she bought a book in a shop. Jane had a lovely time at Peter's party.
Questions 1. Was it Jane's birthday? 2. Did Jane make a cake? 3. Did Jane's mum buy a book? 4. Did Jane go to the party? 5. Did Jane or her mum have any money?	

Note: Anomalous actions are marked with an asterisk.

a precondition and an action. Anomalies in main goals should be more obvious than those in subsidiary goals if children discriminate between more and less important information. The distance between the violated precondition and the inconsistently fulfilled goal was also varied, in the expectation that anomalies would be less obvious when separated from the precondition than when they immediately followed it. We expected that skilled comprehenders would show awareness of anomalies both implicitly (slower reading times for sentences when they were inconsistent with the rest of the story than when they were consistent) and explicitly (high ability to recognise anomalous sentences when asked to find inconsistencies), particularly when the inconsistencies were most salient (i.e. when the inconsistency occurred in the main goal, and when it immediately followed a precondition which it violated). The less-skilled children may be comparatively less likely to note inconsistencies explicitly, if they perform similarly to the younger group of children in the study by Harris et al. However, they were expected to show slower reading times for inconsistent sentences, particularly in the conditions where the anomalies were most salient.

Method Sixteen children in each group took part in this experiment. The materials comprised eight stories. Each began with a title and information about the setting. This was followed, in varying order, by two goals and two preconditions of those goals. One goal was central to the story (it was the goal of the main character, and was referred to in the title) and one was subsidiary (it was either the goal of a minor character, or a peripheral goal of the main character, and was not part of the main topic mentioned in the title). In each story, a precondition of either the main goal or the subsidiary goal was violated (e.g. a girl who wants to buy a present has no money). The stories all contained a filler phrase. In the 'remote' condition, the filler separated the goal and the violated precondition, to increase memory load, while in the 'immediate' condition, the filler appeared later, so that the violated precondition immediately followed the mention of the goal. We used four different lists of materials, and every story appeared once in each of the four conditions: main goal-immediate, main goal-remote, subgoal-immediate and subgoal-remote. Table 6.2 shows one of the stories in each of these four conditions. The stories were designed so that there were minimal differences between a particular line when it was consistent and when it was inconsistent with the story, and so that neither action was more unusual than the other: for example, buying a cake is about as likely as making one. These features facilitated comparison of reading times for the two types of line with minimal confounding due to complexity or plausibility. In the example shown in Table 6.2, for the main-goal violation conditions, 'bought' was replaced by 'made', and in the subsidiary-goal violations, 'looked at' was replaced by 'bought'. The table also shows the relative positions of the information about goal and precondition in the variation of memory-load. The anomalous event appeared either immediately after the unfulfilled precondition, or as the third line following it, by appropriate insertion of filler information. As Table 6.2 shows, slight changes in wording were used to maintain the coherence of the text.

Subjects were randomly assigned to one of the four lists. The story contexts were presented in a fixed order (e.g. the example shown in Table 6.2 was always the first experimental story). There were also two consistent stories of similar length and style presented as the first and sixth stories of each list. The first story provided a practice in the method of reading (see below) while the sixth story was used to assess whether the children would report false positives: detecting errors in stories that were not designed to be anomalous.

Before starting the experiment, each child read through a list of 116 of the words used in the story, to ensure that they knew the vocabulary. The list included all the crucial verbs (e.g. 'made', 'bought') to avoid the (unlikely) possibility that differences in reading times could be attributed to differences in difficulty of decoding these words. The method of presenting the stories was adopted from that used by Harris et al. (1981). Each story was typed on a card, and the children placed a card immediately below the line they were reading, so that they could see that line and all the preceding lines of the text. This procedure ensured that the children could check preceding information, since they might look back at the precondition when reading the inconsistent goal. They moved the card from one line to the next at their own pace while the experimenter unobtrusively recorded a tap on a tape recorder to mark the points at which children moved on to and past the crucial lines (lines 5 and 8 of each story).

After each story, the children were asked five questions. Examples are shown in Table 6.2. All questions had yes/no responses, and the questions were worded so that different patterns of yes/no responses appeared in each story, and there was an equal number of positive and negative responses across all the stories. These questions appeared in the same form and order for all subjects, after each story. Three questions (1, 3 and 4: see Table 6.2) tested memory for the story, and intervened between two other questions, one about the inconsistent event (2) and one about the precondition (5). This separation was designed to make the contradiction between the latter two questions less obvious to children who had not already noticed it. Answers to the questions enabled us to see whether children had implicitly resolved the inconsistent information (for example, by saying that Jane did have some money), or whether they answered questions correctly according to the text, but maintained the inconsistency (agreeing both that Jane had no money and that she bought a cake).

The instructions did not lead the children to expect errors, but just noted that they would be reading stories and answering questions. After reading all the stories and answering the questions, the children were asked if they had noticed anything odd about any of the stories (some children had already spontaneously commented on inconsistencies, and we recorded all such comments). The experimenter showed the cards on which each story was written, and for each one in turn, asked whether there was anything odd. If the child did not point out the inconsistency, the experimenter pointed to the inconsistent event and asked whether it was odd, and recorded the child's response. For each story, children were given a score from 0-3: 3 if the anomaly was spontaneously noticed during reading, 2 if it was noted given the general prompt after reading, 1 if it was noted given the specific prompt, and 0 if not noticed at all.

There were thus three different measures of anomaly detection: responses to questions about the anomaly, anomaly-detection scores, and reading time for anomalous information.

Results *Responses to questions.* The children did well on the questions after each story, with an average score of over 83% for less-skilled, and 92% for skilled children. We noticed that sometimes children answered the questions as if the story had been consistent. Thus, they would give a wrong answer either to the question about the anomalous goal, or to that relating to the unfulfilled precondition. To counteract the possibility that such responses were due purely to lack of attention, rather than an implicit correction of the anomaly, we only counted such responses if children had given correct answers to all the other questions for that story. Less-skilled comprehenders gave 16% of such responses and skilled children gave 10%. All these cases were evenly distributed throughout the story types.

Monitoring scores. Monitoring responses were scored from 0 to 3, as described above, and were analysed using analysis of variance, with skill group between subjects. As predicted, skilled children were more likely than less-skilled ones to notice inconsistencies, with an average monitoring score of 1.69 out of 3, compared to only 0.97 for the less-skilled group, $F(1, 30) = 15.06$, $p < .0005$. Although there was a tendency for salient anomalies to be noticed more – anomalies in main goal and anomalies appearing immediately next to a violated precondition – the effects fell short of significance. The effect of distance yielded $F(1, 30) = 3.56$, $p < .07$, and for goal type was $F(1, 30) = 2.77$, $p < .10$. The interaction of these two factors was not significant, $F(1, 30) = 2.55$, $p < .12$, and all other Fs were less than 1. As the mean scores in Table 6.3 show, children tended to score lower on the least obvious anomalies, those concerning subsidiary goals that were remote from the violated precondition.

The distribution of the scores across the four response categories, shown in Table 6.4, is also revealing. The most common response type for less-skilled children was not to notice an anomaly at all, whereas skilled children detected anomalies more than half the time when given just a general prompt.

It seems unlikely that less-skilled children were reluctant to point out mistakes. Only two children, both good comprehenders, said that they had noticed anomalies during reading but had not commented because they were not quite sure they had understood. Children were quite willing to point out errors or oddities, even if these were not the errors they were intended to find. For example, half of the subjects argued that one of the control stories was odd. This story was about a girl who woke up on Christmas morning hoping for a BMX bike, although she didn't yet know how to ride one, who then received a red bike. Four poor comprehenders and two good ones found this odd, because they thought it unlikely either to want a bike if you couldn't ride one, or for a girl, rather than a boy, to want a bike. This is an example of what Baker (1985) calls a standard of external consistency: these children thought that the girl's goal was unlikely, given their general knowledge about why people want things. Three poor and four good comprehenders criticised the story because it lacked

Table 6.3. *Mean anomaly detection scores for each anomaly type in each group (max = 3)*

	Less-skilled			Skilled		
	Immediate	Remote	Mean	Immediate	Remote	Mean
Main goal	1·06	1·09	1·08	1·81	1·69	1·75
Subsidiary goal	1·03	0·69	0·86	1·81	1·44	1·63
Mean	1·05	0·89	0·97	1·81	1·56	1·69

Table 6.4. *Mean percentages of monitoring scores in each scoring category for each skill group*

	Response score and type			
	3 Spontaneous recognition	2 General prompt	1 Specific prompt	0 Anomaly not noticed
Less-skilled	5·5	32·0	16·4	46·1
Skilled	13·3	57·0	14·8	14·8

information: either not specifying that the bike she got was a BMX one, or not specifying where she went on the bike. Only three children, all good comprehenders, used a standard of internal consistency. These children all rather ingeniously pointed out that it would have been difficult to practice riding the bike because the roads were probably covered with snow. If attempting to resolve inconsistencies in the experimental stories, children would occasionally try to modify the goal (e.g. suggesting that a character who drives his car when there is apparently no petrol might have had a tiny bit of petrol left) or to concentrate on subtle aspects of wording, e.g. in a story about a boy who is apparently looking at some photographs in complete darkness, one child argued that 'he could look at them, but not see them', or as in the case of one poor comprehender, simply argued that the character must have been lying!

Reading times. Inspection times for the two crucial lines were scored from the tape by the experimenter, and by a rater blind to skill group. A reliability check showed an average discrepancy of 0.18 of a second: the times reported here are for the blind rater. We looked at the differences between study time for inconsistent and consistent lines, which differed only in the verb used (e.g. 'bought' versus 'made'); that is, the inconsistent line in the main-goal-inconsistent condition and the corresponding consistent line in the subsidiary-goal-inconsistent condition. An analysis of variance, with skill group between subjects, and goal type (main or subsidiary), distance (immediate or remote) and consistency (consistent or inconsistent) within subjects, showed one significant effect: an interaction of goal type and distance, $F(1, 30) = 4.40$, $p < .05$. The interaction of group with consistency yielded $F(1, 30) = 3.56$, $p < .07$. To investigate the possibility of group differences, we analysed the data separately for each skill group.

The less-skilled comprehenders showed no significant effects or interactions. All Fs were less than 1 other than for goal type, $F(1, 15) = 1.3$, n.s. For skilled comprehenders, on the other hand, there was a significant interaction of goal type distance and consistency, $F(1, 15) = 10.14$, $p < .01$. Table 6.5 shows the difference in study times between consistent and inconsistent lines for each group separately, for each goal type and distance condition. As the table shows, skilled children showed a significant difference between consistent and inconsistent lines for the most obvious type of anomaly, main-goal-immediate. There were no significant differences between conditions for less-skilled children. They showed no increase in study times for inconsistent lines: some of the data were in the opposite of the predicted direction, although not significantly so.

Correlations of monitoring score and reading time. If slower reading times indicate that comprehension monitoring is taking place, then we would expect reading times to be related to monitoring scores. To test this conjecture, we correlated study times and monitoring scores for each group. For less-skilled children, there was no evidence of a relation, $r(14) = 0.04$, n.s. For skilled children the correlation was moderately positive, $r(14) = 0.44$, $p < .05$, one-tailed test. However, the difference between the two correlation coefficients was not significant, Fisher's zr transformation $= 1.10$, $p < .11$.

Relation between responses to questions and monitoring. The high level of performance on the comprehension questions meant that the children often gave answers that were correct, and consistent with the information given in the story, but internally contradictory. In the cases where anomaly questions were answered wrongly, children could respond so as to be internally consistent in two ways: by changing the precondition (e.g. saying that Jane had some money when the story stated that she did not) or by being inconsistent and incorrect (e.g. saying that Jane had bought a cake, when this was incorrect, and that there was no money, when this was correct). In both these cases, the anomaly could either be noticed or not noticed. Although there were too few data for cases with anomaly questions answered wrongly to perform a reliable statistical analysis, there appeared to be interesting differences between the skill groups, and so we tabulated the patterns of responses in such cases. In doing so, we adopted a lenient criterion of anomaly detection, and considered only a score of 0 as failure to detect an anomaly. The most common pattern of response for both groups was to make the story consistent, as shown in their responses to the

Table 6.5. *Mean differences in study times (seconds) for consistent and inconsistent lines in each story condition for each skill group*

	Less-skilled		Skilled	
	Immediate	Remote	Immediate	Remote
Main goal	0·11	−0·27	1·51*	0·44
Subsidiary goal	−0·54	−0·69	−0·30	0·81
Difference	0·65	0·42	1·81	−0·37

Notes: A negative number indicates that the mean time for inconsistent lines was less than that for consistent lines.
* $p < 0{\cdot}05$ (Tukey's HSD).

questions, and to notice the anomaly. However, this pattern was far more common for skilled children (65% of their responses) than for less-skilled ones (33%). Conversely, answering questions consistently and never noticing the anomaly was more common for poor comprehenders (30% of responses) than for good ones (17% of responses). Furthermore, in 21% of cases, less-skilled children gave inconsistent responses without ever detecting the anomaly, but this was never the case for the skilled group. The two groups answered inconsistently and detected the anomaly at about the same rate (15% for less-skilled and 17% for skilled children).

Discussion The text-inspection times indicated that only skilled children slowed their reading when encountering inconsistencies, and then only for the most obvious examples. This is in agreement with the work of August et al. (1984), mentioned earlier, which showed that some less-skilled children did not slow their reading times for stories in which information had been omitted. Our two groups of subjects also differed in the extent to which they overtly detected errors.

The results raise questions about the relation between constructive processing, as measured by reading time, and comprehension monitoring. Our studies of reading time described in Chapter 5 did not show a close association between reading time and comprehension outcome. For example, Experiment 5.3 showed differences between the skill groups in reading time, but both groups performed equally well on questions tapping comprehension. This may have been because the task could have been performed as well using rote strategies. In the present study, skilled children, but not less-skilled ones, showed a correlation between reading time for anomalous information and anomaly detection. However, other studies have been singularly unable to demonstrate such a relation. Harris et al. report a correlation of 0.23 between their two measures for the sixteen 8-year-olds in the first experiment and 0.18 for the thirty-six 8-year-olds and 0.33 for thirty-six 11-year-olds in their second study. Zabrucky and Ratner (1986) reported negative correlations between reading time and anomaly detection in twenty third and twenty sixth graders (rs = -.32 and -.04 respectively). The latter authors argued from their results merely that there are different components of evaluation. Harris et al. used the lack of evidence of a correlation to support a distinction between constructive processing and comprehension monitoring, which they argued was obscured in some of the work by Markman. By using separate measures of these two functions (reading time and anomaly detection respectively), Harris et al. showed that there was no age change in use of constructive processing, but an increase with age in use of comprehension monitoring. Moreover, Baker and Anderson (1982) did not find much consistency between reading time and detection of major or minor anomalies by college students, although they did not report the size of correlations between the two measures. They concluded from their results that people who spent longer reading an anomalous sentence had noticed the inconsistency, but there were also people who detected it without showing longer reading times. Thus, the balance of evidence does not support a relation between reading time and anomaly detection. However, it is possible that any effects of comprehension monitoring may not be detected immediately, but have an influence later on, perhaps in increasing reading time for a subsequent sentence. This may have been true for the less-skilled children in our study, and possibly subjects in other studies, but further investigation is needed to resolve this issue.

The differences between the two groups in the sorts of errors they made in answering questions about the stories provide interesting indicators of the nature of the differences between the groups. Poor comprehenders did sometimes 'fix' the anomaly by making unwarranted inferences, as did some of the less-skilled children in the study by August et al. (1984). However, it was less likely that such implicit detection led to explicit anomaly detection in our less-skilled than in our skilled group. It seems that poor comprehenders may make repairs to stories but do not mark the inferences they have made as hypothetical or unwarranted. We also found that poor comprehenders sometimes answered questions correctly, but in a way that was internally contradictory, but did not point out the inconsistency even when asked directly. Skilled children never did this. It seems, then, that our less-skilled children showed on different occasions both patterns identified by August et al. (1984): failure to integrate the text and hence failure to detect anomalies, and also integration of the text without explicitly marking inferences as unwarranted.

We have already seen that measures of explicit anomaly detection require cautious interpretation. In our study, we used three different methods of assessing comprehension monitoring: reading time, explicit recognition and question-answering. On each of these measures, it appears that less-skilled children performed differently from skilled ones. We are therefore somewhat confident that poor comprehenders are less likely to detect inconsistencies in text than good comprehenders are. However, anomaly *detection* is only one aspect of comprehension monitoring. Once an anomaly has been noticed, some form of remedial action is required to maintain comprehension. In the following experiment, we presented children with anomalies that could be resolved, using information given elsewhere in the text, in order to investigate whether children in the two groups could repair anomalies once these had been detected.

Experiment 6.4: *Effects of processing load on the resolution of anomaly*

In some experiments reported in Chapter 4, we suggested that less-skilled comprehenders fail to make inferences as they are reading, and build a less detailed mental model of the text than skilled children do. Further evidence of differences in integrative processing is provided by our study of comprehension monitoring, in which less-skilled children were considerably less likely than skilled ones to point out anomalies in stories. Skilled children also paused on encountering the more salient anomalies. The absence of effects on reading time in less-skilled children is consistent with the finding that they failed to notice anomalies at least half the time. However, since they so rarely detected anomalies, we could not examine the effects of different processing demands on their comprehension monitoring. In the following study, anomalies were designed to be so salient that most or all of them would be detected. This procedure enabled us to examine the effects of different processing demands on the way anomalies, once detected, were dealt with.

If an anomaly is detected, the reader has several options: referring to the previous text to resolve the inconsistency, scanning forwards for information that might resolve the inconsistency, trying to formulate a resolution from knowledge external to the text, or ignoring it, in which case the text will not be fully comprehended. The difficulty of resolving inconsistencies may be influenced by factors that place varying demands on working memory. Ackerman (1984) tested this idea by presenting 6- to 10-year-olds with stories containing obvious anomalies (e.g. a child is rewarded for being placed thirtieth in a race) that could be resolved using information presented elsewhere in the story (e.g. there were 300 runners in the race), and by assessing the children's ability to integrate the anomaly with its resolution. The processing load was varied in terms of two factors: distance – putting the resolving information immediately adjacent to or two sentences distant from the anomaly, and position – placing the resolving information either before or after the anomaly.

Ackerman described the distance factor as a storage load and the position factor as a processing load, but we considered that both constituted processing loads of different types, and we use the term 'processing load' accordingly.

We used a similar method to compare anomaly resolution in the two skill groups. We expected anomalies in the 'distant' and 'after' condition to be most difficult. For the manipulation of position, Ackerman predicted and found the opposite: that resolution information placed before the anomaly would be more difficult to use than that placed afterwards. He argued that resolution information read before the anomaly would have to be reinterpreted, to address the comprehension problem raised by the anomaly. However, it could also be argued that giving resolution information after the anomaly requires the anomaly to be resolved retrospectively, whereas presenting the resolution first allows the reader to understand the anomaly immediately: in fact, the anomalous information no longer constitutes an anomaly. This position is supported by evidence from previous work in text processing. For example, Bransford and Johnson (1972) found that explanatory titles helped adult readers to recall highly abstract texts when placed before, but not when they were placed after, the text. Similarly, Harris, Mandias, Meerum Terwogt and Tjintjelaar (1980) found that presentation of setting information helped 8- and 10-year-old children's story recall when presented before but not after the story. Provision of context after reading produced recall no better than that when no supporting context was provided, suggesting that children did not use context retrospectively to reinterpret the text. In our experiment, there were two main predictions: first, that the children would be less able to resolve inconsistencies under conditions of high processing demand, and second, that the less-skilled children would be particularly affected by high processing demands.

Method Nine children in each skill group took part in the experiment. The materials comprised twelve six-line stories about adults' responses to children's actions. The condition of interest was the Inconsistent Resolving (IR) one: an adult responded inconsistently to a child (e.g. blaming a boy for sharing his sweets with his little brother), but this anomaly was resolved (the little brother was on a diet). There were two control conditions: Inconsistent Non-resolving (IN: no anomaly resolution) and Consistent Non-resolving (CN: no anomaly and no resolution). These controls checked that children were not simply reluctant to disagree with adults' anomalous actions, that they agreed with the norms involved (e.g. sharing) and also provided a mix of anomalous and non-anomalous stories. There was only a 7% error rate for questions about these control stories, and they will not be mentioned further.

Each child read the twelve stories after practice on three stories. No feedback was given for the practice or for the experimental stories. The processing load was varied in the same way as in Ackerman's study, using distance and position of anomalous and resolving information. Table 6.6 shows examples of a story in the four different conditions of processing load, all in the IR version. After the experimenter had read each story to the child, she asked three questions. The memory question checked that the child remembered the adult's anomalous response correctly, and the norm question that the child agreed with the norm involved. The measure of particular interest was the consistency question, where the child had to judge whether or not the adult's response was right, and to explain why. A correct response was scored when the child said that the adult's apparently anomalous response was right, referred to the resolving information in justifying the adult's response, and agreed with the norm involved in the story. Each subject heard two stories of each type (IR, CN and IN) for each of the four processing-load conditions.

Results The results were analysed using analysis of variance, with group between subjects and processing load (distance and position as separate factors) within subjects. There was a tendency for the skilled children to score higher than the less-skilled ones, $F(1, 16) = 4.20$, $p < .057$ a main effect of distance, $F(1, 16) = 4.71$, $p < .05$ and an interaction of distance with group, $F(1, 16) = 4.71$, $p < .05$. As Table 6.7 shows, the two groups performed similarly in the adjacent condition, when nothing intervened between the anomaly and its resolution, but the less-skilled children were significantly worse than the skilled ones in the separated condition, when an additional memory load was imposed by the interposition of two sentences. The main effect of position fell short of significance, $F(1, 16) = 4.11$, $p < .06$, but was in the expected direction. Children tended to use resolving information less when it appeared after, rather than before, the anomaly.

Discussion The results indicate that both groups of children were capable of resolving textual anomalies, but that the less-skilled children were more adversely influenced by an increase in processing demand. Their failure to use the resolving information was not due to a reluctance to question the adults' responses in the stories, or to failures in recognition of anomalies, because they did both these things in the inconsistent-nonresolving condition. Their difficulty lay in repairing comprehension failures. Thus, even if poor comprehenders do sometimes notice inconsistencies in their reading, they will be less able than good comprehenders to resolve them.

Less-skilled comprehenders do not completely fail to perform comprehension monitoring: they are just less likely to detect and resolve anomalies, and are influenced to a greater extent than skilled children by increased processing demands. They also show differential recall of information according to its importance in a story. We have some evidence, both from our study of anomaly

Table 6.6. *Example of inconsistent story with resolving information in each of four processing-load conditions*

Adjacent – before
Tommy had been out to the sweetshop.

*Tommy didn't share his sweets with his little brother.
†Tommy's brother was very fat and he was on a diet.
‡When their mother saw this, she was very pleased with Tommy.
Tommy got out his train set.
He played with his trains all morning.

Separated – before
†Tommy's brother was very fat and he was on a diet.
Tommy had been out to the sweetshop.

*Tommy didn't share his sweets with his little brother.
‡When their mother saw this, she was very pleased with Tommy.
Tommy got out his train set.
He played with his trains all morning.

Adjacent – after
Tommy had been out to the sweetshop.
*Tommy didn't share his sweets with his little brother.
‡When their mother saw this, she was very pleased with Tommy.
†Tommy's brother was very fat and he was on a diet.
Tommy got out his train set.

He played with his trains all morning.

Separated – after
Tommy had been out to the sweetshop.
*Tommy didn't share his sweets with his little brother.
‡When their mother saw this, she was very pleased with Tommy.
Tommy got out his train set.

He played with his trains all morning.
†Tommy's brother was very fat and he was on a diet.

Memory question: Was Tommy praised or blamed for what he had done?
Consistency question: Should he have been? Why?
Norm question: Would someone usually be praised or blamed for not sharing their sweets?

Notes: * = child's action, † = resolving information, ‡ = adult's inconsistent response.

Table 6.7. *Mean percentages of correct resolutions for each processing load in each skill group*

	Processing load condition					
	Adjacent		Separated			
	Before	After	Before	After	Mean (before)	Mean (after)
Less-skilled	77·78	66·67	33·33	0·00	55·56	33·33
Mean	72·22		16·66			
Skilled	66·67	66·67	77·78	55·56	72·22	61·11
Mean	66·67		66·67			

detection and from our earlier reading-time studies, that poor comprehenders do not vary their study times in response to differences in processing demands to the extent that skilled children do. As Harris et al. (1981, p. 229) note, as readers develop their skills, they may increasingly modify their reading strategy according to the results of comprehension monitoring activity, and monitoring can be seen as a fundamental part of comprehension rather than an epiphenomenon of more basic processes. Poor comprehenders' implicit recognition of differences in importance level may provide a base on which comprehension-monitoring skills could be developed and trained.

Reflecting on language: linguistic awareness

So far in this chapter, we have looked at children's abilities to reflect on their own performance, in general terms of what is important in comprehending text, and more specifically, in their understanding of whether they have understood a particular text adequately. We also assessed their skills in reflecting on the relative importance of different parts of a text. Our primary focus was on the achievement of an internally consistent representation of a text, as opposed to a confused, non-integrated representation. However, there are some uses of language that rely for their effect on the possibility of constructing two internally consistent interpretations that conflict with each other. Non-literal uses of language such as joking, irony, sarcasm and lying are examples of such uses. Appreciating a riddle, for example, requires the hearer to construct two alternative interpretations of a piece of text. The ability to reflect on different interpretations of text has been seen as a *metalinguistic skill* (e.g. Hirsh-Pasek, Gleitman and Gleitman, 1978), or as demonstrating linguistic awareness. In the second part of this chapter, we investigate this aspect of metacognitive skill.

Several studies have traced age changes in the ease with which riddles are grasped, using various classifications of the different ways in which riddles require linguistic awareness (see Shultz, 1974 and Yalisove, 1978 for more details). Riddles provide a useful tool for studying children's ability to reflect on language, because their humour depends on some sort of linguistic ambiguity. So, by observing children's ability to understand riddles, their competence at reflecting on various aspects of language can be assessed. The 'point' of a riddle is that either the question sets up a particular linguistic interpretation that is different from that required to understand the answer, or the answer can be interpreted in two different ways. We 'get' the riddle if we understand the two different interpretations.

Two studies have related riddle comprehension directly to reading skill. Hirsh-Pasek et al. (1978) compared the ability to explain riddles in good and poor readers from grades 1 to 6. Reading skill was assessed by the school reading specialist, although the authors acknowledge that the range of skill was restricted, and that the 'poor' readers were probably about average when compared to the normal population. Poor readers in all age groups were less able to explain riddles than good readers were. Fowles and Glanz (1977) also found an age-independent relation between reading ability and riddle comprehension. They asked fourteen children aged between 6 and 9 to retell and explain riddles read out by an experimenter. Half the children were identified by teachers as above-average readers, and half were below average. Although no statistical tests are reported, the good readers were better at explaining riddles than the poor ones, while there was apparently no difference in the groups' ability to retell riddles. These two studies both suggest that there is a relation between riddle comprehension and reading skill, but in both cases, the measure of reading skill was not specified very precisely, and probably included aspects of decoding, comprehension and general verbal ability.

Hirsh-Pasek et al. attempted to specify the relation between reading skill and riddle comprehension more precisely by varying the types of riddle used. They argued that different types of riddle demanded different sorts of linguistic awareness. They described six types of ambiguity on which riddles may rest, which we adapted and extended for our studies. Three of their categories involved phonological characteristics of words: *phonological* (two words differing in one sound, e.g. quackers/ crackers), *morpheme boundary* (an ambiguity interpretable as a single morpheme or a sequence of morphemes, e.g. engine ears/engineers), and *morpheme boundary with phonological distortion* (a combination of phonological and morpheme-boundary types, e.g. let's hope/ let's soap). A further category rested on semantic characteristics of words: *lexical* (one sound with two meanings, e.g. bark), while the other two categories were concerned with grammatical features: *surface structure* (a word sequence interpretable in different ways, e.g. man eating fish/ man-eating fish) and *underlying structure* (a word sequence resulting from two different grammatical transformations, e.g. make me a milkshake interpreted as 'make a milkshake for me'/ 'make me into a milkshake'). The authors predicted that riddles relying on semantic properties of language (lexical and underlying structure ambiguities) would be easier to explain than those relying on superficial representations of the sentence (phonological and surface-structure ambiguities), because it is more natural in normal language use to focus on meaning rather than on syntactic form. This expectation was generally borne out. However, they pointed out that the difficulty of phonological ambiguity depends on how the ambiguous words are presented: it is considerably easier to see the point of such riddles if the correctly biased pronunciation is used. For example, in the riddle 'Bob coughed until his face turned blue. Was he choking? No, he was serious', the need to use the appropriately biased version (*choking*), rather than the wrongly biased one (*joking*) marks the distortion and makes the judgement task artificially easy. Caution is therefore needed in interpreting results from such riddles.

Contrary to their predictions, however, Hirsh-Pasek et al. did not find any interactions between reading ability and riddle type: they had anticipated that poor readers may have found ambiguities resting on surface features of language particularly difficult, in keeping with their suggestion that verbally skilled people are more able to focus on syntactic properties of language and ignore semantic ones (see also Gleitman and Gleitman, 1970). However, they suggest that this may have been because even their 'poor' readers were probably above average in reading skill. Fowles and Glanz did not find any interactions of reading skill with riddle type, although the authors suggest that this was due to the restricted age range used (6–9-year-olds).

Experiment 6.5: *Preliminary study*: *Understanding riddles*[2]

As there seem to be no studies of riddle comprehension in relation to reading *comprehension*, and no generally agreed classification of riddles, we chose to concentrate on a small set of riddle types that could be classified clearly and that were common to several of the previous studies. The four types investigated we termed phonological, lexical, grammatical and metacognitive. We did not make any specific predictions about the relative difficulty of the different types, because we considered all types of ambiguity to require some form of linguistic awareness. We therefore expected less-skilled children to be generally poorer at retelling and explaining riddles than skilled comprehenders.

In much of the previous work on riddles, children have been asked to retell and explain riddles. Although these measures are not direct measures of comprehension, they are useful indicators of it. Incorrect retellings, particularly those that reproduce most of the original words but 'miss the point', are a sign of incomprehension, although correct repetition does not, of course, indicate comprehension. Explanation shows the reverse picture: many adults find 'explaining' riddles a difficult task, even though they may understand the point of them. Thus, correct explanation demonstrates comprehension, but incorrect explanation does not necessarily mean that the subject has not understood. We assessed the children's understanding and appreciation of the riddles using three criteria: retelling, funniness ratings and explanation.

Method As this was a pilot study, only four children in each skill group completed the experiment.

The riddles used were collected from a variety of published sources, and represented each of the four types: phonological, lexical, grammatical and metacognitive. Each of these, except the lexical ones, could be further subdivided into two categories that can be easily compared with typologies of previous work. This classification gives seven subtypes of riddle, as shown in Table 6.8. Phonological riddles were subdivided into those that required interpretation of single words and those that crossed word-boundaries (Hirsh-Pasek et al.'s 'phonological' and 'morpheme boundary without phonological distortion' types respectively). Grammatical riddles included surface- and deep-structure riddles. Metacognitive riddles comprised riddles that we termed 'metalinguistic', in that they required reflection on the form of a word as a linguistic symbol rather than as a semantic item, and riddles termed 'pragmatic', which involved some violation of expectations about the speaker's intent: for example, the 'fireman' riddle in Table 6.8 suggests that the speaker is focusing on the colour of the firemen's braces, whereas the answer implies that it is the presence (or absence!) of braces that is important.

Subjects were told that their task was to make a child from the same class laugh by posing some riddles, previously given by the experimenter. Unknown to the subject, the listeners were previously chosen and instructed to pretend not to understand any of the riddles. They made comments such as 'I don't get it – tell me why it's funny', and were asked not to laugh until the subject provided some explanation. Listeners played their parts very well, and provided plausible rationales for the need for the subject to retell and explain the riddles. The situation of telling and listening to riddles seemed to prove sufficiently amusing that subjects appeared not to become annoyed with or overtly suspicious of the listener who always needed the riddles explained.

The procedure was as follows: the experimenter told a complete riddle to the subject, who rated how funny it was by giving a thumbs-up, thumbs-horizontal, or thumbs-down, in descending order of funniness. Subjects could also inspect the riddle written on a card, until they thought they could remember it. Pilot work showed that most children felt more confident if they had this written support, and Yalisove (1978) reported no difference in third graders' riddle comprehension for written and aural presentations. For riddles that rested on homophones, the incongruent spelling was used, e.g. 'What's black and white and *red* all over?', rather than '*read*'. The subject, wearing a small tie-clip microphone, then went behind a partition to the waiting listener to retell and explain the riddle. Where necessary, the experimenter probed the riddle explanation further.

Results As this was only an exploratory pilot study, the results were considered as suggestive rather than definitive.

Retellings. Children's recounting of each riddle was scored as correct or incorrect according to whether the essential ambiguity of the riddle was maintained. Skilled children scored 96% correct and less-skilled ones only 75%. There were no striking differences in performance for the different riddle types, and in most cases the skilled children showed higher accuracy.

Funniness ratings. Despite the less-skilled comprehenders' poorer performance on retelling, they reported the riddles to be just as funny as skilled children

Table 6.8. *Examples of each type of riddle*

Phonological:	
(within word boundary)	
	If you put three ducks in a box, what do you get?
	...a box of quackers
(across word boundary)	
	Why can't you starve in the desert?
	...because of the sand which is there
Lexical:	What is black and white and red all over?
	...a newspaper
Grammatical:	
(surface)	What has four wheels and flies?
	...a dustbin lorry
(deep)	How do you stop fish from smelling?
	...cut off their noses
Metacognitive:	
(metalinguistic)	What is at the end of everything?
	...the letter 'g'
(pragmatic)	Why do firemen wear red braces?
	...to keep their trousers up

did. The mean funniness ratings were 1.14 and 1.0 for less-skilled and skilled children respectively, where 3 was the maximum (thumbs-up) score. Less-skilled comprehenders rated a riddle as very funny on seven occasions when they had retold it wrongly, whereas this type of inconsistent response occurred only once in the skilled group. This finding suggests that funniness ratings cannot be considered good indicators of riddle comprehension, for less-skilled children. We discuss the interpretation of these ratings in more detail below.

Explanations. These were scored as adequate or inadequate. We adopted a fairly lenient criterion of adequacy, because it is difficult even for adults to articulate why a riddle is funny. Adequate explanations either mentioned both interpretations of an ambiguity or referred less explicitly to the way in which the riddle violated an expectation. An example of the first, for the riddle 'What is black and white and red all over?' (a newspaper), follows:

> You're meant to think RED?? Black and white and RED all over? So it must be it makes them think and then they won't know and then you say a newspaper because it's READ being read all over when someone's read it.

Obviously, when homophones are involved, some interpretation is involved in deciding which meaning is referred to, and the spellings in the above example reflect our interpretation of what the child said. We made this interpretation on the following basis: the child had presumably interpreted 'red' with the usual bias (the colour 'red'), but had also detected the alternative reading, because her description ('a newspaper... when someone's read it') would not make sense otherwise. A more implicit form of explanation, for the riddle 'Why do firemen wear red braces?' was: 'Keep their trousers up – you wouldn't think of that.' Inadequate explanations were usually 'don't know' responses, simple reiterations of the punchline, and irrelevant attempts to provide a rationale, as in this explanation of the riddle 'What do you get if you put three ducks in a box?': 'You get three crackers cos they're magic'. Use of the form 'crackers', rather than 'quackers', does not indicate resolution, since the subject is just repeating the form given in the answer, but she does not focus on this word-play as the source of humour.

The percentages of adequate explanations for each riddle type in the two groups are shown in Table 6.9. Skilled children scored 44.6% on average, compared to only 23.2% for less-skilled children. As Table 6.9 shows, less-skilled children explained phonological and lexical riddles less successfully than skilled children did, although the difference was smaller for within-word phonological items. They also seemed to find metalinguistic riddles more difficult. For the two types of grammatical riddle and the pragmatic ones, both groups did very poorly.

It is also possible to look at the relation between funniness ratings and explanation scores, as a way of investigating the basis on which children judged the riddles as funny. In order to examine this, we looked at the number of riddles explained appropriately as a percentage of those found funny (combining funniness ratings of 2 and 1, so as to compare riddles rated quite or very funny against those rated not funny) for each riddle. Although both skill groups rated about the same proportion of riddles as funny (about two-thirds), for skilled children these were more likely to be the ones they explained (61%) than for less-skilled children (34%), and this difference was significant, $t(6) = 2.10$, $p < .05$.

Discussion The most striking aspect of these results was that, despite the very small sample size, skilled children performed significantly better than less-skilled ones in explaining riddles. This was despite the fact that poor comprehenders rated two-thirds of the riddles as quite or very funny – about the same proportion as in the skilled children. Funniness ratings and explanation scores appeared to be more closely related in the good than in the poor comprehenders. For the skilled children, it seems, the entertainment value of a joke did rely on whether they understood it or not, but for less-skilled children it did not. This difference could be related to the potential differences in metacognitive awareness that we have discussed through this chapter. Skilled children may be more aware of their own comprehension of a riddle: if they understand it, they rate it as funny, and if they fail to see the point, then it is not funny. This was not the case for poor comprehenders, who showed no clear

Table 6.9. *Percentages of acceptable explanations as a function of riddle type and skill group*

	Riddle type (see Table 6.8)						
	Phonological		Lexical	Grammatical		Metacognitive	
	Within	Across		Surface	Deep	Meta.	Prag.
Less-skilled	25·0	0·0	12·5	25·0	25·0	37·3	37·5
Skilled	50·0	87·5	75·0	12·5	0·0	75·0	12·5
Difference	25·0	87·5	62·5	−12·5	−25·0	37·5	−25·0

relationship between explanation and funniness ratings. It is likely that all the children would rate at least some of the riddles funny, purely because it may have seemed expected in the experimental situation, but even so, a relation between the two measures would be expected. It is possible that the poor comprehenders rated funniness by some other criterion. Informal observation suggested that some children rated riddles as funny if there was an element that was humorous on its own: for instance, the idea of someone's trousers falling down (see the 'pragmatic' riddle in Table 6.8) was enough to send children into gales of laughter, but not necessarily because the answer violated the expectation set up in the initial question.

The results for explanation are perhaps more indicative of children's riddle comprehension than the funniness ratings. The general pattern showed less-skilled children to be poor overall, while skilled children performed better, but still found grammatical riddles particularly difficult to explain. In contrast to the results of Fowles and Glanz, metalinguistic riddles gained the highest explanation scores of all. This may reflect the fact that we were lenient in our scoring criteria, and for this type of riddle in particular, any mention of violated expectations was credited. However, such a response could reflect children's general awareness that riddles are surprising, rather than a specific understanding of the type of violation contained in metalinguistic riddles. The difference between the groups was particularly marked for phonological and lexical riddles. Our data should be treated with some caution, particularly as there were only two examples of each riddle type, and only eight subjects. The results do, though, give an interesting indication of differences between the skill groups, and encouraged us to investigate further.

Experiment 6.6: *Recall and explanation of riddles*[3]

The results of the previous experiment suggested that less-skilled children in particular found lexical riddles hard to explain. We were somewhat surprised at this, because it would seem to be easier to reinterpret a sentence when the meaning of a single word changes than when, for instance, the grammatical structure is altered. It therefore seems prudent to check whether poorer performance on riddle explanation could be accounted for to some degree merely by poor understanding of ambiguous words. To investigate the extent to which mere knowledge of lexical ambiguity contributes to riddle performance, we assessed the children's understanding of a set of ambiguous words. We restricted ourselves to the four main types of riddle used in the pilot study, omitting the subdivisions within each type. Examples of the four types of riddle are shown in Table 6.10. As in the pilot study, we investigated the relation between comprehension skill and riddle comprehension, as well as checking whether riddle comprehension could be accounted for by understanding of ambiguous words. On this occasion, because of time constraints, we used a different method from our usual one, as explained in the following section.

Method Sixty-nine children from two Brighton primary schools were screened initially. They were all tested on the Neale Analysis, and twenty subjects were chosen, as described below, to participate in the study. The subjects were not divided into matched groups of skilled and less-skilled comprehenders, as in most of our other experiments, but measures of their reading ability were correlated with the measures of interest. Their reading accuracy scores ranged from 6;5 to 9;11 years (mean = 7;11), and their comprehension scores between 6;8 and 9;6 years (mean = 7;10). Their chronological ages ranged between 7;5 and 8;5 years (mean = 7;11).

In order to show that performance on the riddles, or on particular types of riddles, is related to comprehension skill, and not just to reading ability in general, we need to show that it correlates with comprehension skill *but not with decoding accuracy*. To ensure that there was a similar *a priori* chance of finding correlations with accuracy and comprehension scores, we selected subjects so that the standard deviations of the group accuracy and comprehension scores were approximately equal (8.47 and 8.45 months respectively).

The sixteen riddles used were selected to provide clear examples of each of the four types. Four riddles were included in each category. The classification into the four categories was confirmed by two raters who were blind to intended category. The sixteen ambiguous words were selected as having a clear distinction between their possible meanings, e.g. 'hare–hair', and avoiding ambiguous words that also occurred in the riddles. All of the words had at least two common unrelated meanings.

Table 6.10. *Examples of each type of riddle*

Phonological:	Where do you weigh a whale? ...at a whale-weigh station (railway)
Lexical:	How do you know there was fruit on Noah's Ark? ...because the animals came in pairs (pears)
Grammatical:	What is out of bounds? ...an exhausted kangaroo
Metalinguistic:	Why is there so little honey in Brighton? ...because there's only one 'B' in Brighton

The test of ambiguity was presented first – the children were asked if they could think of 'two different meanings that the word might have'. Two examples were discussed with each child, before the presentation of the sixteen test items. If any child was unable to provide two definitions they were prompted with 'can you think of anything else the word might mean?' before the next word was presented.

The riddles were then presented in a set random order, starting with two examples. Following the aural presentation of each riddle, the child was asked to rate the riddle for funniness, by choosing one of five faces depicting varying degrees of amusement, from unamused to extremely amused. They were then asked to retell the riddle, and tell the experimenter why they thought it was funny. If they had rated the riddle as not funny the experimenter asked instead: 'can you tell me why you think it should be funny?'. This question, despite its apparent oddness, was designed to elicit any explanation of the riddle that the children might be capable of producing, if their funniness ratings did not reflect their ability to comprehend the riddle.

Results *Test of ambiguity*. Performance on this test was assessed on a five-point scale, as follows:

5 = two correct meanings given for the word
4 = one correct meaning, one feasible attempt
3 = one correct meaning (and one wrong attempt)
2 = attempt at one or two meanings, but incorrect
1 = 'don't know' response.

The responses in this test, and the scores of riddle understanding, below, were assessed by two raters. The second judge did not have access to the children's reading scores, and was not present at the time of testing. Any discrepancies between the two raters' scores were resolved by discussion. Performance on the test of ambiguity was uniformly high: the mean score was 4.3 out of 5.

Neither reading accuracy nor reading comprehension correlated with performance on the word meaning task (both correlations $< .14$). The relation between performance on this task and the various measures of riddle understanding was also assessed, but there were no significant correlations.

Riddle recall. Again, each child was given a score for each riddle, with a maximum score of 5, as follows:

5 = exact recall
4 = meaning same, but different words
3 = some of the same words, but recalled riddle makes no sense
2 = completely inaccurate
1 = 'can't remember' response

Recall of the lexical and phonological riddles was best (with mean scores per riddle of 3.6 for both categories), followed by recall of metalinguistic riddles (3.0) and grammatical ones (2.6). Our current interest, however, is not in the relative difficulty of the different types of riddles, but how performance relates to reading ability. Because the measures of riddle understanding tended to correlate both with word-recognition skill and with chronological age, these correlations were taken into account when calculating the correlations with comprehension age, by computing higher-order partial correlations.

The results showed that even with the effects of age and reading accuracy partialled out there was a significant relation between comprehension and recall of riddles overall ($r = 0.48$, $p < .05$: degrees of freedom here, as in the correlations in the rest of this section, = 67). Within the different categories of riddle, the higher-order partial correlations showed significant correlations of comprehension skill with recall of the metalinguistic riddles ($r = 0.64$, $p < .01$), with the lexical ambiguity riddles ($r = 0.46$, $p < .05$) and with the phonological ambiguity riddles ($r = 0.45$, $p < .05$). The correlation with recall of the grammatical riddles was not significant ($r = 0.29$).

The correlation between reading accuracy and recall of riddles was positive, but non-significant ($r = 0.36$) and none of the within-category correlations with reading accuracy was significant.

Riddle explanation. Again, a five-point scale was used for scoring, as follows:

5 = accurate explanation – gist grasped
4 = not completely clear explanation, reasonable attempt
3 = incorrect, but good attempt
2 = completely incorrect
1 = 'don't know' responses

The extreme categories, 5 and 1, are self-explanatory. A score of 4 was assigned when there was some indication of understanding, but not a complete explanation. For example, one child's response to the phonological joke shown in Table 6.10 was 'You get on trains at a whale station'. The child seems to have noted the ambiguity of whale/rail, but did not mention the weigh/way ambiguity. A score of 3 was given for an explanation that had some plausibility as an account of an inconsistency in the riddle, but did not explain the ambiguity. For example, in the 'newspaper' joke (see Table 6.8), one child explained that 'You don't get red newspapers, only black and white'. An explanation scoring 2 for the same riddle was 'It looks funny if it was red'.

As in the recall task, performance was best on the lexical and phonological categories (mean score = 2.6 and 2.7 respectively), and was poorer for the grammatical (2.3) and metalinguistic riddles (2.2). There was a weak correlation between overall ability to explain the riddles and comprehension skill ($r = 0.43$, $p < .10$), but the higher-order partial correlation (see above) was not significant ($r = 0.37$). Although the explanations of the lexical ambiguity and metalinguistic riddles were moderately correlated with comprehension skill (the higher-order partial correlations were 0.31 and 0.37 respectively), none of the within-category correlations was significant.

Reading accuracy only correlated with ability to explain the lexical ambiguity sub-group of riddles ($r = 0.53$, $p < .02$), but not with explanation scores overall.

Funniness ratings. Responses were scored on a 1–5 scale where 1 = 'not funny' and 5 = 'very funny'. The funniness ratings were very similar for all riddle types, ranging from 3.5 to 3.9, with an overall mean of 3.6. Thus, all riddles received quite high mean-funniness ratings. The funniness ratings did not correlate at all with comprehension skill, or with reading accuracy ($r = -0.19$ and $r = -0.12$ respectively), and did not correlate with the ability to recall or to explain the riddles. Neither were there any correlations with the other measures of riddle understanding. It seemed that, as in the previous study, the funniness ratings were not a good index of whether or not children understood a joke. The small range of scores in the present study suggests that the children just tended to give each riddle a 'moderately funny' rating, perhaps out of politeness more than anything else. It should also be noted that the experimental setting was rather more formal and constrained than in the pilot study, in which one child was telling the riddle to a peer, rather than to an adult experimenter.

Discussion Our results confirmed that the ability to understand riddles is related to reading comprehension skill: there was an overall relation between ability to recall riddles and comprehension skill, but no relation with reading accuracy. There were significant correlations between comprehension skill and recall of riddles for *all* categories except grammatical ambiguity. Thus, the easiest riddles, those with phonological and lexical ambiguities, were not too easy for our subjects – they certainly did *not* perform at ceiling level on riddles in these categories. Even though phonological skills and understanding of lexical ambiguity may be well developed in children of this age, such skills may not be brought to bear very directly in riddle understanding. This conclusion is supported by the finding that the ability to explain ambiguous words did not correlate at all with riddle understanding (on any measure). Thus, it may be that it is not simply the ability to *detect* ambiguities that is important, but the ability to reflect on the different meanings of a word and to reinterpret the riddle in the light of them. There may not have been correlations with the grammatical riddles because this riddle type was too difficult. The mean recall score was only 2.6 – somewhere between 'completely inaccurate' and 'riddle recalled makes no sense'. Indeed, Shultz and Pilon (1973) suggest that grammatical awareness of the sort required to understand such riddles only appears around the age of 12.

Performance on the explanation task was only weakly correlated with comprehension skill, probably because explanations were generally poor. The mean overall score of only 2.5 falls somewhere between 'completely incorrect' and 'incorrect, good attempt'. Explanations in the pilot study may have been better than in this experiment because subjects were motivated to explain the riddles to a peer. However, there was a correlation between recall and explanation ($r = 0.70$), indicating both that performance on the explanation task was not so poor as to preclude the possibility of obtaining correlations, and that the recall task was a reasonable way to assess how well children were able to understand the riddles. The funniness ratings were not a good predictor of riddle understanding. As we suggested in the pilot study, good and poor comprehenders may use different criteria for rating funniness, and children in both groups may consider a riddle funny for the 'wrong' reasons.

Reading accuracy only correlated with ability to explain the lexical riddles. The presence of this correlation was unexpected, but may have arisen because three of the four lexical riddles included homophones spelt differently from each other (pear/pair, red/read, bare/bear). Children with higher accuracy may have been more likely to be aware of these different vowel combinations than poorer readers.

General discussion

We have seen in this chapter that less-skilled children cannot be said to lack metacognitive skills completely: like skilled children, they answer questions about important features of a story better than questions about trivial aspects. However, when asked to pick out the main point of a story that they have heard or seen in pictures, they are less unanimous than skilled children or adults in their choice. In common with younger readers, they are also less likely to notice inconsistencies in stories, even when asked specifically to find anomalies. Their pattern of reading times suggest that they do not generate any internal signal when they encounter such information. If, as we concluded in Chapter 4, they do not make inferences as they read or listen to the extent that skilled readers do, then it is hardly surprising that they should be unaware of such inconsistencies. It may be that they would notice inconsistencies of other types. For example, Baker (1984a) suggests that younger and poorer readers tend to place much reliance on a lexical standard of comprehension monitoring, i.e. checking that individual lexical items are understood, whereas more skilled readers also used other standards, such as internal consistency of the text. Even when inconsistencies are made obvious, as in our study of anomaly resolution, less-skilled children are poorer at resolving the anomaly by integrating it with information elsewhere in the passage. This resolution is particularly difficult as concurrent processing demands increase, again demonstrating the influence of working-memory efficiency in text comprehension. Lexical and external standards, of course, do not require information integration over different parts of a text.

The second part of this chapter investigated metacognitive skills which are less obviously necessary for normal comprehension, but may be informative in considering children's approach to text comprehension. As the interviews in the first part of the chapter showed, the two groups of children did not differ markedly in their professed approach to reading, but less-skilled children were more likely to see decoding as a central part of reading. Other research (e.g. Forrest-Pressley et al., 1984) shows that older children tend to include comprehension in their definitions of reading, compared to younger children, who tend to emphasise decoding.

Our studies of riddle comprehension demonstrate a link between reading comprehension and appreciation of riddles, that has not been shown conclusively in previous research, and suggest an association between comprehension and metacognitive skills. The pattern of results is consistent with the suggestion by Tunmer and Bowey (1984) that poor comprehenders, while they have mastered grapheme–phoneme correspondences, fail to bring their syntactic knowledge of the spoken language to bear on the written language, a skill requiring reflection on the structural features of language. Thus, although children may have implicit knowledge of language structure, they cannot address this knowledge in explicit form so as to monitor their comprehension and recover from comprehension failures.

It could be argued that the sophisticated skills involved in explaining riddles are not necessary for adequate text comprehension (or even for riddle appreciation!). There are some aspects of knowledge about reading and language that children, or even adults, would find hard to articulate, and which may not be required for competent language use. An example of the latter is given in a study by Hirsh-Pasek et al. (1978), who investigated people's ways of paraphrasing invented compound terms such as 'house-bird glass', as a means of looking at use of rules for word-combination. Graduate students were much more likely than clerical workers to focus on syntactic structure, rather than on plausibility. For example, students would paraphrase 'bird house-black' in a syntactically correct but semantically implausible way, e.g. 'a blackener of houses who is a bird', whereas clerical workers would give semantically plausible but syntactically incorrect responses such as 'a black bird who lives in the house'. Both groups can be considered competent speakers of English, but differed in the tendency to analyse syntactic properties of language independently of meaning, at least in experimental tasks of the kind used.

It is therefore important to consider whether a particular metacognitive skill is a prerequisite or a concomitant of skilled reading comprehension. For example, we have found that poor comprehenders are as good as skilled ones in one metacognitive skill, picking out important parts of a text, but less good at a different skill, detecting textual inconsistency. The fact that the two groups were found to differ in some of the metacognitive skills assessed suggests that even if such skills are not necessary for skilled comprehension, they may be a good predictor of comprehension skill.

7 Using cohesive devices in narrative discourse

Introduction

In the previous chapters, we have provided evidence from a variety of sources showing poor comprehenders' problems in integrating and making relevant inferences about text. These difficulties are not confined to reading comprehension: we showed in several studies that these children display similar deficits in their listening comprehension. The studies in this chapter extend our investigations to language *production*. We are using this term in a very broad sense: we have not looked at spontaneous production of discourse in the two groups, but at narratives prompted by picture sequences, at responses to questions, and at reproductions of narratives the children had heard previously. We were interested in how the two groups of children use various linguistic devices that foster *cohesion*, such as anaphora, and causal expressions, as well as in investigating more generally the characteristics of story reproductions. We have already suggested that poor comprehenders have difficulty in making inferences and understanding cohesive devices in their listening comprehension, as well as in their reading. We would expect that, if these difficulties are linked to restrictions in efficiency of working memory, then these children's ability to plan cohesive narratives would also be poorer than that of skilled comprehenders. Furthermore, in keeping with our argument that poor comprehenders show a general linguistic deficit, rather than one that is specific to reading, we would expect differences between the groups in their oral language production, as well as in their reading and listening comprehension.

Production and comprehension of cohesive devices

It is clear that even children as young as 4 have some means of introducing cohesion into stories. Poulsen, Kintsch, Kintsch and Premack (1979) demonstrated that children of this age were more likely to mention the essential points of a picture story, as determined by adults, when given pictures in the appropriate order than when the pictures were in a scrambled order. However, 4-year-olds were less likely than 6-year-olds to use narrative conventions such as *once upon a time*, and temporal connectives such as *finally*. Thus, while young children's stories may be cohesive in terms of selection of content, the ability to use linguistic means of promoting cohesion at a local level appears to be a later achievement. Karmiloff-Smith (1985) has described some ways in which the linguistic form, as well as the content, of an event description alters if it is presented as part of a sequence rather than as an isolated occurrence. She suggests that children move from an initial strategy of producing referential links independently of each other to a stage at which they attempt to make intralinguistic links between referential devices, using pronouns in a truly anaphoric way, rather than a deictic one.

Whatever the source of the differences between narratives produced by children of different ages, it seems clear that such differences do exist. Stenning and Michell (1985) studied 5–10-year-olds' narrative descriptions of a picture sequence, and found three main stylistic differences between stories produced by children of different ages. First, there was a striking increase between the ages of 5 and 7 in the production of stories with appropriate use of reference: younger children were more likely either to omit references to characters, just using verbs to describe the main actions, or to use ambiguous pronouns, whereas older children used a successful mix of nouns and pronouns. Second, less than a third of children under 8 used any connectives other than *and then*, and the proportion of children using other connectives increased gradually up to the age of 10. Third, there was a gradual increase with age in the use of the past tense. There is, of course, nothing wrong with using the present tense, and many writers do so to give a sense of immediacy. However, Stenning and Michell argued that use of this tense can also signal a style of running commentary that remains within the narrator's frame of reference, rather than being organised round the framework of the story. In that sense, they claim, use of the present tense is less sophisticated than use of the past tense.

Some of our previous studies of comprehension can be used to make predictions about language production in the two skill groups. Less-skilled children may be more likely than skilled ones to use some of the 'naive' features identified by Stenning and Michell. For example, less-skilled comprehenders are poor at understanding a variety of cohesive devices such as reference, substitution and ellipsis (see Experiment 4.6). Although we had no specific information on which to base a prediction about the children's *use* of cohesive markers such as *because*, it seemed likely that less-skilled comprehenders, if they construct a poorly integrated mental model of a text, with little grasp of the cohesive links, would use such markers less frequently than skilled children.

In a pilot study, we told some children stories (the 'model' stories) in fairly basic language and asked them to retell the stories, using sequences of pictures as a memory aid. We examined the use of connectives such as *and*, *then* and *because* in the retellings, and found little difference between the two skill groups. In most cases, the children were simply repeating the pattern of connectives given in the model stories. This result suggests that even less-skilled comprehenders can recall appropriate connectives that are given. However, there was an interesting exception to this finding. In one of the two stories, the only connectives in the model story were temporal (*and then*, *when*). Many children made the story more cohesive by adding further temporal connectives, or more complex causal and contrastive terms. Twelve of the sixteen skilled children used connectives other than those provided, eight adding further temporal connectives where they had not appeared in the model, one adding a contrastive *but*, and three inserting causal connectives: *because* or *so*. Two of the latter children added contrastive connectives (*but*) as well as causal ones. However, only four of the sixteen poor comprehenders used any novel connectives, and none of these was causal: three of these children added temporal words and one added *but*. Two examples, the first from a poor comprehender and the second from a good one, show the sorts of stories produced. Connectives that were not present in the original story are italicised, and, as in the other narratives we quote in this chapter, punctuation has been added to reflect the rhythm in which the story was told.

(1) Sally was getting up for school. Her mum done her lunchbox. She went to school. She's singing a song. She put her lunchbox down. She's doing her lessons. She's doing her lessons again. She goes and gets the wrong lunchbox. She eats the wrong lunch. Another girl came with hers and they had their lunch together.

(2) One day there was a little girl and she got off... out of bed *because* she... she forgot school. [Here the child seemed to mean that the girl was rushing because she had forgotten it was time for school. The picture showed an alarm clock and a figure jumping out of bed.] Her mum has got... has got her breakfast ready. And then she took her lunchbox and said goodbye to her mum. Then she went to school with her lunchbox la'ing to herself. [The picture shows the girl singing 'lala'.] Then she put her lunchbox on the table and then she did her lessons. *After that*, she... it was lunchtime, she went to get her lunchbox. *But* she got the wrong lunchbox. *So* they went into the room with different lunchboxes. And then she sat down and she said, 'I've got the wrong sandwiches.' Then she went... and another girl came along and said, 'You've got my lunchbox.' *So* they had lunch together. Yum!

Thus, poor comprehenders could reproduce connectives when these were given in the story model, but were unlikely to provide more cohesion than was given in the model, whereas good comprehenders showed more evidence of attempts to add cohesion to a story, even though their stories were as full of false starts and speech repairs as those of the poor comprehenders. The two stories also give some interesting indications of other possible differences between the groups. The first story appears more list-like than the second. This impression is produced by several features: the use of present and continuous verb tenses (*was getting up*, *is doing*), the lack of connectives, and the repetition of events where this does not contribute to the story line (*she's doing her lessons again*). The latter phrase also suggests that the narrator is not recounting a story, but describing in turn the contents of each picture as a separate entity. The second story, on the other hand, is all in the past tense, integrates narrative and descriptive information (*she went to school... la'ing to herself*), uses various connectives (e.g. *but*, *so*), and includes phrases conventionally used in stories (*one day there was...*). This evidence, however, is somewhat impressionistic. The following experiment investigated differences in the two groups' narratives in a more systematic way.

Experiment 7.1: Cohesion in narratives: Effects of presentation method

Our pilot study suggested that less-skilled children did not go beyond a story model in their use of cohesive devices. However, it is possible that they, more than good comprehenders, perceived the task as requiring accuracy in retelling a narrative, and that they might be able to use such devices to a greater extent when given the freedom to plan their own narratives about a picture sequence. In the present study, therefore, the children were required to produce their own stories from picture sequences, rather than being given a model story to reproduce. The study focused on three linguistic features identified by Stenning and Michell as differentiating narratives by children of different ages. First, we examined children's use of referring expressions. Our previous studies of pronouns showed that poor comprehenders were less proficient at interpreting referential ties. If this finding reflects a general misunderstanding of the functions of pronouns and other such ties, then we would expect that this group's stories would either be highly repetitious, if full noun phrases were used instead of pronouns, or ambiguous, if pronouns were used inappropriately. Second, we looked at the sorts of connectives used in stories: were they exclusively simple *and then* constructions, or did children also use contrastive and causal links such as *but* and *because*? Third, we examined tense: would poor comprehenders use the present tense more than good comprehenders did?

In order to investigate further the extent to which children planned cohesive narratives, we varied the mode in which the picture sequences were presented. The children were given sequences with the pictures either all on view simultaneously, or presented serially. In the serial presentation mode, the storyteller does not know what will happen next, or what new characters might be introduced. Such circumstances would disrupt the planning of a cohesive linguistic strategy, e.g. choosing appropriate pronouns, understanding the significance of current events in the light of later ones. Seeing the entire sequence at once should enable the narrator to consider the story as a whole.

Method Twelve children in each skill group took part in this study. We drew our materials from a study by Yussen (1982), who used picture sequences to elicit narratives from fourth to seventh graders. The sequences were from the Picture Arrangement Task (PAT) of the Wechsler Intelligence Scale for Children – Revised Version (Wechsler, 1974), which comprises twelve sets of cartoon-style black-and-white illustrations, with three to six pictures in each sequence. The sequences are ordered in terms of increasing difficulty, according to children's ability to put scrambled pictures from a sequence into the correct order. After some pilot work, we chose six sequences, items 1,2,7,8,10 and 11 of the PAT. Each picture was coloured and mounted on a separate card. For the serial condition, the cards in each story were bound together as a booklet. The subjects told the story as they leafed through the pages. In the simultaneous condition, all the pictures in a sequence were laid out in front of the child at the outset. The children looked at all the pictures first, and then told the story, with the pictures still visible. The six sequences were divided into two sets, with sequences of approximately equal difficulty, according to the PAT ordering, and with one sequence of three, one of four and one of five pictures in each set. A synopsis of each sequence is given in Table 7.1. Half the children in each skill group had Set A presented simultaneously and Set B serially, and the other half had the opposite assignment. The order in which the stories were presented was also counterbalanced for each story set and presentation mode. As a warm-up to the task of telling the stories, the children were first asked to 'tell the story' of the practice item of the PAT.

Results The stories were transcribed and were then scored for use of reference, connectives and tense by two raters, one of whom was blind to skill group and condition. Disagreements were resolved by discussion.

Reference. Following the method of Stenning and Michell (1985), we gave each story production an overall rating according to how referential ties were used. A rating of 0 was given if there were ambiguous or repetitious references (e.g. use of a pronoun without a preceding noun phrase, use of full noun phrases only), and a suitable mixture of nouns and pronouns was coded as 1. We termed these two codings 'embedded' and 'disembedded' respectively.[1] There were only eleven disagreements in 144 stories (8%). We analysed the scores by analysis of variance with presentation condition (simultaneous or serial) within subjects, and comprehension skill, order of story sets and order of presentation condition as between-subjects' factors.

The main effect of skill group approached significance, $F(1, 16) = 4.06$, $p < .06$. The skilled children tended to produce more disembedded patterns of reference than the less-skilled children. The percentages of stories containing disembedded references in the two groups were 67% and 44% respectively. There was also a marginally significant main effect of method of presentation,

Table 7.1. *Descriptions of pictures in each story*

Practice:
(a) Woman approaching weighing scales, shopping bag on floor
(b) Woman standing on scales
(c) Woman with bag walking away from scales

SET A
1. Picnic:
(a) Man and woman walking along carrying basket with chicken leg in it, dog following
(b) Dog standing on hind legs and taking hold of chicken leg. Man and woman looking in opposite direction
(c) Man and woman standing by picnic cloth, staring in horror at empty basket
2. Vain:
(a) Woman with paintbrushes in pocket carrying mirror towards easel
(b) Woman putting mirror on table by side of easel
(c) Woman painting at easel, looking towards mirror
(d) Woman admiring finished picture of an over-glamorised self-portrait
3. Worms:
(a) Woman in garden with spade, pointing to bush in bag, watched by boy
(b) Boy, smiling, digging hole next to bush, worm emerging from hole
(c) Spade and bush lying on ground, boy with fishing rod creeping away
(d) Boy walking through trees, carrying rod and can
(e) Boy fishing in river, can by his side

SET B
1. Boxing:
(a) Two men in boxing ring, spectators, one man punching the other
(b) Other man punching first man, who is falling
(c) First man carried out on stretcher, other man raising arms in victory
2. Rope:
(a) Cowboy looking in shop window containing saddles, hats, rope
(b) Cowboy in shop, pointing out a rope to shopkeeper behind counter
(c) Shopkeeper giving indicated rope to cowboy
(d) Cowboy behind counter taking money from till, shopkeeper tied to chair with rope
3. Table:
(a) Man looking in window of furniture shop with 'Sale' sign
(b) Man outside shop, carrying table, walking behind second man
(c) First man in front of second man, who is hit on head by table
(d) Table on ground, second man, hands on hips, turned towards first man
(e) First man punching second man in the eye, two cheering spectators sitting on table

$F(1, 16) = 4.36$, $p < .053$. When pictures of a story were presented simultaneously, the children were more likely to use a disembedded pattern of reference than when presentation was serial: the percentages of stories with disembedded reference were 62% for simultaneous and 47% for serial presentation. The most interesting result, though, was the marginally significant interaction of skill group and presentation condition, $F(1, 16) = 4.36$, $p < .053$. The skilled comprehenders benefited from being able to see the entire picture sequence at once, but presentation condition made no difference to the less-skilled group (see Table 7.2).

There was also an interaction that we had not anticipated, of story set (A vs B) and presentation condition, $F(1, 16) = 14.67$, $p < .002$. Inspection of the data showed that the tendency for serial presentation to induce disembedded reference less often than simultaneous presentation was more marked in Set B than in Set A, as shown in Table 7.3. Consideration of the two story sets suggested a potential source of this difference that we had not considered at the outset – the number of characters of the same sex appearing in the picture sequences. In Set B, the characters within each story are of the same sex, while in Set A, there are either two characters of different sexes or only a single character in each story. Appearance of two same-sex characters in the sequential condition led to repetitious and ambiguous use of referring expressions characteristic of an embedded style. For example, the story below shows how one child used repetitious noun phrases to distinguish two male characters:

There was these two boxers and there was one in red shorts and one in blue shorts, the one in blue shorts was fighting down the one in red and then the one in blue shorts fell down and and the one in red shorts thought he was gonna be the winner and the one in red shorts did win because he knocked the blue one down and he had to be put on the thing [a stretcher].

Other children solved the problem of reference more elegantly, for example, referring to the characters by role (*a shopper, the winner*) or using linguistically distinct descriptions (consistently using *he* for the main character, and *the man* for a male appearing later in the story), or by consistent use of deixis to distinguish between the characters, as in the following example:

This man is boxing and he beats that man cos that man keeps on losing and getting cuts everywhere cos he's too worn out, they're taking him to hospital or somewhere to get better.

Connectives. We made a slightly finer differentiation of connectives than Stenning and Michell did, by recording the number of uses of connectives of three types – *and then* only, temporal and contrastive links (e.g. *when, until, but*) and causal connectives (*because* and *so*). For each story, the children received a score of 0 if they used only the first type, 1 if they included one or more examples of the second type, and 2 if they included the third type. As the list of connectives was exhaustive, there were no disagreements in ratings.

Analysis of variance with skill group, presentation mode and presentation order showed no significant effects or interactions, all $Fs < 1$. Despite our finding, described earlier, that skilled children tended to add connectives to stories to a greater extent than less-skilled ones, we did not find any differences between the groups in the sophistication of connectives used. About 45% of the stories by each skill group included at least one causal connective. However, the

Table 7.2. *Mean percentages of stories containing disembedded reference in the two presentation conditions for each skill group*

	Presentation condition		
	Serial	Simultaneous	Difference
Less-skilled	44·3	44·3	0·0
Skilled	50·0	83·3	33·3*

Note: * $p < 0{\cdot}05$ (Tukey's HSD).

Table 7.3. *Mean percentages of stories containing disembedded reference for each story set in the two presentation conditions*

	Presentation condition	
	Serial	Simultaneous
Set A	69·3	72·3
Set B	25·0	55·7
Difference	44·3*	16·6

Note: * $p < 0{\cdot}05$ (Tukey's HSD).

poor comprehenders' scores tended more towards a bimodal distribution than the good ones' scores. Six of the twelve poor comprehenders used only one or no causal connectives at all, over all the six stories they were given, compared to only two good comprehenders. At the other end of the distribution, three less-skilled children used more than nine such connectives over the six stories, compared to only one skilled comprehender. Thus, the majority of good comprehenders used causal connectives in moderation, whereas the poor comprehenders tended to use either very many, or none at all. Over both groups, 51% per cent of the stories contained at least one causal or contrastive connective.

Tense. We classified stories according to the predominant tense used, past or present. There were seven cases (5%) in which equal numbers of past and present tense verbs occurred, and these were categorised according to the prevailing impression of which tense was primary (e.g. stories starting and ending with past tense, and with a present-tense description of a single sequence in the middle were classified as 'past' even though there may have been an equal number of verbs in each tense).

Stenning and Michell found that about half their 7-year-olds consistently used the past tense in their stories, whereas virtually all 10-year-olds did. In our

Table 7.4. *Mean percentages of stories containing predominantly past tense as a function of story set and comprehension skill*

Story set:	A	B
Less-skilled	31·0	8·0
Skilled	56·0	58·0
Difference	25·0	50·0*

Note: $*p < 0{\cdot}05$ (Tukey's HSD).

Table 7.5. *Mean percentage of stories containing predominantly past tense as a function of presentation order and comprehension skill*

Order of presentation:	A first	B first	Difference
Less-skilled	19·0	19·0	0·0
Skilled	94·0	19·0	75·0*

Note: $*p < 0{\cdot}05$ (Tukey's HSD).

study, we found first, and most strikingly, that the skilled comprehenders used the past tense much more often than the less-skilled comprehenders, $F(1, 16) = 11.76$, $p < .004$. Only 19% of the less-skilled children's stories used the past tense, compared to 57% of the skilled children's stories. Comprehension skill also interacted with story set, $F(1, 16) = 5.79$, $p < .03$. The less-skilled comprehenders' tendency to use the present tense was particularly marked in Set B, as shown in Table 7.4. The first story in Set B was about a boxing match (see Table 7.1). This story tended to elicit a 'running commentary' style from many of the poor comprehenders, and use of the present tense was part of this style. Furthermore, an interaction between comprehension skill and set presentation order, $F(1, 16) = 11.76$, $p < .004$, showed that the skilled children were even more likely to use the past tense if they saw Set A before Set B, rather than the reverse order, while this was not the case for the less-skilled comprehenders (see Table 7.5). The less-skilled children used the present tense predominantly, regardless of presentation order. Surprisingly, the children did not use the past tense more for simultaneous than for serial presentation. For these stories at least, comprehension skill and story content seemed more potent factors in determining tense choice.

Discussion The analysis of the reference scores showed that the less-skilled comprehenders had difficulty in making use of appropriate reference in their own narratives. This tendency is not parallel to their performance in comprehending referential ties (Experiment 4.6): for example, one child, who participated in both studies, gave a female referent for a male pronoun in Experiment 4.6, but did not make such mistakes in her story-telling for the present study. This finding underlines the point that less-skilled comprehenders are not deficient in basic linguistic knowledge (e.g. that *she* refers to a female), but in their ability to interpret cohesive devices in context. This difficulty includes using referential ties provided in a text and producing such ties in narratives. The results also showed a striking difference in tense usage in the two groups. As in the case of reference, poor comprehenders' use of tense was more like that of younger children than the good comprehenders' was. The results also suggested other factors in story structure that contribute to variations in tense use: present tense was more often associated with a particular story content, and with the order in which stories were presented. Unlike our pilot study, this experiment showed no group differences in the types of connective used, although the good comprehenders seemed to use causal connectives more uniformly across stories than the poor comprehenders did.

Experiment 7.2: Cohesion in narratives: Effects of referential distinctiveness

As we mentioned above, the poor comprehenders' tendency to use an embedded style of reference was particularly marked in stories with same-sex characters, because it was more difficult to refer to characters distinctively. We investigated this issue more thoroughly by carrying out a further study of story-telling in which we varied the sex of the characters systematically. For practical reasons, we tested slightly older children (8–9-year-olds), as we had selected groups of good and poor comprehenders, matched in the usual way, for another experiment. Because these older children would probably find our task less difficult than the younger children we had tested previously, we used only the more difficult, serial presentation condition.

Method There were fifteen children in each skill group. The materials were sequences 8, 12, 10 and 11 of the PAT, which provided, respectively, two stories of four pictures (the 'rope' story shown in Table 7.1 and a story about a girl who gets soaked by the rain after ignoring her mother's warning that there are storm clouds[2]), and two stories of five pictures (the 'worms' and 'table' stories described previously in Table 7.1). For one story of each length, both characters appeared in the first picture and for the other, only one character appeared in the first picture. We varied whether the two main characters were the same or different sexes by the simple expedient of altering the pictures.

Each child was given four stories, two with different-sex characters and two with same-sex characters. The order of presentation and the sex of characters in each story were counterbalanced. Thus, children saw the same-sex stories first or second, and a particular story was presented either with same-sex or different-sex characters to different subjects. As in the previous study, children were first given a warm-up task: telling a story about the practice item of the PAT. All the stories were presented serially, with the pictures bound into a book.

Results *Scoring*. As in the previous study, we investigated the use of reference, connectives and tense. We also investigated the frequency of other cohesive devices – ellipsis and substitution – as these seemed more likely to appear in the narratives of 8–9-year-olds than they had in the younger children we had tested earlier. A rater, blind to skill group, scored each story according to the details given under each subheading below. A second rater independently scored transcripts from four subjects selected at random (i.e. sixteen stories) with under 5% of disagreements in each category, which we considered to show adequate reliability. The data for the first rater were used. We analysed the data by analysis of variance, with skill group between subjects and referential distinctiveness (different- or same-sex characters) within subjects.

Reference. Each occurrence of a reference to either of the two main characters was scored as embedded or disembedded (as defined in the previous experiment). Embedded references were of two types: those that would not distinguish two characters for a listener who could not see the pictures, e.g. beginning a story with *he*, or using *she* to refer to both of two female characters without otherwise indicating linguistically which was meant. The second sort of embedded reference involved the use of definite references when a character was first mentioned, e.g. beginning a story with *the boy* without signalling that this was a new character, rather than introducing the character by a phrase such as *once there was a boy*. Introductory references of the type *this boy* were not considered to be embedded, because the use of *this* as an indefinite article was frequent in the speech of many of the children (e.g. *there was this boy, and he*...). The number of embedded references in each story was then expressed as a proportion of the total number of references to main characters.

As expected, there was a greater proportion of embedded references for same-sex than for different-sex stories, $F(1, 26) = 8.12$, $p < .01$. There were on average 15% of such references for same-sex stories, compared to 8% for different-sex stories. Neither the main effect of group nor the interaction of group and referential distinctiveness reached significance, $Fs(1, 26) = 2.21$ and 2.05 respectively. The less-skilled children used embedded reference 13.5% of the time, compared to 9.6% for the skilled children. Despite the lack of a significant interaction of group and referential distinctiveness, the correlation of reference score and comprehension age was greater for same-sex stories ($r = -.395$, $df = 27$, $p < .02$) than for different-sex stories ($r = .087$, $df = 27$, n.s.). The difference between these correlations, taking into account the correlation between the two reference types ($r = .154$), was significant, $T^2 = 2.03$, $p < .05$.

Connectives. There was at least one causal connective in 37% of the stories, and this figure was the same for both skill groups. These figures are, surprisingly, a little lower than those for the 7-year-olds in the previous experiment. We analysed the data by looking at the number of causal connectives as a proportion of the total number of all connectives used for each story production. However, there was no significant difference between the skill groups: causal connectives formed 11% of all the connectives used by the less-skilled children, compared to 14.5% for the skilled children. Nor was there any difference between use of causal connectives for same- and different-sex stories, average percentages = 12.5% and 12.6% respectively. All Fs were less than 1.

Tense. As in the previous study, we rated each story in terms of the predominant tense of verbs. The less-skilled children used the past tense less frequently than the skilled children did (in 39% of stories vs 59%), but this difference was not significant, $F(1, 26) = 1.33$, n.s. (In comparison, the previous study showed 19% and 57% use of past tense by poor and good 7-year-olds.) There was no effect of sex of story characters on tense use, $F < 1$, and no significant interaction.

Ellipsis and substitution. We had not investigated ellipsis and substitution in our previous studies of narratives because such usages were quite rare. However, as the children in the present experiment were somewhat older than those we had used before, we examined the stories for instances of these two types of cohesive tie. In order to do this, the stories were divided into 'units' (that is, each phrase containing a tensed verb constituted a unit). Both groups made about the same use of ellipsis: the number of ellipses used as a percentage of the number of story units was 18% for less-skilled children and 16.5% for the skilled ones. Rutter and Raban (1982) found that under 3% of sentence units contained ellipsis in their 6- and 10-year-olds' written productions. However, their criteria for ellipsis were stricter than ours. They did not include noun-phrase ellipsis, the type we found most commonly: deletion of the subject before a verb, as in *the girl went out and* [] *played in the rain*, where [] marks an ellipsed reference to the girl.[3] Halliday and Hasan (1976, p.174) call such examples 'operator ellipsis'. However, many linguists would not consider this category 'true' ellipsis, compared to verb-phrase ellipses such as *He thought it was great fun planting the tree but he didn't really want to* [], where [] marks *plant the tree*. There was only a handful of such 'true' ellipses in our data. Nor did the two groups differ in the percentages of substitutions used: these were very rare, at under 1% of units (representing only nineteen uses in all 180 stories), a similar figure to that found by Rutter and Raban.

Discussion The differences between good and poor comprehenders found previously were not as apparent for these older children. However, there was still a link between the use of embedded reference and comprehension skill.

Furthermore, referential devices were used more effectively in stories where characters were of different sexes, a manipulation that minimised difficulties in using distinctive reference. The less-skilled children still used the present tense more frequently, although the difference between skill groups was not significant.

Discussion of narrative production studies

The assessment of the narrative skills of poor comprehenders is a new theme in our investigation: we have already shown that such children's difficulties are not restricted to reading comprehension, but also extend to listening comprehension. The story-telling studies show that there were also differences between the groups in some aspects of their language use. Both the studies above showed that poor comprehenders used more embedded patterns of reference than good comprehenders, although the older children did not show a significant difference. However, use of appropriate reference is not all-or-nothing: children were affected by characteristics of the story, in this case the presence or absence of two characters of the same sex. The 7–8-year-old less-skilled children also performed more similarly to younger children (Stenning and Michell, 1985) in their greater use of the present tense. We did not find clear evidence that the groups differed in their use of causal links, except in the study of prompted productions.

The difference between the groups might be described in stylistic terms, in that the less-skilled children told stories that were more like running commentaries. In some cases, this may have been an effective stylistic device, but in others, it seemed more to reflect the fact that the children were describing a series of apparently unrelated events (what Yussen, 1982, called a 'reactive chain'), rather than constructing an integrated sequence of statements. For some of the poor comprehenders, it did seem that 'every picture tells a story'.

There is no suggestion that the differences in language use reflect children's general linguistic competence. For example, less-skilled children are quite capable of producing verbs in the past tense. The difference between the groups lies in the choice of language forms for narrating stories, and can perhaps be illustrated more vividly by two typical accounts of the 'picnic' story (see Table 7.1), from a poor and a good comprehender respectively, in Experiment 7.1:

A man and a lady is walking along and the doggie is behind them and there's some chicken hanging out of their bag and the dog bites it and they have a picnic and all the food is gone.

Once there was a man and a lady and a dog and they went for a walk to have a picnic and they took two legs with them. When they came near the spot they were gonna have their picnic, the dog was trying to get their food because he thought the food was for him so he ate the food, and when they got to their picnic spot they looked in and everything was gone and they were so surprised they went home and got their dinner at home.

Table 7.6. *Examples of materials for empirical and deductive uses of 'because'*

Empirical
1. Pictures: Mary finds a mouse in her bed. Mary is hiding in the corner.
Questions: Mary is scared isn't she?... Why is Mary scared?
Completion: Mary is scared because...
2. Pictures: John falls off his bike. John's leg is in plaster.
Questions: John has got a broken leg, hasn't he?... Why has John got a broken leg?
Completion: John's leg is broken because...

Deductive
1. Pictures: Mary gets soaked. Mary is sneezing.
Questions: Mary has got a cold, hasn't she?... How do you know Mary has got a cold?
Completion: We can tell that Mary has got a cold because...
2. Pictures: John bumps into Mary. There is a puddle of milk on the floor.
Questions: Mary spilt the milk, didn't she?... How do you know Mary spilt the milk?
Completion: We can tell that Mary spilt the milk because...

As well as illustrating some of the differences between skill groups in language use (e.g. choice of verb tense), these stories show the contrast between a typical reactive chain story (the first example, above) and a more cohesive narrative style. The second narrator seems to have some general plan in mind, as she mentions the couple's intention to have a picnic, and their approach to the picnic spot, which only appears in the final picture of the sequence. This planning requires the narrator to look ahead, and to modify the description of the current picture with respect to what will be said about subsequent ones. This more complex style presumably makes more demands on working memory during production. The first narrator merely describes one or two aspects of each picture, and could presumably focus on each picture in sequence, to provide an external place-marker of where she is in the story. It may be that less-skilled children, despite having some knowledge of cohesive devices, are constrained by working memory limitations in the sorts of stories they can produce (see Chapter 5). It is also notable that the central point of the story is not clear in the poor comprehender's story. There is no indication that the couple are surprised at the disappearance of the chicken, and it is not even clear why 'all the food has gone': without seeing the pictures, a listener might assume that the couple ate the food themselves. As we described in Chapter 6, poor comprehenders were not very good at picking out the main point of the stories.

Experiment 7.3: Comprehension and production of causal expressions[4]

As we have seen in the story-telling studies, causal expressions are an important means of establishing cohesion between ideas in a text, and of expressing the causal structure of a story. One of the most common linguistic devices for expressing causal links is the word *because*. Our studies of story production did not give clear support to our hypothesis that poor comprehenders would use *because* less often than good ones. However, it is possible that the less-skilled children are proficient in some uses of the word and not others. Support for this possibility comes from an extensive study by Donaldson (1986) of children's comprehension and production of *because*. She distinguished between different uses of the word. The most common 'empirical' use is as a causal link between two events, e.g. 'Mary spilt the milk because John bumped into her.' However, *because* is also used deductively, to introduce evidence for a conclusion, as in the sentence 'We can tell that Mary spilt the milk because there is a puddle on the floor.' Donaldson assessed comprehension and production of empirical and deductive *because* by showing 5–10-year-olds pictures of simple causal sequences (e.g. John bumping into Mary, who is carrying a milk jug; a puddle of milk on the floor). Then she asked them questions to elicit *because* either in its empirical form, e.g. 'Why did Mary spill the milk?', or its deductive form, 'How do you know that Mary spilt the milk?'. In another condition, Donaldson checked children's interpretations of *because* by asking them to complete sentences that invited either deductive or empirical usage, e.g. 'We can tell that Mary spilt the milk because...' versus 'Mary spilt the milk because...'. The children were largely correct in their empirical uses, but tended to interpret invitations for the deductive uses as if they required an empirical response, e.g. saying 'because John bumped into her', rather than 'because there is a puddle on the floor'. For the question task, 8-year-olds scored only about 50% correct for deductive items, and even 10-year-olds were only 64% correct. All children showed a greater bias to respond empirically on the completion task than on the questions.

All the examples of *because* we encountered in the previous studies in this chapter were clearly empirical. However, we thought it was important to assess children's appreciation of deductive *because*: this usage seems particularly relevant in reading comprehension because it concerns the relation between evidence and conclusions. While it is possible to draw conclusions from reading text without being aware of how those conclusions were reached, comprehension failures can best be resolved if the reader is aware of the course of reasoning. Only then can the reader recognise the source of a misunderstanding, or interrogate the text to find evidence for an inference.

Method Twelve children in each group were given eight sequences in the questions task, and then a further eight for the sentence completion task, using the same simple causal sequences as Donaldson did. Some examples are shown in Table 7.6, including instructions for each task. Each item was accompanied by two coloured pictures showing the events described. Within each task, half the items were deductive, and half were empirical. We derived four different lists of randomly-ordered materials, so that each material appeared once in each mode (empirical and deductive) in each task (question and completion). All children were given the question task before the completion one, which was preceded by a single, non-causal practice item showing a simple sequence of events that was described to the child, followed by an incomplete sentence mentioning the first part of the sequence only.

We had noticed in pilot work for this study that some children seemed to expect all items to be empirical, without listening carefully to the exact form of the question or partial sentence. We therefore included some new 'pictorial cue' instructions which were designed to emphasise the difference between empirical and deductive items by focusing attention on pictures as sources of evidence for the deductive items. These instructions were used for deductive items, and took the form: 'How do you know *from the picture* that Mary spilt the milk?', or for the deductive completion task, 'We can tell *from the picture* that Mary spilt the milk because...'. Half the subjects in each group were given the tasks with the standard instructions used by Donaldson, as shown in Table 7.6, and half were given the pictorial-cue instructions.

Results We classified the children's responses as empirical or deductive: no child answered 'don't know' to any of the items. Responses were scored as correct if they used the appropriate mode. We analysed the results from both tasks with groups and instructions (standard or with pictorial cue) between subjects, and mode (empirical or deductive) within subjects.

Answers to questions. There were main effects of group, $F(1, 20) = 6.66$, $p < .02$, and mode, $F(1, 20) = 67.48$, $p < .0001$, as skilled comprehenders gave more correct answers, and empirical items were easier than deductive ones. There was also an interaction between skill group and mode, $F(1, 20) = 13.18$, $p < .002$. As the upper half of Table 7.7 shows, both groups performed well on the empirical items, but the less-skilled comprehenders were significantly poorer than the skilled comprehenders on the deductive ones. The pictorial-cue instructions also had a beneficial effect on performance, $F(1, 20) = 6.66$, $p < .02$, and instruction type interacted with mode, $F(1, 20) = 13.18$, $p < .002$. As we expected, the pictorial-cue instructions increased children's performance for the deductive items, but not for the empirical ones, as shown in Table 7.7.

Sentence completions. The results for completions were very similar to those for the question task. There was a marginal main effect for skill group, $F(1, 20) = 4.05$, $p < .058$, and a main effect of mode, $F(1, 20) = 60.80$, $p < .0001$, and an interaction between these factors, $F(1, 20) = 7.36$, $p < .002$. Again, this was because the difference between modes was more marked for the less-skilled comprehenders than for the skilled comprehenders, as the lower half of Table 7.7 shows.

As in the question task, there was a main effect of instruction, $F(1, 20) =$

Table 7.7. *Mean numbers of correct responses as a function of instructions, mode and comprehension skill (max = 4)*

	Question–answers					
Mode:	Empirical			Deductive		
Instructions:	standard		pic. cue	standard		pic. cue
Less-skilled	4·00		4·00	0·83		2·00
		4·00			1·42	
Skilled	4·00		3·67	2·00		3·67
		3·83			2·83	
Difference		0·17			1·41*	

	Completions					
Mode:	Empirical			Deductive		
Instructions:	standard		pic. cue	standard		pic. cue
Less-skilled	4·00		4·00	0·33		2·50
		4·00			1·42	
Skilled	3·83		3·83	1·67		3·50
		3·83			2·58	
Difference		0·17			1·16*	

Note: $*p < 0{\cdot}05$ (Tukey's HSD).

16.18, p < .001, and an interaction of instruction with mode, F (1, 20) = 16.55, p < .001, because the pictorial-cue instructions enhanced performance on the deductive items but not on the empirical ones (see Table 7.7). No other effects were significant, all Fs < 1.

Discussion The less-skilled children tended to interpret *because* as empirical to a greater extent than skilled children did, and in this respect, their performance was similar to the younger children studied by Donaldson. Our revised instructions did curtail this tendency to some extent, but the difference between groups still remained. The poor performance on deductive items could be interpreted in different ways: it may indicate a failure to map the linguistic item on to an existing conceptual knowledge of the relation expressed by deductive *because* or may reflect a conceptual failure to understand the relation expressed by the word. In either case, it represents a handicap to reading comprehension. If poor comprehenders misinterpret deductive *because*, they will be unable to construct an adequate mental model of the text.

We suggested in our introduction to this experiment that misunderstanding of deductive usage may reflect a conceptual deficit in relating evidence to conclusions. We see this ability as *metacognitive*, i.e. it involves a judgement about one's own knowledge, in this case, the source in the text of one's knowledge. Unless readers are aware of how a conclusion has been reached, or an inference made, they cannot go back to the text and trace the source of any misunderstandings that may arise. Even if less-skilled children have some conception of the relation between the text and their interpretation of it, they are less able than skilled children to articulate their understanding.

A further clue as to the nature of poor comprehenders' problems with deductive *because* is provided by their better performance with the revised instructions. It is important to note that these instructions did not give the children any specific information about the content of the correct answer: the phrase 'from the picture' could have referred to either of the two pictures. The pictorial-cue instructions merely suggested to children a general procedure they could use to reach the correct answer. Even so, this minor change produced a marked increase in the number of correct responses to deductive items. This result suggests that at least part of the children's problem with deductive sentences was of focusing attention on the relevant source of evidence. They seem to have some capacity to understand deductive relations, but fail to use this capacity appropriately. This interpretation is similar to Bereiter and Scardamalia's (1982) argument that children's difficulties with written composition often stem from 'executive problems' such as difficulty in attending to relevant aspects of the writing task. These authors found that they could improve children's written composition by various forms of 'procedural facilitation', such as reminders to switch attention between generating text and evaluating it, and minimising the attention required to run executive processes, by being given a set routine for generating text. Our revised instructions for deductive items could be seen as a form of such facilitation.

Effects of referential continuity on story-retelling
Experiment 7.4

In the final experiment of this chapter, we explored how the groups cope more generally with referential links in coherent discourse. The method we used was to investigate how the presence or absence of such links affects children's *memory* for text. If children appreciate the cohesive function of the linguistic forms we have discussed in this chapter, then they should be in a good position to understand the logical structure of a text, and therefore better able to reproduce a cohesive text from memory. As we pointed out in Chapter 2, the *referential continuity* of a text can affect how easy it is to understand. For instance, the absence of referential continuity may mean that pronouns lack any plausible antecedents. The three examples of texts in Table 7.8 that we used in the present experiment illustrate our point. The first example shows the original story, and the second is a version in which the order of sentences has been

Table 7.8. *Example story from Experiment 7·4*

David was playing with his big, coloured ball in the garden. He bounced it so hard that it went right over the fence. The people next door were out so he climbed over to get it. He found his ball and threw it back. David carried on with his game. (original)
He found his ball and threw it back. The people next door were out so he climbed over to get it. David carried on with his game. He bounced it so hard that it went right over the fence. David was playing with his big, coloured ball in the garden. (random)
David found his big coloured ball and threw it back. The people next door were out so he climbed over to get it. He carried on with his game. He bounced his ball so hard that it went right over the fence. David was playing with it in the garden. (revised)

randomised. This procedure completely disrupts referential continuity. However, it also disrupts the causal sequence of events in a story. Such stories may be hard to understand because of the disruption in either referential or causal continuity. The effect of referential continuity alone can be investigated since it can be restored independently of the event sequence of a text, as shown in the third story in Table 7.8. Garnham, Oakhill and Johnson-Laird (1982, Experiment 1) provided evidence to show that both referential continuity and event structure of a text contribute to the ease with which a text can be recalled.

We thus examined the groups' recall of normal text, and the effects on recall when (a) both event structure and referential coherence are disrupted by randomising the order of sentences, and (b) event structure is disrupted but the coherence of a passage is maintained by rewriting the randomised stories to restore referential continuity. We expected the skilled comprehenders to remember more than the less-skilled ones from the normal texts, as a direct result of their superior comprehension. If, as we hypothesised, the groups differ in their ability to make use of the referential ties in a text to aid their recall, then skilled children should recall more of the revised stories, but should not differ from the less-skilled ones in recall of random stories.

Method Six passages, each five sentences in length (forty-eight to fifty words), were written in a suitable vocabulary. In each passage the main person and object occurred in the first sentence, and were pronominalised thereafter, except in the fourth sentence, where the object was reintroduced, and in the fifth sentence, where the person was reintroduced. A second version of each passage was constructed in which the same sentences occurred in a random order. A different random order was used for each passage. A third version was then constructed by replacing the noun phrases of the randomised passage, where necessary, so as to re-establish the referential continuity of the story. In each case, the number of words per passage was not changed. An example of a passage in each of its three versions is shown in Table 7.8.

There were twelve subjects in each skill group. All the children received two stories in each of the three experimental versions: normal, random and revised. There were three sets of materials, such that each passage occurred in each of the three versions, and equal numbers of subjects in each skill group were assigned to each set. Three different orders of presentation of the three versions were used to control for practice effects between versions.

The children were told that they would be given six short stories to read, and, after they had read each story, they would have to repeat as much of it as they could remember. They were told to try to recall the exact words of the story if possible but, if they could not do so, to put what they could remember into their own words. The children had as much time as they wanted to recall the stories: the next story was not presented until they had said that they had finished their recall.

Results Six independent adult judges divided each story into nine 'idea units', and the children's recall protocols were scored in relation to those units – for the most part simple surface clauses – on which at least four of the judges were agreed. A child was deemed to have remembered an idea unit provided that its gist was correct, i.e. synonymous terms were treated as correct, and there was no penalty for omitting adjectival or adverbial modifiers, articles and other items that were not essential to meaning. Table 7.9 presents the mean numbers of idea units recalled by each group for the three sorts of passage. The skilled group recalled more ideas overall than the less-skilled one, min F' $(1,21) = 8.70$, $p < .01$; the version in which a story occurred had a significant effect on the number of ideas recalled, min F' $(2,18) = 4.65$, $p < .025$; and there was an interaction between comprehension ability and the version of the story, F_1 $(2,44) = 3.32$, $p < .05$, F_2 $(2,10) = 5.22$, $p < .03$. The nature of this interaction was investigated using Newman–Keuls tests with p set at .05. This analysis revealed that the skilled comprehenders recalled more of the original and revised random stories than did the less-skilled comprehenders, but there was no reliable difference between the two groups in their ability to recall the unrevised random stories. Comparisons within groups showed that the skilled group recalled more of the original stories than the revised random stories, and more of the revised random stories than the unrevised random stories. The less-skilled comprehenders recalled more of the original stories than the revised random stories, but they did *not* recall reliably more of the revised random stories than of the unrevised random ones.

Discussion The results demonstrate that only the skilled comprehenders were able to take advantage of the restoration of referential continuity in randomised stories. Their superior abilities helped them with understanding and remembering the original and the revised random stories. But, if the task was to recall a

Table 7.9. *Mean number of idea units (max. = 9) recalled in each skill group as a function of passage version*

	Passage version			
	Normal	Revised	Random	Mean
Less-skilled	5·2	3·5	3·9	4·2
Skilled	7·4	6·2	4·8	6·1
Mean	6·2	4·8	4·4	5·2

jumbled story in which there was no referential continuity, comprehension skill made little difference to performance. Additionally, the less-skilled group did not recall reliably more from the revised than from the random story versions, whereas the skilled group showed a significant improvement between random and revised, and between revised and normal versions. The finding that the less-skilled comprehenders found the random and revised passages equally difficult is understandable when one considers their performance in the experiments on anaphor comprehension in Chapter 4. If they were unable to perceive and use the referential links between the propositions in a story, they would experience no advantage when referential continuity was restored to the random passages. The finding that the less-skilled comprehenders were poor on revised passages might also be attributable to their inability to infer plausible causal links in a text where the event sequence has been disordered. Differences in the quality of the two groups' reproductions seemed to support this idea.

We sought to quantify the differences between the groups in coherence by rating each recall protocol for coherence on a scale of 0 to 4, where 0 = completely incoherent and 4 = completely coherent. Two raters, both blind to skill group, showed good consistency in the relative ordering of stories, with correlations varying from .81 to .93 and averaging about .90. However, the raters differed in the absolute classification: that is, one rater gave all the stories consistently higher ratings. The results reported here are based on the average of the two ratings.

The mean coherence scores for each story are shown in Table 7.10. Not surprisingly, stories tended to be more coherent when the text to be recalled was referentially and/or causally coherent. More interesting, though, were the differences between the groups. Skilled children reproduced the normal and revised random stories in a more cohesive form than the less-skilled children. The lack of group differences in rated cohesion for the random stories may have been because the relations between the propositions were so obscure as to defeat the inferential capabilities of both groups.

Table 7.10. *Mean coherence ratings for story recall by each group in each passage version (max. = 8)*

	Passage version		
	Normal	Revised	Random
Less-skilled	4·91	3·12	3·54
Skilled	6·67	5·37	4·33
Difference	1·76*	2·25*	0·79

Note: $^{*}p < 0{\cdot}05$ (one-tailed t, df = 22).

A second factor seems to be operating here which Bartlett (1932) termed the 'effort after meaning': when the sentences are out of order skilled comprehenders do not simply give up, but try to make some sense of the jumbled text, often providing inferences to link apparently unrelated propositions. For example, one good comprehender given the revised random version of the story shown in Table 7.8 produced the following:

David found his coloured ball next door. He climbed over the fence to get it. He bounced it so hard that it went right over and he went on with his game.

In the version this child heard, the story begins with a boy throwing a ball 'back', fetching it and then throwing it over the fence again. In her recall, this child manages to make the story appear as if the ball was only thrown over the fence once, from the neighbour's garden, where David found it, back to David's own garden, where he could play with it. She mentions the fence earlier than in the version she heard, making the reference to the ball 'going right over' more understandable. She also mentions the boy carrying on with his game later in the story, again making it more coherent. Another of the revised random stories mentioned that a boy was sad, and later mentioned the fact that was given in the original version as the cause, that he scratched his bike. This causal relation was no longer clear from the ordering of the sentences. A good comprehender maintained the random ordering of the sentences but added coherence by making the boy's sadness the *reason* why he went to ride his bike, rather than the *result* of it. A similar phenomenon was reported by Rumelhart (1975) who found that text recall was often distorted by the addition of new information, so that the story became more congruent with available schemata. He also found that subjects moved sentences around to make better sense of a passage, and added words to justify the existence of a sentence in an unpredictable position. A common way in which the good comprehenders introduced greater coherence into the revised random stories was to use verb forms that showed a late-appearing sentence to be an explanation of what has already been mentioned, as in the first example below. Failure to make such repairs can lead to a completely incoherent sequence of events, as in the second example below.

Mother went shopping. Mark carried the shopping. He carried it through the park. He put it down and went off. When he came back the shopping had gone. His mother was very cross. He *had gone to look* for conkers. (skilled comprehender)
Peter went shopping and he put the bag down for a while and when he got home it was gone and his mother was very cross and he *went back to go and find* the conkers. (less-skilled comprehender)

This experiment showed that the poor comprehenders' difficulties in recalling the gist of a short story were not due to a straightforward inability to recall sentences, because they showed no significant difference from skilled children in their recall of randomised stories. The problem seemed to be that the less-skilled group were less aware of, or less able to use, the referential features of texts to facilitate their understanding and memory. This conclusion is consistent with our experiments on anaphor comprehension, reported in previous chapters.

General discussion

The experiments in this chapter have approached the question of use of cohesive devices in a variety of ways. Experiment 7.3 showed that less-skilled children are less able than skilled ones to use causal connectives appropriate to a given context, supporting the suggestion that they do not take full advantage of the cohesive import of causal connectives. Some of our other studies also suggest that poor comprehenders may have difficulty with a variety of cohesive devices. Experiments 4.4 and 4.5 showed that poor comprehenders made more errors in assigning the referents of pronouns, and Experiment 4.6 demonstrated their difficulties with other types of links: ellipsis, substitution and lexical cohesion. In some cases, children drew completely misleading conclusions. These experiments required some awareness of how particular lexical items bring cohesion to a text.

Another way we examined knowledge of cohesive devices was to investigate how children used cohesive ties in their own narratives. Skilled children were more likely than less-skilled ones to add connectives to their reproductions of a narrative where these were absent in the original text, although there was no overall difference between the groups in their use of the more sophisticated connectives (temporal, contrastive and causal) when they narrated their own stories from pictures. This lack of a difference is not inconsistent with our study of *because*: in that study, less-skilled children showed poorer performance than skilled ones only on the *deductive* use of *because*, whereas all the uses in children's narrative productions were empirical.

A further indicator of skilled children's greater facility with cohesive ties is their ability to take advantage of the restoration of referential continuity in their recall of scrambled stories. Poor comprehenders had no general difficulty in recall: they remembered as much of the unrevised random stories as good comprehenders did. However, they were not helped when stories were scrambled but referential cohesion was maintained. Further analysis suggested that skilled children made a greater attempt to introduce cohesion into the scrambled stories, resulting in more cohesive stories in the revised random versions than the less-skilled children could produce. Skilled children's reproductions of normal stories were also rated more cohesive.

Our studies of text production and reproduction do, then, support some of the results from our studies of text comprehension. Particularly in the case of referential ties, poor comprehenders show difficulty in their reading, listening and production of cohesive text. So their difficulties are not confined to understanding written or spoken text, but are also reflected in their ability to tell stories. We suggested that at least part of the difference in performance could be attributed to stylistic differences, and it may be that under some circumstances, poor comprehenders could be induced to tell stories that are referentially more cohesive than some of those they produced in our studies. It certainly seems that some of the difficulties poor comprehenders have are not due to a basic lack of knowledge (for example, about the potential referents of personal pronouns), but that they fail to put this knowledge into practice. The next chapter addresses the possibilities of training poor comprehenders to use their knowledge more effectively when reading.

8 Methods of improving poor comprehension

Introduction

Nearly all of the studies we have described so far used the same general procedure of comparing groups of good and poor comprehenders, matched in important aspects of reading ability, for the reasons we gave in Chapter 1. However, the evidence this provides is essentially correlational: such evidence cannot show a *causal* link between poor comprehension and deficiency in a particular skill. Training procedures can be used to test hypotheses about cause more directly, as well as being a potential source of convergent evidence for our claims. The experiments presented in the previous chapters have isolated several specific skills in which poor comprehenders are deficient. The next step was to train both good and poor comprehenders in such skills. If trained poor comprehenders improve to the level of good ones, then there are good grounds for inferring that the comprehension deficit was *caused* by the failure to employ the skills trained. This conclusion would be further strengthened if skilled children were to show no improvement after training, because this would suggest that they were already using the skills in which they were being instructed. This point is expanded by Campione and Armbruster (1984), who discuss in detail the possible outcomes of remediation studies, and their interpretations.

Training studies obviously also have important practical implications: if successful, they could be used in education. Two types of approach could be adopted to potential problems: devising general methods of comprehension instruction to form part of any normal reading instruction, or identifying which children will have difficulties at some later point, and designing more specific types of help for these children. As we argued above, an approach that helps poor comprehenders specifically is more interesting from a theoretical perspective than a general approach. Our experimental evidence provides a description of the specific differences between the two groups, and guides the development of instructional techniques to alleviate the factors we believe to have causal roles in poor comprehension.

Improving inferential and monitoring skills

The main differences we have identified between good and poor comprehenders fall into three categories: working-memory efficiency, inferential ability and comprehension monitoring. Previous research has addressed primarily the second and third of these categories: training in comprehension monitoring may include activities such as inducing children to ask themselves questions about what they have read (e.g. Palincsar and Brown, 1984), while inferential training more typically requires children to answer questions that have already been provided (e.g. Hansen and Pearson, 1983). It is less obvious how working-memory efficiency might be increased by direct tuition. It might be improved less directly by requiring readers to make summary statements during reading (e.g. Taylor, 1982) or to use mental imagery (e.g. Levin, 1973), as a means of improving the efficiency with which text is represented in memory and of reducing the load during reading. Processes such as rehearsal and use of mnemonic strategies might also be used (e.g. see Brown and Campione, 1978). We would not expect the effects of these different types of training to be independent: training inferential strategies, for instance, should improve working-memory efficiency, because information from connected text can be stored more economically in a mental model rather than as a set of propositions.

Before describing our own forms of training, we will first look briefly at previous training studies. Some of these are empirically driven attempts to find educationally useful ways of teaching comprehension, and not all of them are methodologically adequate (e.g. some lack appropriate control groups). We have not reviewed previous work exhaustively because recent comprehensive reviews already exist (Pearson and Gallagher, 1983; Tierney and Cunningham, 1984), and many of the studies are concerned with general techniques for improving comprehension, rather than remediation of poor comprehension specifically. However, there are some studies that are particularly relevant to our concerns.

Hansen and Pearson (1983) developed a method of training inferential skills for fourth-grade poor readers whose comprehension performance was about one year behind their age. The approach was intended to encourage children to relate textual information to their own previous experience. This aim was addressed in two ways. Before reading a text, the children were encouraged to use their own previous experience in relation to the topic as a source for generating hypotheses and predictions about the text. After reading the text, the children took part in a discussion led by the teacher, who asked questions about information not explicitly mentioned in the text. The control groups were given general reading instructions from the teacher's manual of the reading scheme used, and discussed eight literal and two inferential questions after each text. Inferential training improved poor readers' performance on specially designed comprehension tests up to the level of a group of good readers given normal comprehension instruction. The improvement occurred for inferential but not for literal questions. The results suggest that poor comprehenders may have the competence to make inferences, but need to be encouraged to use their inferential skills when reading.

Brown, Palincsar and Armbruster (1984) focused on the effects of training metacognitive skills in seventh grade children with average reading-accuracy skills but poor comprehension, using a Soviet psychological approach that emphasises the importance of the gradual transfer of responsibility for learning from teacher to apprentice. Children were taught in groups, first by fairly direct instruction, and then taking over the teacher's role, so that they regulated their own activities in four areas: summarising, questioning, clarifying and predicting. This method produced improvements on various measures of comprehension, including performance on classroom comprehension exercises and on tasks devised by the experimenters to test whether the skills taught could be transferred to different but related tasks.

Another relatively large-scale project for improving reading comprehension that also focuses on metacognitive skills has been developed by Paris and colleagues (see e.g. Paris and Oka, 1986; Paris, Cross and Lipson, 1984). Their reading programme, Informed Strategies for Learning (ISL), involves not just provision of reading strategies, but also an emphasis on applying the strategies appropriately. ISL presents an explicit analogy of reading as the detection of meaning. Subjects are encouraged to approach a text as if they were a detective looking for clues, or a driver attending to signs to 'stop and think' or 'slow down'. As we have seen, less-skilled comprehenders seem particularly poor at understanding the relation of evidence to conclusions (see Experiment 7.3 on understanding of *because*). This deficit may make it difficult to see how words are evidence or clues to meaning, and could explain why less-skilled children can scan text for information that is presented explicitly, but cannot recognise information that would help them to make inferences and reach conclusions. In a sample of well over a thousand 8- and 10-year-olds, the ISL procedure produced significant improvements in the Index of Reading Awareness, a test of knowledge about factors that improve reading, towards which the training was directed. This benefit was similar for children at all levels of comprehension skill, so the results do not suggest any deficits that might be specific to poor comprehenders. It is interesting to note that, for the younger age group, comprehension skills were the main predictors of reading achievement (performance on the Gates–MacGinitie comprehension test), whereas in older children, motivation and awareness of strategies were more influential.

All the above studies were carried out as long-term projects administered by teachers in normal classrooms. Our training studies were less ambitious, in that they were quite short-term and training was administered by an experimenter to small groups or to individual children. Our methods have not been put to the stringent test of whether they are effective in the less controlled setting of a real classroom. However, they had the advantage of being directed quite specifically at a particular group of poor comprehenders, about whose deficits we already knew a substantial amount from our experimental studies. This precision may account for the high quality of the results we obtained considering the modest scope of our procedures. In our two medium-term training studies, we also adopted a more stringent criterion of evaluation than much of the other research, by assessing the effects of training on a standardised comprehension test (the Neale Analysis) rather than purely on tasks related to those used in training.

Experiment 8.1: *Effect of instructions to increase inference awareness*

As we have shown, poor comprehenders' difficulties are particularly evident in their inability to make inferences from text. Previous training studies have concentrated mainly on improving inferential skills in a very general way, using analogies such as 'reading as detection'. This type of strategy seems well-suited to the older children (8–12-year-olds) used in previous studies, but we suspected that our 7-year-olds would find such general guidance hard to put into effect without extensive practice. Some informal evidence gained from inspecting children's performance on the Neale Analysis suggested a form of training that might be relatively simple for the age group we were using. We had noticed that poor comprehenders often responded wrongly to questions in the Neale test that rely on an inference from just a single word. For example, the second story in Form C includes the sentence *A surprise parcel for Peter and Jane arrived on Saturday*. One of the questions is *How do you know that the children were not expecting the parcel*? The answer to this question depends entirely on inferring the story characters' ignorance from the single word *surprise*. This question was particularly difficult for less-skilled comprehenders. Out of a sample of two groups of 42 children for whom we have detailed response data, 39 of the poor comprehenders failed to give a correct response, in comparison with 21 of the 42 skilled children. This discrepancy was even larger than the usual, expected discrepancy between the groups in number of errors. (The response also requires the deductive use of *because*, which poor comprehenders find difficult: see Experiment 7.3.) The main aim of the training was therefore to induce children to make inferences from single words. In order to emphasise the utility of making such inferences, we presented the children with stories that were deliberately somewhat obscure: much of the information about the setting and activities relied on inferences from only a few words. In normal texts, there is greater redundancy: if an inference is not drawn from one word, then other parts of the text will usually enable the same inference to be drawn. The primary aim of the current experiment was to assess whether inferential training improved poor comprehenders' ability to answer comprehension questions: such training was not expected to enhance the performance of good comprehenders.

There was also an element of comprehension monitoring included in the instruction, in that children were guided in the sorts of information they should be looking for in each story. This was done by giving a preliminary statement of the issues that were crucial in understanding the story. Comprehension questions after each story addressed the information that had been primed by this preliminary statement, and other information that had not been primed. This procedure enabled us to assess which aspects of comprehension were most affected by the training: it might help children to make inferences about the central aspects of the story, but might not generalise to other aspects of the story.

In addition to assessing comprehension, we also looked at recall of the main ideas, and subsidiary details, of the stories. As we had previously found that poor comprehenders perform adequately in recall tasks, no overall difference was expected between the groups. Our study of importance levels (Experiment 6.3) showed that poor comprehenders were as sensitive as good ones to variations in importance of information, so we expected both groups to recall main ideas better than subsidiary ones.

Method From ten children in each skill group, half were randomly selected to be trained, and the others formed a control no-treatment group. The control and trained groups within each skill group were not significantly different on any of the selection criteria, unrelated t-tests (18) all ps $> .20$.

Eight stories[1] were written in a highly abstract style, so that particular words became important clues to meaning. Table 8.1 gives examples for a practice and an experimental story. The stories were fifty to seventy words in length, with suitably simple vocabulary, and each consisted of ten idea units, used when scoring recall. Although the stories were not written according to any particular story grammar, there were three main ideas in each one: a setting or problem, an initiating event and a main consequence. These categories of information are said to play an important role in story comprehension (Stein and Glenn, 1979). For example, in the practice story shown in Table 8.1 (which we did not score), the main ideas would have been (a) a bathroom, (b) a boy reading a book and (c) the boy dropping the book into the water. The other seven idea units were termed 'subsidiary'. Each story had an associated 'puzzle statement', used for the instructed subjects only. This statement raised two issues that were judged central to story comprehension: for example, where the story took place (setting) and what the main event was (consequence). Five comprehension questions were also devised for each story. Two of these concerned information that was highlighted in the puzzle statement. For example, Questions 1 and 2

Table 8.1. *Examples of abstract stories*

Practice story

Tommy was lying down looking at a reading book.
The room was full of steam.
Suddenly Tommy got some soap in his eye.
He reached wildly for the towel.
Then he heard a splash.
Oh no! What would he tell his teacher?
He would have to buy a new one.
Tommy rubbed his eye and it soon felt better.

Puzzle: where Tommy was and what happened to the book
Clues: about the location: lying down, steam, soap, towel, splash
about the book: splash, oh no, buy a new one
Questions:

1. Where was Tommy?
2. What was Tommy doing?
3. What happened to the book?
4. What did Tommy plan to do about the book?
5. How did Tommy make his eye feel better?

Experimental story

Lucy saw the ground below her. It seemed very far away. She heard the cat and tried to move, but she realised it was unsafe. What could she do? Then she saw her father walking towards the house. She called loudly to him. Father looked up and saw Lucy, then he ran towards the tree.

Puzzle: Where Lucy was and what she was doing
Questions:

1. Where was Lucy?
2. Why was she there?
3. Why couldn't she move?
4. Who did she see from the tree?
5. Where did her father go?

of the experimental story shown in Table 8.1 address the same information as the puzzle statement ('Where Lucy was and what she was doing'). Such questions were termed 'primed'. The other three questions were unprimed.

Each child was seen individually, and given two practice stories, followed by the eight experimental stories. After each story, the children were asked to recall as much of the story as possible and then to answer five comprehension questions. The trained children were given the following additional instructions:

All of these stories have a puzzle in them, that makes them a bit hard to understand. I'm going to tell you something to help you work out the puzzles, so listen carefully. The stories don't actually say exactly what is happening, but they give you some clues. You must look for the clues, and make some guesses about what is going on. First we can practise together.

After the trained children had read the first practice story, the experimenter told them what the clue words were and explained what each word told about the story. For example, the first story shown in Table 8.1 is about a boy reading a schoolbook in the bath. He gets soap in his eye and drops the book in the water. The main consequence, the book falling in the water, is not stated explicitly, but can be inferred from particular words suggesting the setting, indicated by the clues that the room was *steamy*, the boy was *lying down*, there is *soap* and a *towel*. Given that the boy is reading in the bath, then the clues to the main event, the *splash* and the boy's exclamation of horror, enable the inference that the book fell in the water. This inference is supported by his worries about what to tell the teacher and his plan to buy a new book. A full causal account of the event would also include the fact that he dropped the book as he reached for the towel to rub the soap from his eye.

For the second practice story, these children were given the puzzle statement and had to provide and explain the clue words themselves, with the experimenter adding any clue words not mentioned. For the eight experimental stories, the instructed children were just given the puzzle statements before each story (see the second story in Table 8.1 for an example). No help was given, either in the form of clues or feedback. By using this procedure for the experimental stories, we did not give the children any specific information that would help them to answer the questions, but merely guided them in what aspects of the story were most important. The children in the control group just read the practice and experimental stories and performed the recall and comprehension tasks, without any guidance to clues or puzzles.

Results Two raters, one of them blind to skill group and condition, independently scored transcripts of the responses. We scored comprehension by giving each answer a score of 2 if it was completely correct, 1 if it was partially correct and 0 for a wrong answer or no response. For recall, we gave a maximum of 2 for correct recall of each of the ten idea units, and a score of 1 for any unit that was only partly recalled. The scorers achieved reasonable levels of agreement, with coefficients of concordance of .94 for comprehension and .89 for recall.

Comprehension. We analysed the comprehension scores using analysis of variance, with skill group and treatment (control or trained) between subjects. The skilled group, not surprisingly, were better overall, $F(1, 16) = 4.78$, $p < .05$. They scored an average of 86% correct, compared to 76% for the less-skilled children. There was also a main effect of treatment, $F(1, 16) = 7.57$, $p < .01$, with trained children doing better (86% correct) than control children (77% correct). The mean percentages of correct comprehension responses in each condition are shown in the upper part of Table 8.2. Although the interaction of skill group and treatment was not significant, $F(1, 16) = 1.28$, $p > .25$, we used planned comparisons (t-tests with p set at .01) to inspect

Table 8.2. *Mean percentages of correct responses for comprehension and recall as a function of treatment group and comprehension skill*

	Treatment group		
	Control	Trained	Difference
Comprehension			
Less-skilled	72·0	84·9	12·9*
Skilled	83·0	88·4	5·4
Recall			
Less-skilled	56·0	59·2	3·2
Skilled	51·0	61·5	10·5

Note: $^{*}p < 0{\cdot}05$ (planned comparisons).

predicted differences. These comparisons showed that the effect of instruction was significant for the less-skilled comprehenders but not for the skilled comprehenders. Thus, less-skilled children who received instruction almost reached the level of performance of the good comprehenders.

The source of the effect of instruction can be investigated in more detail by looking at the sorts of questions that children in the trained and control groups answered correctly. One possibility was that the 'puzzle' statements primed the children to seek the sort of information that was asked for in particular questions. If this was the case, then the training effect should be confined to responses to questions about the 'primed' information. We therefore analysed the comprehension responses according to whether or not they had been primed by the puzzle statements. The comprehension data for the two skill groups were analysed separately, with question type (primed or unprimed) within subjects and treatment group between subjects. As before, the less-skilled comprehenders showed a treatment effect, $F(1, 8) = 5.23$, $p < .05$, as trained children scored higher than untrained ones. There was a main effect for question type, unexpectedly showing that poor comprehenders in both treatment groups answered unprimed questions better than primed questions, $F(1, 8) = 6.28$, $p < .05$, as shown in the upper half of Table 8.3. The results suggest that this effect of question type was less striking for trained than for control children in this skill group. Although there was no interaction of treatment with question type ($F < 1$), the difference between the control and trained poor comprehenders for performance on primed questions was somewhat larger than the difference between the two groups for unprimed questions. The primed questions were primarily those for which an inference was required, whereas most of the unprimed questions were factual.[2] The skilled children showed no significant effects or interactions, all $F\text{s} < 1$ other than for treatment condition, $F(1, 8) = 1.52$, n.s. (see lower half of Table 8.3).

Table 8.3. *Mean percentages of comprehension questions correct for unprimed and primed questions as a function of treatment group and comprehension skill*

	Unprimed	Primed
Less-skilled		
control	77·1	64·1
trained	87·1	81·6
Mean	82·1	72·9
Difference	10·0	17·2*
Skilled		
control	82·1	84·4
trained	89·4	86·9
Mean	85·8	85·7
Difference	7·3	2·5

Note: * $p < 0{\cdot}05$ (Tukey's HSD).

Table 8.4. *Mean percentages of idea units recalled for main and subsidiary ideas as a function of treatment group and comprehension skill*

	Idea type		
	Main	Subsidiary	Difference
Less-skilled			
control	62·8	53·2	9·6
trained	69·0	53·0	16·0
Mean	65·9	53·1	
Skilled			
control	62·0	45·8	16·2
trained	73·0	55·8	17·2
Mean	67·5	50·8	

Recall. The recall data were analysed by analysis of variance with treatment and skill group between subjects. The mean percentages of idea units recalled in each condition are shown in the lower half of Table 8.2. We also included the extra within-subjects' factor of idea type (main and subsidiary), as described in the procedure section. These results are shown in Table 8.4. There was no main effect for skill group, and no interactions involving group, all Fs < 1. Less-skilled children were as good as skilled ones in remembering the stories, achieving an average recall score of 59.5%, compared to 59.2% for the other group. Although trained children gained slightly higher recall scores than control children (63% and 56% respectively), the effect of instruction was not significant, $F\ (1,\ 16) = 2.3$. Main ideas were recalled better than subsidiary ideas, $F(1, 16) = 38.11$, $p < .0001$, with mean percentages correct of 67 and 52 respectively. The interaction between idea type and skill group was not significant, nor was there a significant three-way interaction of these two factors with treatment condition, both Fs < 1. However, as Table 8.4 shows, while skilled children in both treatment groups remembered main ideas better than subsidiary ones, within the less-skilled group, the effect was more marked for trained children than for control children.

Discussion This initial training study showed some interesting results. Firstly, there was a surprisingly clear effect of training, given the brevity of the instruction. Poor comprehenders who were trained performed significantly better than a control group, and also attained the same level of performance as a group of skilled children. This pattern of evidence provides support for the claim that the instructions influenced a factor playing a causal role in poor comprehension. This effect of instruction was only assessed on a task in which children had received training: it would be informative to examine whether the training had more general effects on comprehension performance.

The comprehension data also showed that the two skill groups differed in the sorts of questions they were able to answer correctly. The poor comprehenders were less likely to answer the primed questions correctly than the unprimed ones, whereas the skilled children were just as good at both types of question. This result is probably because the primed questions were more difficult, a greater proportion of them requiring inferences from information in the text, rather than memory for a relevant piece of text close to its exact form. This pattern of results fits our previous data very well, in that the groups differ markedly in inferential skills (e.g. see Chapter 4). However, the finding that the trained poor comprehenders performed significantly better than the controls for the primed questions suggests that the instruction did improve the children's inferential skills.

It is also interesting that the training had no overall effect on the children's ability to recall the stories, nor did the two skill groups differ in their recall performance. It should be noted that, to a large extent, the primed questions concerned information expressed in the main ideas of the story, rather than the subsidiary ideas. Thus, the priming information given to trained poor comprehenders improved their understanding of the stories, but had no overall effect on their recall. Furthermore, main ideas were recalled better than subsidiary ones for both skilled and less-skilled children, suggesting that both groups were sensitive to differences in importance of information. However, this generalisation might be further qualified, because the advantage of main idea recall in the less-skilled group was significant only in the trained condition and not in the control group. The training seems to have helped poor comprehenders to focus on the appropriate parts of the story, as well as helping them to answer comprehension questions about those aspects. Thus, the effect of the training appears to be twofold: not only did it help children to address the important aspects of the story, but it also encouraged them to make inferences from particular lexical items.

Experiment 8.2: Training in inferential and monitoring skills

Our instructional study suggested that inferential skills could be encouraged fairly readily. However, we did not address directly the other main difficulty we had identified: comprehension monitoring. Our next study was designed to facilitate both inferential and monitoring skills. In addition to the clue-words approach, we included training designed to improve comprehension monitoring. Another way in which we extended the training was to continue it over several sessions. We compared this extended training with two different control conditions. In one of these, we used a common type of comprehension exercise: requiring children to answer questions about a text they had just read. This procedure is a more implicit way of teaching comprehension skills than our training procedure, because the questions pick out which aspects of the text require inferential processing to be understood, but do not give any guidance as to how comprehension should be achieved. The second control condition involved training in rapid decoding. Although there is some evidence that such training is not helpful in improving comprehension (Fleisher, Jenkins and Pany, 1979), we included this control as it could give further evidence against the 'decoding bottleneck' hypothesis, described in Chapter 2, as an account of our poor comprehenders' difficulties. This control group also acted as a control for various incidental features of the other two treatments which may have enhanced performance, such as individual attention, familiarity with the experimenter, and practice at reading texts. Any of these features could improve performance on the post-test independently of the essential aspects of the training.

Method This study was carried out in two consecutive terms, to allow sufficient time to recruit enough subjects for each of the three conditions. There were twenty-eight children in the first term (Autumn 1985) and a further twenty-four in the second term (Spring 1986), with the groups matched in each term, according to our standard procedure. In each term, the children were assigned to the treatment groups randomly, with the proviso that the children within each skill group were adequately matched between treatments. In the first term, seven skilled and seven less-skilled children received the training, and the same number in each group were given comprehension exercises. In the second term, six children in each skill group were trained and six given practice in rapid decoding.

Table 8.5. *Examples of inference training materials*

Anna tried and tried to turn the key. But the castle had been empty for too long. The old witch laughed wickedly and ran up behind her. Now Anna was trapped! But suddenly they were dazzled by headlights. It was Peter! Anna jumped into his van and sighed with relief. The witch gave an angry shout and disappeared into the clouds.
Examples of clue words and inferences:
key: may be the key of a door
tried and tried: suggests it was difficult to open the door
castle: presumably the door in question is the door of the castle
empty ... too long: implies it had been empty so long that the keyhole was rusty

The training, divided into seven sessions, had two main components:
Lexical inference. This activity was included in every training session. We instructed children in how to look for clue words that would help them to understand a text, and demonstrated what sorts of inferences could be made from selected words in a sentence. This task was explained with sentences such as the following:

Sleepy Tom was late for school again.

Each child had to pick a word and to say what information it provided about the sentence. For example, we know from *Tom* that it is about a male person, and combined with the word *school*, that he is probably a pupil, since his first name is given, rather than a title such as *Mr Smith. Sleepy* suggests that he overslept, perhaps because he stayed up late the previous night, and suggests why he was *late. Again* suggests that he has been late before, perhaps because he habitually stays up late. After some practice sentences of this sort, the children applied these techniques to some of the short, abstract stories used in the instructional study described above. The children progressed from inferences about single words to inferences that connected words together: for example, the location inferred from the word *steam* in the practice story of the previous study (Table 8.1, above) can be used to guess that the *room* was a bathroom, and that the *splash* meant some object had fallen into the water. After this, the children picked their own clue words by highlighting words in text, and then explaining what inferences they could draw from the words they had marked. This technique was also intended to improve the efficiency of working memory: if inferences are made during reading, then an integrated model of the text can be built up and the memory system will not become overloaded. A more extended example of the clue-word approach is given in Table 8.5, and demonstrates how the children were encouraged to draw inferences across sentences.
Question generation. The children were introduced to the idea of question words

(*who*, *where*, *why*, *when*, etc.) and given examples of how these words could be used to formulate questions about text. They then practised generating their own questions. For example, in the story about Lucy, shown in Table 8.1, the children might produce questions such as 'Who was Lucy?', 'Where was she?' and 'Why was she there?'. The children took turns to 'be the teacher', by asking a self-generated question of each other child in the training group. The other children could then use their inference training to find the answers. The question-generation procedure was intended to increase the children's awareness of the extent of their own comprehension of a text, and to help them to formulate questions to guide comprehension. It was included in four training sessions, and a further session was used to demonstrate how the general question 'What happens next?' could be used to generate predictions. We did this using a kind of 'macro-cloze' task: children read texts in which some sentences were obscured by removable tape, and had to guess what each hidden sentence was, based on clues from surrounding sentences. The children could then reveal the sentence and check their predictions. This procedure was to encourage children to make predictive inferences as they read. An example from one of the later training studies is as follows:

Kerry wanted cereal for her breakfast.
[hidden sentence]
So she had to have toast instead.

The missing sentence was then revealed as:

But there wasn't any left.

Control conditions *Comprehension exercises.* After discussing the importance of comprehension with the instructor, children in this condition read aloud the text for the session and then answered comprehension questions in strict rotation. The instructor did not give detailed feedback on responses, but did correct answers that were obviously wrong. The children also often discussed the answers and corrected each other. The questions asked by the instructor were similar to the sorts of comprehension exercises commonly found in school textbooks, comprising a mix of literal and inferential questions.

Rapid decoding practice. We drew up a word list for each of the set texts, containing the words most difficult to recognise (based on pilot work). The lists contained about 20% of the words in each text. In the first session, the instructor explained the importance of rapid word recognition. For each session, the instructor then read through a list of words from the set text and each child practised reading the list as quickly and accurately as possible. Then children shared the reading of the set text. Finally, each child read the word list again, and the instructor recorded the time taken, using a stopwatch. In the subsequent session, the instructor again timed children reading the previous word list.

Measures of change All the children had been given Form C of the Neale test as part of the selection procedure. The main measure of change was the difference between their initial comprehension age on this test and on a post-test using Form B of the Neale test. As all the tests were administered and scored by the instructor, who knew which group children were in, the tests were audiotaped and rescored by a rater blind to skill-group and treatment condition, with over 98% agreement. The disagreements were resolved by discussion.

In order to discover whether the rapid decoding training had any effect, the children in that condition, and the matched groups given inference training, were given a test in their final training session. They read the word list from the second session as quickly and accurately as possible, after one practice.

Results *Changes in comprehension age.* Preliminary analysis showed no significant main effects or interactions involving time of test (Autumn or Spring term), so the data for the inference-trained groups in each term were combined. The data were analysed by analysis of variance with the two skill groups (poor and good) and three treatment groups (rapid decoding, comprehension exercises and inference training) as between-groups' factors. The average increase in comprehension age from pre- to post-test for each group is shown in Table 8.6. The main effect of treatment group was not significant, $F < 1$, while that for skill group approached significance, $F(1, 46) = 3.13$, $p < .08$: poor comprehenders showed an average increase across all treatment conditions of 13.76 months, compared to 6.81 months for good comprehenders. Of greater interest given our predictions, the interaction of group and treatment approached significance, $F(2, 46) = 2.65$, $p < .08$. We performed planned comparisons, using t-tests and correcting for unequal sample sizes as appropriate, to investigate possible differences between the treatments in each skill group. As Table 8.6 shows, the less-skilled comprehenders tended to improve more than the skilled ones did, but the difference between the skill groups was greatest for inference training. Furthermore, the less-skilled comprehenders who were trained improved more than those given decoding practice, as shown on the right-hand side of Table 8.6. Also, the advantage of training over decoding was greater for the less-skilled comprehenders than for the skilled comprehenders (critical difference on Scheffe's test = 15.35, $p < .10$). As Table 8.6 shows, all groups made gains in comprehension age of at least five months over the two months of training, perhaps simply because they had already had practice on the Neale test. However, the important point is that trained poor comprehenders showed an average increase of over seventeen months. This brought them on average to within six months of the skilled comprehenders, and well above their chronological ages. Although the test does not provide standard scores that are applicable to our subjects, and so increases in comprehension age cannot

Table 8.6. *Mean improvements (months) in comprehension age as a function of treatment group and comprehension skill*

	Treatment group						
	Rapid decoding (n = 6) D	Comprehension exercises (n = 7) E	Inference training (n = 13) T	Difference between treatments Mean	E–D	T–D	T–E
Less-skilled	6·00	13·71	17·38	13·76	7·71	11·38**	3·67
Skilled	10·33	5·43	5·92	6·81	−4·90	−4·41	0·49
Mean	8·16	9·57	11·65				
Difference between skill groups:	−4·33	8·28	11·46		12·61	15·79*	3·18

Notes: n = number of subjects in each skill group.
* p < 0·10 (Scheffe's test).
** p < 0·05 (planned comparison).

reliably be translated into real units of time, the increase still represents a substantial improvement in terms of number of questions answered correctly.

Rates of improvement were quite variable, so it is also important to look at the outcomes for individual children. We classified each child on the basis of post-test Neale test performance, as 'low' (comprehension age below accuracy and chronological ages), 'high' (comprehension age above accuracy and chronological ages) or 'intermediate' (comprehension age above either accuracy or chronological age, but not both). Table 8.7 shows the post-test comprehension status of the children in each skill group. Nine of the thirteen poor comprehenders given inference training were in the 'high' group, compared to only three poor comprehenders in the other two treatment conditions. A comparison of the inference-training group with the other two treatments, combining the children with low and intermediate post-test status, showed that the frequency distribution for the less-skilled children was significantly different from chance, chi squared (1) = 5.57, $p < .05$. Treatment condition had no effect on the skilled group, as all but three children from this group were high comprehenders in the post-test.

Reading accuracy. In order to check that comprehension improvements had not occurred simply because of improvements in accuracy, we also analysed changes in accuracy age. Preliminary analysis showed that children in the Autumn term improved more than those in the Spring term, presumably because there is a greater jump in progress after the long summer holiday. Because of this finding, data for the two terms were analysed separately. There

Table 8.7. *Post-treatment comprehension status as a function of treatment and skill group*

	Comprehension status			Combined data	
	low	intermed.	high	low/intermed.	high
Less-skilled					
Decoding	4	2	0	{10}	3
Exercises	2	2	3		
Inference-trained	2	2	9	4	9
Skilled					
Decoding	0	0	6	{1}	12
Exercises	1	0	6		
Inference-trained	0	2	11	2	11

Notes: low = Neale comprehension age below accuracy and chronological age.
intermediate = Neale comprehension age above either accuracy or chronological age.
high = Neale comprehension age above accuracy and chronological age.

Table 8.8. *Mean improvements (months) in Accuracy age as a function of treatment group, term and comprehension skill*

	Treatment group		
Autumn term	Comprehension exercises (n = 7)	Inference training (n = 7)	Mean
Less-skilled	6·14	6·14	6·14
Skilled	3·86	5·29	4·57
Mean	5·00	5·71	5·35
Spring term			
	Rapid decoding	Inference training	Mean
	(n = 6)	(n = 6)	
Less-skilled	2·83	2·17	2·50
Skilled	3·17	2·17	2·67
Mean	3·00	2·17	2·58

Note: n = number of subjects in each skill group.

were no significant differences between any of the four subgroups of children in each term, all t-values < .50 (see Table 8.8). It is still possible that comprehension improvements were mediated by accuracy improvements, because the number of questions attempted in the Neale test depends on how many stories the child reads. This means that accuracy age and comprehension age are not completely independent. However, the number of stories children read was very similar for all subgroups, and there were no significant correlations between improvements in accuracy and comprehension. Pearson correlation coefficients within each of the subgroups were all non-significant, ranging from r (5 or 6) -.09 to .41. (The value required for significance at $p <$ .05 for a sample of this size is .67.) Correlations for the whole sample were not significant either, r (27) = .29, (Autumn) and r (23) = .09, (Spring).

Decoding speed. The lack of differences between treatment groups in accuracy improvement suggests that training in rapid decoding did not help general reading accuracy. We have already seen that such training fared less well than inference training in improving comprehension skill. This finding raises the question of whether decoding training conferred any advantages in reading speed. A comparison of reading speed on the test given to children at the end of the Spring term showed that the children given decoding practice read the list more quickly than inference-trained children (mean times = 29.8s and 56.6s respectively), t (20) = 3.22, $p < .005$.[3] It is also interesting to note that there was little evidence for the idea that less-skilled comprehenders are slower readers than skilled comprehenders: in fact, the skilled comprehenders tended to take slightly longer than the less-skilled comprehenders to read the word list, with mean times of 33.8s and 25.0s respectively, although this difference did not reach significance, t (21) = 1.65, $p < .20$. Also, a comparison of the time taken to read the word list given to the children in the decoding-practice condition in their second session (data for the first session was incomplete) showed that the skilled comprehenders were, if anything, slightly slower than the less-skilled comprehenders (means = 43.7s and 27.0s respectively), t (10) = 1.52, $p < .20$.

Discussion The pattern of results was similar to that in the previous instructional study: the less-skilled comprehenders given inference training improved almost to the level of skilled comprehenders, who were unaffected by form of training. Moreover, this effect was found on a standardised reading test, which suggests that the training has a general facilitative effect on comprehension, and not just on stories for which children were trained, as in the previous study. The training effects were not attributable to improvements in decoding, nor was there any evidence that the good comprehenders were generally superior to the poor ones in speed of decoding: in fact, the results were in the opposite direction.

It is not possible to tell from these results, though, what particular aspect of the training was helpful, nor do we have a detailed picture of how the effects arise. However, some clues about the process of improvement can be found by investigating the pattern of results. Firstly, it seems that the less-skilled comprehenders' deficits were not due to slow decoding. Despite increasing their decoding speed, children given this form of training did not improve their comprehension to the same degree as those given inference training. This finding agrees with the results we cited in Chapter 3, which showed no evidence of decoding problems in less-skilled comprehenders. It is of course possible that *some* children show poor comprehension because of slow decoding, but this does not appear to be a causal factor in our sample.

Secondly, it seems unlikely that improvement occurred through some incidental feature of training, because the decoding and exercise training groups acted as controls for such features. It could be argued that the inference training was more motivating than the repetitive tasks of the decoding group or the less novel activities of the exercise groups. However, observations of the different groups' behaviour makes us think this possibility is unlikely, and even that the reverse might be true. The decoding groups seemed to enjoy their training: the rapid reading task was challenging and provided an objective index of success, and the children always succeeded in improving their time for each list. In many respects, the inference training was less satisfying: there was no objective index of success, and the 'correct' answer to a question was often left unresolved, although the children did discuss the relation of alternative answers to the text. The question-generation task was particularly difficult, perhaps because it lacked sufficient structure.

The training in comprehension exercises was more structured than the inference training, and may have been more popular because of this feature. There were, though, no significant differences between improvements following comprehension exercises and the other treatments. Comprehension exercises shared some features with inference training: in both, the children discussed stories and answered questions about them. Exercises were more similar to the post-test, and perhaps in some respects a better preparation for it than the other treatments: both exercises and post-tests required the children to answer literal and inferential questions from a previously read text, although in the Neale test the text is not available when the questions are asked. Also, the children in the exercise group had a model of the sorts of questions that are asked in the Neale test, whereas the inference-trained children only had the example of questions generated by children in the same skill group: these questions were often less relevant to the story, and less related to the forms of question in the post-test. It is all the more surprising then that the trained children showed such a marked improvement, particularly considering that the post-test was a general standardised test of comprehension, rather than a test specifically designed to tap the skills that were being trained. If this form of training was put into practice, it might be even more beneficial for the poor comprehenders if they were trained in groups containing some skilled children, who might model more relevant questions. This possibility is supported in the training studies performed by Brown et al. (1984), who noted that one group of children they trained included two children who performed quite well from the start of training, and the poor students in this group improved rapidly compared to children in other groups.

Experiment 8.3: *Comparison of inference and monitoring training*

The previous study shows that a short period of training can bring significant benefits to poor comprehenders when they are tested immediately after training. The present study examined whether these effects would be maintained over a longer period of time.

Both our instructional study (Experiment 8.1) and the training study above incorporated two distinct aspects of treatment. The more prominent feature in both cases was the procedure of making inferences, either from single words or word sequences. Children's ability to make a variety of such inferences, once they had been made aware of the possibility of doing so, seemed intuitively to be the most useful aspect of the training. However, the treatments we used also contained other elements. These were less precisely defined than the lexical inference procedure, but can be summarised under the general heading of comprehension monitoring activities. In the instructional study, the children were told what sorts of information they should look for in the stories. While this did not give them any specific procedure to recognise the relevant parts of the text, it may have helped them in allocating their attention to certain aspects of the stories. This suggestion is supported by the results of the recall test and the comprehension data: less-skilled children who had been given instruction were both significantly more likely to recall main ideas from the texts than subsidiary ideas, and they also showed significantly better comprehension performance than control children on questions that addressed central aspects of the texts. In Experiment 8.2, above, trained children were also shown how they could generate questions about a text, and use their inferential skills to answer the questions. This procedure enabled them to monitor their own comprehension activities. They also practised filling in missing information in texts, to answer the general question of predicting 'what happens next'. The nature of our post-tests did not enable any investigation of whether this aspect of the training was more or less effective than the inference-training procedure or, indeed, whether both parts of the training were required to achieve the effects we found. The purpose of the present experiment was to separate the two main aspects of the training – inference training and comprehension-monitoring – in order to clarify whether each aspect was helpful in itself, or whether it was the combination of activities that led to the training effects we had found previously. This experiment also examined the long-term influence of training on comprehension skills.

Method In this study, as in the previous one, children were recruited over two terms. Twenty-seven children in each skill group were assigned randomly to the three treatment groups described below, with the restriction, as before, that the different groups were adequately matched.

There were three treatment conditions: decoding, inference training and comprehension monitoring. As it became apparent at the end of the first term that the monitoring group had shown little improvement, this treatment was not used in the second term. Instead, the sample size in the other two treatment conditions was increased by dividing subjects in that term between those two conditions. This meant that in each skill group, there were fifteen children in the control condition, six in the monitoring condition and sixteen in the inference-training condition.

The *decoding practice* groups had rapid decoding training, as before, together with instruction in a different phonic pattern each session. They were asked to find examples of a particular pattern in the reading material, and to generate new examples of their own. The *inference-trained* groups had practice in finding clue words, as described for the previous training study, and guessing missing sentences. The *comprehension monitoring* groups were given cards with 'question words' on them (such as *why*, *what*, *when*) and were taught how to construct questions about the training materials, using these words. In both forms of training, the children progressed from short, highly abstract texts to longer, more normal stories. They were also induced to perform the training activities first overtly, at specific points in the text, and later in their heads, as they were reading. As in the previous training study, the texts used in training were identical for each treatment group.

Measures of change. As in the first training study, the children's scores on their initial Neale test were compared with post-tests using alternate forms of the test. There were two post-tests: one two weeks after the training, and one six months later, using Forms B and A respectively of the Neale Analysis.

Results The results were scored and analysed as in the previous study, using analyses of variance with skill group and treatment condition between subjects, and changes between post-tests within subjects. There were no significant changes between the two post-tests, so for simplicity, we report here just the changes from the initial assessment to the second post-test, spanning a time period of six months. The average changes are shown in Table 8.9.

The pattern is less clear-cut than in the previous study, because the less-skilled comprehenders in all conditions showed substantial improvement in all conditions. This result is reflected in the significant main effect of skill group, $F(1, 68) = 16.66$, $p < .001$. The overall effect of treatment did not reach significance, $F(2, 68) = 2.16$, $p < .13$, nor was the interaction of group and treatment condition significant, $F < 1$. However, the pattern of results show some similarities to the first training study, as shown in the planned comparisons given in Table 8.9. The poor comprehenders given inference training showed an average improvement of about sixteen months, over five months greater than the gain by those given decoding practice (t-test for planned comparison,

Table 8.9. *Mean improvements (months) in Comprehension age six months after treatment as a function of treatment group and comprehension skill*

	Treatment group						
	Rapid decoding (n = 15) D	Comprehension monitoring (n = 6) M	Inference training (n = 16) Mean	Difference M–D	T–D	T–M	
Less-skilled	10·93	12·70	16·32	12·73	1·24	5·39*	4·15
Skilled	4·40	1·63	6·78	5·05	−2·77	2·38	5·15
Mean	7·66	7·16	11·55				
Difference between skill groups:	6·53	10·5	9·54	7·68	4·01	3·01	−1·00

Notes: n = number of subjects in each skill group.
* $p < 0{\cdot}05$ (planned comparison).

p < .05) and greater than the skilled comprehenders' gains in any treatment condition. The less-skilled comprehenders given comprehension-monitoring training did not differ markedly from the other groups of poor comprehenders. The subgroups of skilled comprehenders showed little difference between conditions.

As in the previous training study, it was clear that the improvements in comprehension were not mediated by gains in reading accuracy scores, and none of the differences between accuracy scores at the initial and the second post-test was significant.

Discussion Although there were no significant differences between the different types of training, the comprehension-monitoring condition failed to produce comprehension improvements of the same magnitude as the combined method of training used in the earlier training study. This may have been because longer training was required in such skills, or the skills are more difficult to teach than inferential skills are, or such training is necessary but not sufficient for comprehension improvement. Inference training was, however, effective in comparison with decoding practice, and we have already shown the benefits of such training even when used in a short instructional study. Our experimental work does suggest, too, that less-skilled children are deficient both in making inferences and in comprehension monitoring. It may be that there are individual differences in this respect, some children having more difficulty in inferential skills and others in comprehension monitoring, and that in future, training could cover both aspects, or be tailored to meet the needs of specific subgroups.

Inference training seemed to be more effective than the other treatments we used. It was particularly interesting to find that such training was more effective for less-skilled than for skilled children, bearing out our hypothesis that poor inferential skills may be one of the causes of poor comprehension. Neither of the two training studies above showed that training in rapid decoding improved children's comprehension. This finding suggests that less-skilled comprehenders' deficits are not a result of slow decoding. Not only were the less-skilled comprehenders equal, or even superior to skilled comprehenders in rapid decoding, but the children trained in rapid decoding showed a significantly smaller comprehension improvement than the inference-trained group, despite an improvement in decoding speed. This finding is consistent with the evidence we presented in Chapter 2 that decoding insufficiency is not responsible for these children's comprehension difficulties.

Inference training did not produce significantly greater improvements than did standard comprehension exercises or comprehension monitoring exercises for poor comprehenders. The lack of a significant difference between inference training and comprehension exercises may have been partly due to the fact that children in the exercise group often corrected each other and discussed their answers. These incidental activities may have been helpful in increasing their awareness of their own comprehension. In some respects, the comprehension exercises were a better preparation for the post-test. Both the exercises and the post-test required children to answer mainly inferential questions on texts just heard or read, although in the Neale test the text is not made available while questions are asked. Also, the questions asked in the comprehension exercises were sometimes much more relevant to story comprehension than the subject-generated questions in the inference-trained groups. This difference in question quality would be particularly great for less-skilled comprehenders, as they heard questions posed by other less-skilled children, and presumably had poorer questions modelled than skilled children given comprehension exercises did. We showed in two earlier studies that poor comprehenders focus on different sorts of story information than good comprehenders (Experiments 5.2, 6.1).

Other approaches to comprehension improvement

Our training studies concentrated on the influence of primarily verbal strategies in altering processes at a high level. In those studies, the children were instructed to pay close attention to particular words, and to derive inferences from these words that would enable them to build a more detailed representation of the text. We did not investigate whether the two skill groups differed in their non-verbal comprehension skills, or whether it was useful to provide children with an organising framework to help them coordinate information in text. We addressed these issues in two further training studies. The first was designed to induce children to integrate information in text by providing them with 'advance organisers', a technique frequently used with college students (e.g. Ausubel, 1968; Mayer, 1979). The subsequent study looked more closely at whether children could be induced to produce their own visual organisers, in the form of mental imagery. These studies represent a new direction in our research, as we had not previously studied differences between the groups in their use of pictures or mental imagery.

Experiment 8.4: Effects of visual and verbal organisers on text integration[4]

We have already seen that good comprehenders can select and coordinate information from text by applying their prior knowledge appropriately, and using the organising features provided in the text, such as cohesive devices and story structure. In addition to these features of the text itself, stories for children are also often illustrated. Pictures are presumably provided in part because they are thought to enhance retention and comprehension of the accompanying text. Such an assumption has empirical support, as recent reviews (Rusted, 1984; Schallert, 1980) have shown. Two types of illustration seem to predominate in children's books: large pictures which summarise the whole story, or its main events, and smaller pictures illustrating parts of the story, scattered through the text and usually placed next to the relevant piece of text. Larger pictures may serve to show how separate elements or events in the story can be integrated. If the reader can make use of this information, then such pictures would presumably help text comprehension more than smaller pictures that do not integrate different parts of the story. There is some support for this position in the results of a study by Bransford and Johnson (1972). They asked adults to recall a highly abstract text, in which individual sentences made sense, but the text as a whole appeared meaningless, because it described an unlikely situation in an obscure way (a man is serenading a woman in her fifth-floor room by playing a guitar, with an amplifier supported at the woman's window by some balloons). Subjects given a so-called 'meaningful' picture, which represented the objects in the text in the correct spatial configuration, recalled the text better than subjects given no picture at all, suggesting that integrated pictures are helpful. Furthermore, subjects given a non-integrated picture, containing the same elements as the other one, but not in the correct relationship, did not recall any more of the text than subjects given no picture at all. This finding suggests that pictures are helpful only when they provide an overall framework within which the ideas in the text can be integrated.

In an experiment which used the above paradigm with children, Arnold and Brooks (1976) read short texts to second- and fifth-graders, describing unusual situations such as three children flying through the air on a swan. The texts were accompanied by a picture that integrated the elements (the children are shown riding on the swan) or depicted them in a non-integrated way (the swan and the children are shown in separate parts of the picture). Both second- and fifth-graders made more correct inferences in their recall of short texts with integrated pictures than the same texts with non-integrated pictures.

However, in both the above experiments, the texts used were unintelligible without pictures. Furthermore, the non-integrated pictures were either misleading, as in the study by Bransford and Johnson, in which incorrect spatial relations were shown, or they depicted physical impossibilities, such as people flying through the air unsupported, as in the study by Arnold and Brooks. Thus, these studies show only that integrated pictures are helpful in comparison to misleading or distracting pictures. Indeed, Peeck (1974) found that, when presented with stories that had pictures conflicting with the text, fourth-grade children tended to retain the pictorial information rather than the text. Since illustrators presumably try to produce pictures that reflect what is actually happening in the text, it would be useful to know whether different types of *accurate* picture vary in their facilitative effect. We therefore compared the effect of one large, summarising picture with a series of smaller pictures depicting individual elements.

In the experiment already mentioned, Arnold and Brooks found that verbal organisers, as well as pictorial ones, could facilitate gist recall of text. Children were given titles for the texts, which either integrated the elements of the text (e.g. 'this story is about two boys and a girl *riding* a swan') or simply listed the main characters ('this story is about two boys and a girl *and* a swan'). Although integrated titles did not help verbatim recall, they led subjects to make more correct inferences than non-integrated titles did. In a similar manipulation, Harris, Mandias, Meerum Terwogt and Tjintjelaar (1980) showed that titles providing setting information led to greater gist recall of text by 8- and 10-year-olds than titles simply listing the characters. Although no measure of comprehension was used, children reported that stories with setting information made more sense to them than stories with character information only.

The above experiments show that both visual and verbal organisers can facilitate text comprehension. In our own research, we have found that poor comprehenders often fail to integrate information in text. It is therefore possible that text organisers could go some way to remedy this deficit. The following experiment was designed to test this idea, and had two main aims. Firstly, we wanted to find out whether less-skilled comprehenders in particular would be helped by the provision of an integrated framework within which to comprehend text. Secondly, we investigated the effects of two different modalities: visual and verbal, to see whether both had the same effect on comprehension. The questions are also relevant to wider issues in the field of advance organisers: much previous work has explored the use of organisers for average readers, but we investigated whether there were different effects for different groups, and more specifically, whether the facilitative effects of advance organisers arose

Table 8.10. *Example of story with integrated and non-integrated titles and pictures*

Billy was crying. His whole day was spoilt. All his work had been broken by the wave. His mother came to stop him crying. But she accidentally stepped on the only tower that was left. Billy cried even more. 'Never mind,' said mother, 'We can always build another one tomorrow.' Billy stopped crying and went home to his tea.

Non-integrated title: Billy and his mother
Integrated title: Billy's sandcastle gets broken by the wave
Non-integrated pictures:
(1) Billy crying (2) Mother shrugging shoulders (3) Broken sandcastle
Integrated picture:
Billy, crying, sitting next to broken sandcastle with mother, shrugging, standing on one tower
Questions:
1. Where was Billy?
2. Why was Billy crying?
3. What had the wave broken?
4. Why did his mother go to him?
5. What did she do by mistake?

mainly from their effect on less-skilled children. We also took the opportunity to investigate what sorts of information children would recall, by categorising each text proposition as central or peripheral to the main story line.

Method Twelve children from each skill group took part in this experiment. The stories we used were the same as those described in Experiment 8.1, and were designed to be abstract and hard to understand without some form of organiser. Each story was divided into ten idea units. Although we did not write the stories to fit a particular form of story grammar, we identified in each story three main ideas: the setting, or main problem, the initiating event, and the direct consequence. For the story about Billy, given in Table 8.10, these three ideas were, respectively, that Billy's castle was broken by the wave, that he was upset when his mother broke the last tower, and that his mother suggested they could build more sandcastles the next day. The other seven units were classified as subsidiary ideas. Each story was accompanied by a picture and a title which could be integrated or non-integrated. The pictures were simple black-and-white line drawings with either one picture to the right of the story (integrated) or three smaller pictures interspersed through the text (non-integrated). The title of each story either described the main consequence (integrated) or listed the characters (non-integrated), and was typed in capitals at the top of the page for each story. Table 8.10 shows examples of each type of adjunct. Each of the stories appeared in one of four versions, comprising each picture-title combination. We constructed four different booklets of stories, each containing the eight stories, two in each condition, in random order for each booklet, and randomly assigned three matched pairs of children to each of the four booklets.

Each child was asked to read aloud the eight stories, to remember as much of the stories as they could, and to answer questions about them. The experimenter emphasised that it was more important to understand the stories than to remember them, and that it was not necessary to remember the story word for word. The children read the stories, including the title, at their own pace and were given help with reading as required. Most had little difficulty in reading, because of the simple language used. No specific instructions were given to attend to the pictures or titles. After each story, the experimenter removed the book and asked the child to remember the story, until the child replied negatively to the prompt 'Anything else?'. Then the children were asked five comprehension questions, as in the examples in Table 8.10.

Results Two judges, blind to story condition and skill group, scored transcripts of each session for comprehension and recall, as in Experiment 8.1, with coefficients of concordance of .91 for comprehension and .80 for recall.

Comprehension. The comprehension scores were analysed by analysis of variance with skill group between subjects and picture and title type within subjects. There was a main effect of group, $F(1, 22) = 7.74$, $p < .01$. Not surprisingly, the skilled comprehenders scored higher than the less-skilled comprehenders, with mean percentages correct of 88 and 75 respectively. There was also a main effect of title type, $F(1, 22) = 10.19$, $p < .005$. The children understood stories with integrated titles better than those with non-integrated titles, means = 84% and 78% respectively. The scores for each skill group and each condition are shown in Table 8.11. Although the interaction of skill group and title type did not reach significance, $F(1, 22) = 1.56$, the results of planned comparisons using t-tests showed that, as predicted, the difference between the two title types was significant for less-skilled comprehenders, but not for skilled comprehenders (see Table 8.11).

Although there was no main effect of picture type, $F(1, 22) = 1.15$, $p > .25$, picture type interacted with skill group, $F(1, 22) = 4.73$, $p < .05$. Planned comparisons using t-tests showed that the difference between picture types was significant for the less-skilled group, but not for the skilled one, which showed a slightly lower mean score for integrated than non-integrated pictures (see Table 8.11). There were no other significant interactions, $Fs < 1$.

The lack of effects in the skilled group could be attributed to a ceiling effect, given that this group scored on average 88% correct. However, analysis of data from the six lowest scoring skilled comprehenders (mean score = 82%, standard deviation = 3.13) showed no main effects or interactions, all $Fs < 1$.

Recall. The recall scores were analysed in the same way as comprehension scores, with the added within-subjects' factor of idea type (main or subsidiary).

Table 8.11. *Mean percentages of comprehension questions correct as a function of title and picture type and comprehension skill*

	Title type			Picture type		
	Non-integrated	Integrated	Diff.	Non-integrated	Integrated	Diff.
Less-skilled	70·60	78·95	8·35**	71·85	77·70	5·85*
Skilled	86·25	89·90	3·65	89·05	87·10	−1·95

Notes: * $p < 0{\cdot}05$.
** $p < 0{\cdot}01$ (planned comparisons).

Table 8.12. *Mean percentages of idea units recalled for main and subsidiary ideas for each title and picture type*

	Title type			Picture type		
	Non-integrated	Integrated	Diff.	Non-integrated	Integrated	Diff.
Main ideas	60·10	65·62	5·52	65·62	60·10	−5·52
Subsidiary ideas	36·17	34·44	−1·73	33·65	36·96	3·31

As expected, there were no main effects or interactions involving skill group. However, there was a main effect of idea type, $F(1, 22) = 113.77$, $p < .0001$, main ideas being recalled better than subsidiary ones (63% vs 35%). Idea type also interacted with title type, $F(1, 22) = 4.44$, $p < .05$ (see Table 8.12). Integrated titles were associated with greater recall of main ideas than non-integrated titles were, but the results showed a tendency in the opposite direction for subsidiary ideas. The interaction of idea type and picture type fell just short of significance, $F(1, 22) = 3.88$, $p < .06$. In this case, the pattern of results was the opposite of the case for title type: integrated pictures produced higher scores than non-integrated ones for subsidiary ideas, but the results were in the opposite direction for main ideas. There were no other significant effects or interactions.

Discussion The results showed clearly that although the groups did not differ in their recall of the texts, poor comprehenders in particular gained significant benefits from the presence of integrated cues. For both pictures and titles, less-skilled children performed significantly better given an integrated cue than a non-integrated cue, while skilled children showed no significant differences between the two types of cue. This finding is consistent with our earlier work in two respects. Firstly, we have already found that the two groups do not differ in their ability to recall text verbatim, and the stories in the present study were short enough to enable a substantial part of the text to be recalled almost verbatim. Secondly, the results support our findings that poor comprehenders do not integrate text to the extent that skilled children do (see Experiment 4.1). The present study demonstrates that we can provide children with a framework within which the story can be interpreted, and this leads to better comprehension.

The results do not tell us exactly how this effect might work. Pictures could act as aids to memory in several different ways: in constructing a mental image of the text that can be used later to answer questions, or in the concurrent processing of text – as children read, they could refer to the picture to interpret each phrase – or in providing an initial framework in which text comprehension occurs. Titles could act as prior organisers or as mnemonic devices after the text is read. Work in adults suggests that integrated aids are more helpful if they are provided before the text is read, rather than after (e.g. Bransford and Johnson, 1972), but further work is needed to assess more precisely how children use such information during reading, particularly when it is pictorial. In the present study, we did not even direct the children's attention to the pictures, and it is possible that training children to use pictures constructively would produce even greater facilitative effects than we found here. A difficulty specific to investigating effects of pictures is that there is no simple, generally accepted, way of describing pictorial information that would enable researchers to compare the informational content of different pictures (see Schallert, 1980).

We did not replicate the finding of Arnold and Brooks that integrated cues facilitated recall more than non-integrated cues. For the case of pictures, this may be because in our study we used two types of accurate picture, and both were helpful, unlike the study by Arnold and Brooks, which included an accurate and a jumbled picture. The integrated cues in our study may have helped by providing frameworks within which to interpret the text while it was being read, thereby freeing capacity for integrating other information not given in the titles or pictures. This view is compatible with our previous account of the role of working memory in reading comprehension.

The finding that both groups remembered main ideas better than subsidiary ones shows that, despite their poorer comprehension, less-skilled children are still able to be selective in what they recall from a text. This is consistent with the work on recall for information varying in importance, described in Experiment 6.1. Stein and Glenn (1979) have shown that settings, initiating events and direct consequences are the best-remembered categories of information in narrative text, and our results suggest that this conclusion holds for readers differing fairly widely in comprehension skill.

Most children are eventually able to read and understand normal text without the presence of external cues such as pictures and titles to integrate the text. However, less-skilled comprehenders, who are helped by the presence of such cues, cannot rely on such aids being available. It would be more useful for these children to be able to integrate text through their own efforts, using internally generated cues. The next experiment investigated the possibility of inducing children to create their own images of stories as an aid to comprehension.

Experiment 8.5: *Effects of imagery training*[5]

Another way in which children's comprehension might be improved is by teaching them to use mental imagery as they are understanding a text. Such techniques have been shown to be effective. For instance, Pressley (1976) taught 8-year-olds to generate images for sections of stories as they read them. Compared with children who simply read the stories, those who generated images were subsequently better able to answer questions, even though both groups spent a similar amount of time studying the stories. However, the ability to learn to use self-generated images to aid comprehension is not available to children younger than about 8. For example, a study by Guttman, Levin and Pressley (1977) showed that the comprehension of third-graders, but not kindergarteners, could be improved by imagery instructions or by the use of 'partial pictures' (children who were shown the partial pictures were told to use them to help them to construct an image of what was not shown). The same study showed that when complete pictures were used to illustrate stories, children in all the age groups tested (kindergarten, first and third grade) could use them to improve their recall.

Between about 8 and 10 years of age, children cannot benefit from simply being told to use imagery: they need to be instructed in its use. Furthermore, as is the case with other comprehension aids, imagery instructions do not invariably enhance comprehension, even for children older than 9 (see Levin, 1981, for a review). Levin argues that the outcome of studies has varied partly because not all types of image are equally helpful and different types of passage or subject matter may call for different types of image. (We discuss different types of image in more detail below.) In the present study, we addressed the issue of whether imagery is particularly suitable for aiding memory for some sorts of information by asking the children three different types of question. The first type, which we term 'factual', required memory for facts that were explicit in the text. The second main type of question, 'inferential', asked about information that could only be inferred from the story, and the third type, 'descriptive', asked about details that would be particularly likely to come to the reader's attention if an effective image had been formed. These different types of question are illustrated with respect to an example passage in the method section.

Peters, Levin, McGivern and Pressley (1985) suggest that different forms of imagery instruction might be suitable for different passages. They identified two distinct types of imagery which they termed 'representational' and 'transformational'. Representational imagery is the fairly direct translation of the text into an image. In transformational imagery, however, as the name suggests, some aspects of the text are transformed so that the image does not correspond directly to the text, but is used as a sort of mnemonic. Peters et al. argued that this form of imagery might be useful for recalling information that is difficult to remember, such as names and numerical data, which are more prevalent in non-narrative passages, and which do not necessarily lend themselves to representation in an imageable form. An example from the study by Peters et al. provides an illustration of how transformational imagery might be used. Their subjects (8-year-olds) had to remember what each person was famous for, given sentences such as:

Larry Taylor was famous for inventing a house on a turntable.

They were instructed to transform the names into more imageable forms (in this case, a tailor), and to integrate this image with another image of the rest of the sentence. Their results confirmed their prediction: transformational imagery substantially improved the subjects' recall of difficult-to-remember factual information (e.g. names), but was less helpful for information that could be more directly coded into an image. Representational imagery, by contrast, did not significantly facilitate memory for the difficult information. In our experiment, we incorporated training in *both* sorts of imagery technique, in order to optimise the effectiveness of imagery training.

Some work has investigated the effects of imagery training on poor comprehenders specifically, and has shown that they seem to derive special benefit from visual imagery instructions. Levin (1973) tested two groups of fourth-grade poor comprehenders – those with decoding and vocabulary problems (a 'deficit' group, as identified by Cromer, 1970), and those with adequate decoding and vocabulary skills (a 'difference' group). The subjects given imagery instructions were told to try to 'think of a picture in their mind' as they read each sentence. Such instructions improved comprehension (compared with simply reading the story) for the difference, but not for the deficit, poor readers. Indeed, the difference poor readers, when they were given imagery instructions, performed as well as good comprehenders did.

In the present experiment, we also investigated the effects of imagery instructions on good and poor comprehenders, but explored in more detail the particular types of information that imagery might facilitate by asking the subjects different types of question about the passages, as outlined above.

Method Because the age of children we have used in the majority of our experiments (7–8 years) is at the lower end of the range in which children are able to benefit from imagery instructions, we used older subjects in the present experiment (9–10-year-olds). Since this study was the only one we were conducting in a school term, we used a different, and less time-consuming, method to select subjects. We followed the usual procedure of testing whole classes of children on the Gates–MacGinitie Vocabulary Test (1965, survey D, Form 1), to assess their decoding and vocabulary skills. Those subjects who showed average, or above average, performance on this test were then given Form C of the Neale test. In order to provide a quick measure of the children's comprehension, the test was adapted as a group test of listening comprehension. (Previous work, for example Experiments 4.1, 4.6, 6.1, has shown that children who have a reading comprehension problem also have difficulty in their listening comprehension.) Instead of listening to children read the passages aloud, the passages were read aloud *to them* in groups of six. The children were given booklets containing the questions for each passage, with one set of questions on each page. When the experimenter had finished reading the passage, the children turned to the appropriate page in their booklet, and the questions were read aloud to them, one at a time. After each question, the subjects were given time to write a response under the written version of it.

From the ninety subjects who were given the Neale test, we selected twenty-two good and twenty-two poor comprehenders, on the basis of their ability to answer the questions about the Neale passages. Since we did not use the test in the prescribed way, the raw scores cannot be converted to age equivalents. The mean score for the poor comprehenders was 14.26, and for the good group, 24.3 (max = 36), and these scores were significantly different, $t(42) = 9.70$, $p < .001$. The good and poor comprehenders were matched on chronological age (9.7 years for both groups), and on Gates–MacGinitie Vocabulary scores (31.4 and 31.3 respectively out of a maximum of 50). The good and poor comprehenders were subdivided into two matched groups, one of which was given training in imagery. The other children formed a control group. The reading tests scores of the four groups of subjects are shown in Table 8.13.

Nine stories were written using suitable vocabulary, so that all subjects would be able to read them without difficulty. Four of the stories were allocated for use in the training sessions, and the remaining five were used in the test session. We wrote the passages in such a way that the three types of question (inferential, descriptive and factual) could be asked. An example passage, and its accompanying questions is shown in Table 8.14. The inferential questions addressed information that was not explicit in the text, for example, in the passage shown in the table, the information that the ladder was kept in the kitchen, because a cooker is mentioned. The descriptive questions asked about details that would be more likely to be available to subjects using an imagery

Table 8.13. *Reading test scores of the four groups of subjects*

	Comprehension score (max = 36)	Gates–MacGinitie score (max = 50)
Less-skilled comprehenders:		
Trained (n = 11)	14·9	31·3
Control (n = 11)	14·8	31·4
Skilled comprehenders:		
Trained (n = 11)	24·2	31·4
Control (n = 11)	24·5	31·4

Table 8.14. *Example story and questions*

The step ladder was put away safely behind the door which was just to the right of the cooker. The three shelves were up at last and, even with a sore thumb, Terry Butcher was happy. The hammer that had caused the pain was put away in the tool box with the other tools.

Linda, Terry's wife, came into the room with a box of crockery. 'The shelves are for my little model aeroplanes', said Terry with a stern voice. 'We'll see', was the reply from Linda.

A little while later, when Terry was putting away the tool box, he heard a loud scream and the sound of breaking glass and china. Terry walked back into the room and was angry. 'I warned you about those shelves', he said to Linda and sadly went to get the tool box out again.

Questions
(F = factual, I = inferential, D = descriptive)

1. Exactly where was the step ladder put away? (D)
2. In which room was the step ladder put away? (I)
3. How many shelves had been put up? (F)
4. Why did Terry have a sore thumb? (I)
5. Who was carrying the crockery? (F)
6. Why did Linda scream? (I)
7. Describe the scene in the room when Linda screamed. (D)
8. Describe Terry's face when he saw the state of the room. (D)
9. What was the full name of the person who had put up the shelves? (F)

strategy than those who were not, so we expected that performance on these questions might be particularly helped by imagery instructions. The stories also incorporated factual statements, so that straightforward factual questions could be asked.

For each passage, we devised three questions of each type (inferential, descriptive, factual) and the stories and questions were typed on separate sheets of paper and made into booklets. Appropriate representational and transformational pictures were also produced for the training sessions.

In all training and in the final test sessions the subjects were seen in small groups of four or five. The good and poor comprehenders were trained and tested in separate groups. The children were allowed one-and-a-half minutes to read each story for themselves, and then turned to the next page of the booklet, showing the appropriate questions. The experimenter read out each question in turn, and the children were given enough time between questions to write in an answer under the appropriate question in their booklet.

Imagery training. The imagery training took place over three sessions. The first session lasted for thirty minutes, and the second and third for twenty minutes each. The subjects were told that they would be learning to 'think in pictures' as they read stories, to help them to answer questions about the stories. In the first training session the subjects read one of the stories, and the experimenter then produced two drawings: one was a cartoon-like sequence of four pictures which represented the sequence of events in the story. The other was a single picture, depicting the main event in the story (for example, the main event of the story illustrated in Table 8.14 was the crockery crashing to the floor as the shelves collapse). The subjects were shown how each of the pictures related to the story. The subjects were also told that the drawing used to illustrate the main point was called a *representational* drawing because it represented the information in the story. They were then told to imagine that the pictures were in their minds, and that they were to use them to help them to answer some questions about the story. The stories and pictures were taken away before the questions were presented. The subjects were then given a second story to read, and were told to try to form mental pictures as they read it, and to formulate a picture of what they thought was the main event of the story. After the subjects had attempted to answer the questions with the aid of their 'mental pictures' the experimenter asked each subject to describe the images they had used, and gave feedback and suggestions for improving their images. For example they were told 'That's a good picture to imagine' or 'How about including (x) in your picture?', to encourage and extend their ability to create images. Many questions, both general and specific, were also asked, such as 'Did you see colour?', 'Could you describe what (x) looked like?'.

In the second training session, both representational and transformational drawings were used. The children were told that the transformational drawings were specifically designed to help them to remember details from the stories, and the way in which this could be achieved was explained. The subjects were then told that they should try to form three different types of image as they read through a new story: a cartoon sequence with four frames to represent the sequence of events in the story, a representational image of the main event, and a transformational image involving the name of the main character, to help them remember specific details. When they had completed the task and answered the questions, their images were discussed with them, as in the first session.

In the third training session the children were not shown any drawings. The imagery procedure was reiterated, and the subjects read and answered questions about a new story and a final discussion of their 'mental pictures' took place, as in the first two sessions.

Control condition. The subjects who did not receive imagery training saw the same stories, also in three sessions. The subjects read the stories and answered the questions, and their answers were then discussed with them. They were told whether their answers were adequate or not, and learned that the stories had to be read very carefully to gain full marks. Subjects in this condition spent as long with the experimenter as those in the imagery training groups.

Test phase. The subjects were tested in small groups of six to ten children. Those who had received imagery training were tested separately from the children in the control group. The stories and questions were presented in a booklet (again with stories and questions on separate pages), and the questions were read aloud to the children as before. The subjects who had received the imagery training were reminded to form mental images as they read the stories, and to use their pictures to help them to answer the questions. The subjects in the control condition were told to read the stories very carefully, and to answer the questions in as much detail as possible.

Results The questions were given a maximum score of 1, but quarter and half marks were awarded, where appropriate, depending on the level of detail provided. The mean numbers of correct responses are shown in Table 8.15.

The data were analysed by analysis of variance. There were two between-subjects' factors: comprehension skill and training condition (imagery and control), and one within-subjects' factor: question type (inferential, descriptive and factual). All three main effects were significant. There was an effect of comprehension skill with good comprehenders answering more questions correctly than poor ones: $F(1, 40) = 10.64$, $p < .01$. There was a main effect of training condition, the subjects given imagery training performing better than those in the control group: $F(1,40) = 12.32$, $p < .01$. The main effect of question type, although significant, $F(2,80) = 12.41$, $p < .01$, is uninteresting since the questions in the different conditions were not matched in any systematic way.

There was a near-significant two-way interaction between comprehension skill and training condition: $F(1,40) = 3.80$, $p = .058$. As predicted, poor comprehenders given imagery training showed a marked improvement in performance on the questions. This interpretation was confirmed by a comparison of the effects of training on the two groups. The poor comprehenders given imagery training did significantly better on the test questions than the control group of poor comprehenders: $t(40) = 2.24$, $p < .025$, but there was no such difference for the good comprehenders: $t(40) = 0.64$. No other interactions reached significance.

Table 8.15. *Mean post-training question answering scores as a function of comprehension skill, training group and question type (max. = 15)*

Question type:	Inferential	Descriptive	Factual	Mean
Less-skilled				
Control	7·46	6·05	8·32	7·27
Imagery training	8·55	9·82	10·46	9·61
Skilled				
Control	8·96	8·46	11·09	9·50
Imagery training	10·27	9·50	10·73	10·17

Discussion The findings show that imagery training was especially effective for those children who did not possess adequate comprehension skills and that, overall, it was particularly effective in improving performance on questions that required inferences or information of a descriptive nature that was not explicit in the text.

The finding that poor comprehenders benefit from imagery training may arise because it enables them, or forces them, to integrate information in the text in a way that they would not normally do. Several of our studies (e.g. Experiments 4.1–4.3) have led to the suggestion that poor comprehenders do not engage in constructive and integrated processing to the same extent as good ones do. Training in the production of images to represent the information in the stories may have encouraged the poor comprehenders to integrate the information in a way that they did not normally do, particularly the training in deriving an image for the main point of the story.

Our results do not enable us to conclude which sort of imagery training was more effective, or whether the two sorts (representational and transformational) affected memory for different sorts of information from the stories, since all the children who received training in imagery were given both sorts. Further work is needed to address these issues.

The finding that the comprehension of the good group did not improve with imagery training does not *necessarily* mean that they already use imagery and, hence, do not benefit from training in its use. It may be that they have some other equally efficient strategy for remembering information from text, and that training in imagery provides them with no *additional* advantage.

As we said at the beginning of this chapter, techniques that purport to influence the way readers represent a text mentally may be effective because they enable readers to use working memory more efficiently. The effects of imagery may be mediated by working memory, in that it gives poor comprehenders a means of integrating information in the text, and possibly encouraging them to make inferences that they may not normally have made. However, imagery as a strategy has some limitations. For example, Tierney and Cunningham (1984) remark that imagery training has not been proved helpful for young children (below 7 years), for students who do not learn well from pictures, and for longer passages, during which the strategy may not be maintained. Despite these limitations, it may well be a useful strategy for some readers in some situations, as our study shows. It might even be a useful stepping stone to other means of representing information in text.

General discussion

In summary, we have described four different methods for improving text comprehension, focusing on mental imagery, use of text organisers, drawing inferences and comprehension monitoring. Each of these showed some effect on our outcome measures. The results of our inference-training procedure suggested that this training in particular had potential for further development. In our instructional study, inference training showed effects on an immediate post-test of story comprehension after only the minimum of instruction (Experiment 8.1). Our longer-term training studies showed that inference training over a period of weeks was both more beneficial than decoding practice, and more helpful to less-skilled than it was to skilled comprehenders. The advantage of inference training over decoding practice was significantly greater for less-skilled than for skilled children. Inference-trained less-skilled comprehenders also improved slightly, but not significantly, more than those given comprehension exercises or comprehension-monitoring instruction.

The size of the inference-training effect for less-skilled comprehenders was larger than we had anticipated, with an average increase in Neale comprehension age of over sixteen months in a period of two months, and thirteen of the thirty-five less-skilled children given such training were classified as high comprehenders in the post-test, compared with only four of the twenty-eight poor comprehenders in the other treatment groups. This result is particularly striking, since many training studies do not demonstrate improvements on standardised tests, but tend, rather, to measure improvement on tests of the particular skills trained.

The other forms of training that we used – generating imagery and using verbal and visual organisers – both produced improvements in poor comprehenders and no significant increases in performance for good comprehenders. In the study of advance organisers, the training helped less-skilled children to answer questions about information that was not explicit in the text, but did not facilitate verbatim recall. The imagery instructions used in Experiment 8.5 appeared to have a more general effect of increasing performance by poor comprehenders on various types of questions.

We still have only a limited understanding of exactly *how* the training we used affects children. We cannot assume that they adopt wholesale the strategies we had intended them to learn, but that through doing the tasks we set them, they evolved some processes and strategies of their own which later proved effective.

We did not address the issue of working-memory differences between skill groups explicitly in the training, but the various training methods we used could all have helped children indirectly to use working memory more efficiently. For instance, the procedure of making inferences from particular words may have prompted the poor comprehenders to build a model of the text as they read, and so reduced the working-memory load involved in comprehension. This possibility could be assessed more directly by looking at children's reading time, in the way that we did in Chapter 4, before and after training, although there are some drawbacks to this method, that we described previously. The use of integrated titles and pictures may have enabled children to mobilise prior knowledge and expectations before reading, and to make it easier for them to integrate information during reading. Even a brief period of imagery training brought a group of poor comprehenders almost up to the level of performance shown by good comprehenders, suggesting that the less-skilled children were able to make inferences, and just had to be induced to bring their abilities to bear on text that they read. Although basic memory capacity may not be amenable to training, there are techniques designed to improve memory functions, such as rehearsal, that might have indirect effects on working memory (see Brown and Campione, 1978). Further investigation of such techniques in comprehension training might not only increase the efficacy of treatment, but would also help in understanding the role of working memory in reading.

The training techniques we used succeeded, therefore, in producing measurable, general improvement, and for the inference-training technique, improvement on the test that we had used to distinguish the two skill groups in the first place. The methods used were also all general procedures that could be applied to any narrative text, rather than being tied to specific texts. The effects of training also seem to be specific to poor comprehenders. It is possible that there may have been a ceiling effect for good comprehenders, but this seems unlikely, in that this group showed considerably less than perfect performance in all of our training studies. Our methods could be further tested under other conditions. For example, it may also be useful for other types of text, e.g. expository text, or other types of poor reader, or different-aged poor comprehenders.

We should also consider our results in the light of some recent criticism of training studies. Carver (1987) critically reviewed recent training studies, including those by Hansen and Pearson (1983), Palincsar and Brown (1984) and Paris, Cross and Lipson (1984), and argued forcefully that three principles could explain the facilitative effects of training more simply than the accounts given by the proponents of the training schemes. The first principle, *Easiness*, states that comprehension scores will appear to increase if texts given at post-testing are sufficiently easy to read. Carver suggests that subjects in training studies should be given post-tests at an appropriate level of difficulty and cites some cases in which this had not been done. In our studies, use of the Neale test ensures that children read texts only up to their level of competence, since testing stops when a certain number of errors are made. Furthermore, in terms of reading accuracy, our two groups were of course matched, and so the other forms of post-test that we used were presumably of equal difficulty for the two groups.

Carver's second explanatory principle is the *Reading Time* principle. He argues that in many cases, training procedures induce children to read text more slowly than they otherwise would have done, and this in itself increases comprehension. The third principle, *Practice*, is closely related to the second: that subjects will improve on any task given practice. This principle will not provide an alternative explanation of results if appropriate controls are used, and as we already argued above, some of our control treatments, particularly the comprehension exercises, were more similar to the post-test than the experimental treatments were. Thus it seems unlikely that this principle accounted for our results. It could be argued that the reading time principle explains our results. However, this is not a plausible argument in our case. Carver's criticism implies that reading time is a study skill, suggesting that he views reading time as 'study time'. Our subjects simply read texts aloud, and 'time to study the text' before answering questions was not an issue. The reading time explanation therefore seems an unlikely alternative explanation for our results. Out of curiosity, though, we did analyse reading time for the data we had available: times to read the first three stories of Form A of the Neale Analysis for subjects in Experiment 8.2. There were no significant differences between skill groups or treatment conditions, nor any interactions. There is therefore no evidence that any of Carver's alternative explanations account for our results.

Although we would claim that our training studies are not open to the kinds of criticism levelled by Carver at most other recent studies, we would like to add notes of caution of our own here about the interpretation of our training studies. While they do in general support our account of poor comprehension, our failure to find effects of decoding training does not mean that such an effect might not exist, for example, if we improved the training. However, this outcome seems unlikely in view of the fact that the decoding training produced measurable improvements in what it was designed for: increasing decoding speed. We do not wish to make strong claims for the practical applications of our results. It would be encouraging to think that such procedures would be helpful in the real world of classroom instruction, but they need to be tested in a more realistic school context, with teachers being the instructors, and children's performance being assessed in a variety of ways.

The variations in improvement rates in our studies were considerable. Our poor comprehenders are probably not a truly homogeneous group: some children improved markedly with training and others no more than would be expected in the normal course of development. As Tierney and Cunningham (1984, p. 616) note, we need to know how specific training methods interact with characteristics of the reader and of the text. We have gone part of the way towards this end, in studying children who are poor in comprehension but not decoding skills. Obviously we could go further in subdividing our poor comprehenders, but in our present state of knowledge, we feel that it is more useful to ascertain general characteristics of this subgroup, in order to understand the processes of normal comprehension, and then to feed this knowledge of normal processes into a revised training programme. Tierney and Cunningham (1984) caution against training that puts into practice the theorist's prescriptive beliefs about the 'right' way to read, particularly in terms of strategies the reader 'should' adopt: 'teaching children our theories about how they think in order to get them to think better seems to us to be fraught with danger' (ibid., p. 634). We do not know enough about strategy use to make such prescriptions, and there are probably many strategies leading to the same end product. However, what we can do is to try to induce children to develop strategies for themselves leading to the end product: comprehension. We then can examine in more detail the strategies that they adopt.

9 Conclusions

Summary of findings

One of the clearest messages to emerge from our studies of children's text understanding is that comprehension problems are not necessarily due to difficulties in decoding words or accessing their meanings. There is evidence from several different sources that the poor comprehenders we studied do not suffer from a decoding bottleneck. For instance, their comprehension deficit is apparent not just in reading, but also in listening, and training in rapid decoding did not produce marked comprehension improvement. There are several areas in which less-skilled children performed equally to skilled children: short-term memory, vocabulary skills, syntactic skills and recall of the exact wording of sentences and texts. They showed little or no comprehension deficit at the level of single words or sentences. However, poor comprehenders had three main areas of weakness. Firstly, they were less likely than skilled comprehenders to integrate information from different parts of a text, and to make relevant inferences to help them understand a text. We characterised this pattern of deficits by saying that the poor comprehenders do not build such adequate *mental models* of text as do the skilled ones. The lack of integrative processing exhibited by the less-skilled children may have been related to the fact that they were remarkably poor at using the linguistic devices that signal the cohesion of a text: anaphoric links and explicit connectives. They were also less able to reconstruct or repair text that was disorganised or anomalous. Secondly, less-skilled children showed evidence of poorer working-memory efficiency. The process of constructing a mental model requires the use of working memory so that new information can be stored, and integrated with previous parts of the text and with prior knowledge. We have proposed that an inefficient working memory makes it difficult to construct such a model. The third weakness we identified was in metacognitive skills: the poor comprehenders tended not to notice inconsistencies in text, and more generally, they did not realise that they had failed to understand a text, or know how to remedy such a failure if it did become apparent to them.

Our account of comprehension failure is essentially descriptive. It does not in any way *explain* why some children do not develop the comprehension skills we have identified. Nor did we investigate the developmental precursors of these skills. However, our work should provide some useful pointers to the areas in which studies of early comprehension development should be done.

In our training studies we have begun to identify causal factors in poor comprehension. The most effective method of training was that in which children were made aware of the sorts of inferences that could be made from single lexical items. Other forms of training, in which children were guided in using imagery, and pictorial and verbal organisers, also showed some beneficial effects. However, the inference-awareness training had two advantages: it could be applied to any type of text, and is a technique that children can carry round in their heads – they do not need to rely on external aids such as pictures or titles.

Educational implications

We did not start with the assumption that the children we identified as poor comprehenders constitute an educationally significant problem. However, in the course of the research, we inevitably asked ourselves whether such children needed any special help. Less-skilled comprehenders constituted 10–15% of all children in the classes we used in the research. Our sample was restricted mainly to 7–8-year-olds in a single geographical area, but we have no reason to suppose that our sample was atypical. In some cases, 'poor' comprehenders were simply very good decoders and average at comprehension, as our selection procedure was focused on finding children with a lag of at least six months between their accuracy and comprehension ages, with the relation to *chronological* age as only a secondary factor. However, many of the children also showed comprehension skills well below what might be expected for their age, and there was an average lag of about six months between comprehension age and chronological age. As we mentioned in Chapter 1, other researchers have described comparable instances of children who can read well but whose comprehension lags behind their decoding skills.

Our sample of poor comprehenders came from different schools in which various different teaching methods were used. They were distributed fairly evenly across schools, and came from the same classrooms that the good comprehenders did. We therefore have no basis for suggesting that poor comprehension is linked to particular teaching methods. We have little information about what happens to poor comprehenders. It is possible that they just 'grow out of it', although we identified a similar proportion of poor comprehenders in the 8–9-year-olds we tested. Only longitudinal studies can show the extent to which such comprehension problems may persist. Even if poor comprehension is short-lived, lasting only for six months or a year, there could be detrimental consequences. Children will be held back at a time when reading for information is becoming increasingly important, and their motivation to read for pleasure and instruction may be reduced.

Unfortunately, it is quite easy for poor comprehension to go unnoticed. Reading skill is generally and most simply monitored by listening to children read aloud, or by administering tests that involve no more than the comprehension of isolated words or sentences, tests on which our poor comprehenders would have done well. Even the ability to remember chunks of text verbatim, without understanding it, can give the impression that a child has understood.

Our own data, and that of others, shows that, for young children, decoding is the most salient feature of reading. We do not dispute that in the early stages of learning to read, decoding skills are of great importance. It is understandable that teachers may wish to devote their limited resources and time to children who have not mastered the basic decoding skills. Such children can fall rapidly behind, because there may be little time for individual reading tuition in late primary and in secondary education. However, it is also important for comprehension skills to be recognised, and assessed, even during the early stages of learning to read. Given that our poor comprehenders showed deficits in listening as well as reading comprehension, their problems could be picked up before fluent reading is achieved. Indeed, the training techniques described in Chapter 8 could quite easily be adapted to listening comprehension tasks for younger children.

After an upsurge of interest in methods of teaching comprehension (e.g. Tierney and Cunningham, 1984), there have been some signs of disillusionment with the idea that comprehension could or should be taught (Carver, 1987). But many of the instructional studies have been concerned with high-level and quite explicitly used techniques, that could be taught directly as 'study skills'. The sorts of skills we have studied are basic to reading and listening. The ability to resolve anaphors, make simple inferences and remember the gist of a text are not 'optional extras', but fundamental skills. We need to know much more about how the skills we have identified interact, and about their early development. As is often the case, this research raises more questions than it answers. But at least the questions we end with are more specific than the ones with which we set out.

Notes

1 The nature of poor comprehension

1. The burden of proof in such studies is on the experimenter to demonstrate that 'difference' poor readers are in fact as skilled in decoding as good readers, and that the two groups contrast purely in comprehension skills. We think we have overcome the common objections to the claim that such children have a comprehension deficit:

   (a) Regression: Calfee et al. (1976) noted that previous authors had omitted to consider regression to the mean in subject selection. We deal with this issue later in this chapter.
   (b) Decoding speed: Previous researchers have suggested that poor comprehension occurs because of slow, non-automatic decoding. Although we did not use a measure of decoding speed (e.g. reading time) in our subject selection, we have evidence that our poor comprehenders are not slower decoders (see Chapters 3 and 8). They may in some cases even be better in their decoding skills than the skilled children, as shown in the examples we gave earlier.
   (c) Study time: Carver (1987) argued that comprehension is greater when *more* time is spent in reading a text. This would mean that our good comprehenders had an advantage if they spent longer reading. However, Carver seems to mean study time, rather than decoding speed, as he uses 'reading time' and 'study time' interchangeably. Furthermore, time to study the texts is not really at issue in the type of reading tasks we used: children either decoded or listened to a passage, and then answered questions, but could not be said to be 'studying' the text. In fact, we have no evidence for differences between the groups in text reading time (see Chapter 8).

2 Background: reading, remembering and understanding

1. More recently, Perfetti has proposed a more general version of this theory, which he terms the 'verbal efficiency hypothesis' (see Perfetti, 1985, Chapter 6). The core proposal is that comprehension can be limited by the inefficient operation of *any* 'local' processes, such as schema activation, propositional encoding and lexical access.
2. It might be argued that, in order to test causal hypotheses about comprehension failure, it is necessary to compare the results of our two groups with a younger group of 'average' comprehenders who have the same comprehension ability as our older poor comprehenders (see, e.g. the arguments put forward for a reading age match by Bradley and Bryant, 1983, when discussing research on good and poor readers). The point of such a control group is best explained by an example. If, say, our poor comprehenders are found to be deficient in inference making, then this may be

because they have had less experience of successful understanding than their age- and decoding-matched controls, and it is *understanding* that promotes inference skills, rather than vice-versa. Thus, if we had a younger control group (a 'comprehension age match'), and their inference skills were *better* than those of the older poor comprehenders, then we would have better evidence that skill at making inferences is likely to have a causal role in reading comprehension.

However, it is not clear that such a comprehension-age match control group would really tell us anything very interesting, since it is not immediately obvious what they would be matched *for*. Since not being able to understand obviously doesn't prevent a child from *trying* to understand (i.e. a poor comprehender's experience of attempting to understand will not be limited in the same way that a poor decoder's attempts to decode words will be), the older children would probably have had more experience of the latter – not only in their reading but also in their experience of spoken language.

At a practical level, there would also have been considerable problems in finding such a control group for our studies because of the characteristics of the Neale (and related) tests. Because such tests make the (accurate) assumption that comprehension and decoding skills are usually highly correlated, testing is curtailed when the child makes more than a certain number of errors on a passage. Hence, good decoders (i.e. our older groups) would have the opportunity to try to answer more questions simply because they are able to read more passages. Because of this method of testing, a 7-year-old with 'average' accuracy and comprehension would be likely to be a *better* comprehender than a 9-year-old with average accuracy but comprehension at the 7-year-old level because the younger child would have answered a higher *proportion* of the questions offered to them than the older and better word decoder.

3. Many of the studies we describe in this book were carried out in the United States, and the school grade level, rather than the ages of the subjects is provided in accounts of this work. Although exact age equivalents cannot be given, approximate ages can be calculated by adding on five to grade numbers (e.g. grade 3 = 8 years).
4. Cromer's work has been criticised extensively by Calfee, Arnold and Drum (1976), who doubt the existence of people who can decode fluently but not understand what they read. They argue that three basic flaws in Cromer's work undermine the conclusions that can be drawn:

   (a) The 'difference' poor readers (those who have adequate vocabulary, but poor comprehension scores) are an atypical group and, because of the phenomenon of 'regression toward the mean' one would expect that, if they were retested, their comprehension would improve or their vocabulary decline. In fact, on a subsequent test the scores of a substantial number of the difference readers and their controls switched, providing fuel for Calfee et al.'s worries and suggesting that 'The Difference and Difference-controls are two groups of moderately poor readers, not different from one another' (p.32).
   (b) Although Cromer's experimental findings did support the idea that the difference poor readers perform differently from their controls, his statistical analyses are questionable.
   (c) The poor readers took longer than good readers to decode single words, bringing into question whether they were really 'fluent' readers.

3 Processing words and sentences

1. In addition to reporting analyses of variance with subjects as a random factor, we have also, where appropriate, reported the corresponding analyses treating items as a random factor. This procedure, which is common in psycholinguistic research,

enables one to test whether the experimental results could be generalised to a new set of materials. Just as it is assumed that subjects' performance in an experiment is representative of the population of subjects of that type, so the materials used in an experiment should be representative of that type of material. Min F' (see Clark, 1973) provides an estimate of whether the results will generalise *simultaneously* to new samples of subjects and materials.

When we report the results of an analysis of variance, the min F' statistic alone is reported where significant. Otherwise F_1 (subjects as a random factor) and F_2 (items as a random factor) are reported separately. In some cases, it was not practicable to analyse the data by materials because of the small numbers of items used, or because the data were not scored on an item-by-item basis. In such cases, F_1 alone is reported.

4 Inferences and the integration of text

1. We would like to thank Scott Paris for providing the materials on which the stories and questions used in Experiment 4.2 were based.
2. A more plausible characterisation is that subjects make inferences about the possible referents of a word according to the context, rather than that they select one particular meaning for a polysemous word (see Johnson-Laird, 1983). For example, *shark* may be a good retrieval cue for the sentence *it frightened the swimmer*, but could not be said to be a *sense* of *it*.

5 Allocating resources during reading

1. Recent work by Henry (conference paper, 1989) casts doubt on whether the word-length effect for pictures is necessarily a sign that rehearsal has been used. She showed that the word-length effect did not occur for 5-year-olds' recall of picture names for a probed-recall measure, although 7-year-olds did show such an effect in this task. The probed recall did not require full output of the list of names. If the word-length effect is due simply to output processes (the length of time it takes to say the names in the list), then no word-length effect should be expected in the probed recall task. Further work is therefore needed to establish the source of the word-length effect in good and poor comprehenders.
2. Replacement occurred for 13% of the data in each skill group. This procedure means that the variance of the scores is somewhat reduced.

6 Metacognition and reading

1. The following descriptions of judgements about main ideas formed part of two different experiments which we describe in full elsewhere (Experiments 6.1 and 7.2). Both these experiments, in addition to their primary purpose, had a secondary aim of investigating the two groups' abilities in abstracting the main idea of a story, whether presented verbally or as a series of pictures. The results related to this secondary aim are presented together here rather than with each study separately, for convenience of exposition.
2. We report this pilot study here, despite the tiny sample size, because we obtained some interesting and suggestive data that formed the background to our second, larger study reported below.
3. We are grateful to Sharon Bridgman, who carried out this experiment as an MSc project at the Laboratory of Experimental Psychology, University of Sussex.

7 Using cohesive devices in narrative discourse

1. Although Stenning and Michell term these uses 'naive' and 'sophisticated' respectively, what the difference really amounts to is that one style is disembedded, i.e. the narrative would be comprehensible to someone who could not see the pictures, and the other is embedded in the context of two people who can both see the pictures that the storyteller is talking about. It is possible that children who do not use a disembedded style could do so in a situation where it is clearly indicated that the listener could not see the pictures and did not know anything about the story. However, we were interested in the differences between the two skill groups in how they would respond to the same situation, and did not manipulate the context of story-telling. We have therefore termed the two styles of reference 'embedded' and 'disembedded', without meaning to imply that one is superior to the other.
2. This story was in fact the first four pictures of a five-picture sequence. The final picture, which we omitted, showed the girl going out a second time, taking an umbrella. This omission was purely to permit us to balance story length across conditions. The remaining pictures still told a story.
3. We have already noted that there is some debate about classification of some examples of ellipsis. This example could be described as a verb-phrase conjunction, rather than an ellipsis.
4. This experiment was carried out in collaboration with Morag Donaldson (then at the Department of Psychology, Plymouth Polytechnic).

8 Methods of improving poor comprehension

1. These stories were written by Trish Joscelyne as part of an undergraduate project, described in Experiment 8.4.
2. By 'factual', we mean that the answer could be derived fairly directly from the text: for example, questions 3, 4 and 5 in the experimental story in Table 8.1. Categorising each question as factual or inferential, 94% of primed questions were inferential, while 67% of unprimed questions were factual.
3. Data for the final word list were missing for two subjects: a decoding-practice poor comprehender and an inference-trained good comprehender.
4. We are grateful to Trish Joscelyne, who carried out this study as an undergraduate project.
5. We are grateful to Sima Patel, who carried out this study as an undergraduate project.

References

Related publications

Several of our own experiments that are described in this book have also been published elsewhere as individual studies. The following list gives publication details for these experiments. In many cases, the reference gives more detailed or technical descriptions of experiments than appear in this book.

Experiment 4.1:

Oakhill, J.V. (1982). Constructive processes in skilled and less-skilled comprehenders' memory for sentences. *British Journal of Psychology*, 73, 13-20

Experiment 4.2:

Oakhill, J.V. (1984). Inferential and memory skills in children's comprehension of stories. *British Journal of Educational Psychology*, 54, 31-9

Experiment 4.3:

Oakhill, J.V. (1983). Instantiation in skilled and less-skilled comprehenders. *Quarterly Journal of Experimental Psychology*, 35*A*, 441-50

Experiment 4.5:

Oakhill, J.V. & Yuill, N.M. (1986). Pronoun resolution in skilled and less-skilled comprehenders: Effects of memory load and inferential complexity. *Language and Speech*, 29, 25-37

Experiment 4.6:

Yuill, N.M. & Oakhill, J.V. (1988). Understanding of anaphoric relations in skilled and less skilled comprehenders. *British Journal of Psychology*, 79, 173-86

Experiment 5.1:

Oakhill, J.V., Yuill, N.M. & Parkin, A. (1986). On the nature of the difference between skilled and less-skilled comprehenders. *Journal of Research in Reading*, 9, 80-91 [Experiment 2]

See also:

Oakhill, J.V., Yuill, N.M. & Parkin, A.J. (1988). Memory and inference in skilled and less-skilled comprehenders. In M.M. Gruneberg, P.E. Morris, & R.N. Sykes (eds.), *Practical Aspects of Memory*, Vol. 2. Chichester: Wiley

Experiment 5.2:

Yuill, N.M., Oakhill, J.V. & Parkin, A.J. (1989). Working memory, comprehension ability and the resolution of text anomaly. *British Journal of Psychology*, 80, 351-61 [Experiment 1]

Experiment 6.4:

Yuill, N.M., Oakhill, J.V. & Parkin, A.J. (1989). Working memory, comprehension ability and the resolution of text anomaly. *British Journal of Psychology*, 80, 351-61 [Experiment 2]

Experiment 7.3:

Oakhill, J.V., Yuill, N.M. & Donaldson, M.L. (1990). Understanding of causal expressions in skilled and less-skilled text comprehenders. *British Journal of Developmental Psychology*, 8, 401-10

Experiment 7.4:

Garnham, A., Oakhill, J.V., & Johnson-Laird, P.N. (1982). Referential continuity and the coherence of discourse. *Cognition*, 11, 29-46

Experiment 8.1:

Yuill, N. & Joscelyne, T. (1988). Effects of organisational cues and strategies on good and poor comprehenders' story understanding. *Journal of Educational Psychology*, 80, 152-8 [Experiment 2]

Experiment 8.2:

Yuill, N.M. & Oakhill, J.V. (1988). Effects of inference awareness training on poor reading comprehension. *Applied Cognitive Psychology*, 2, 33-45

Experiment 8.4:

Yuill, N. & Joscelyne, T. (1988). Effects of organisational cues and strategies on good and poor comprehenders' story understanding. *Journal of Educational Psychology*, 80, 152-8 [Experiment 1]

Works cited

Ackerman, B. P. (1984). The effects of storage and processing complexity on comprehension repair in children and adults. *Journal of Experimental Child Psychology*, 37, 303-34

Anderson, R.C. & Ortony, A. (1975). On putting apples into bottles: A problem of polysemy. *Cognitive Psychology*, 7, 167-80

Anderson, R.C., Pichert, J.W., Goetz, E.T. Schallert, D.L., Stevens, K.V., & Trollip, S.R. (1976). Instantiation of general terms. *Journal of Verbal Learning and Verbal Behavior*, 15, 667-79

Anderson, R.C. and Shifrin, Z. (1980). The meaning of words in context. In R.J. Spiro, B.C. Bruce and W.F. Brewer (eds.), *Theoretical Issues in Reading Comprehension*. Hillsdale, N.J.: Lawrence Erlbaum Associates.

Anderson, R.C., Stevens, K.V., Shifrin, Z., & Osborn, J.H. (1977). *Instantiation of Word Meanings in Children*. Technical Report No. 46, Center for the Study of Reading: University of Illinois

Appel, L.F., Cooper, R.G., McCarrell, N., Sims-Knight, J., Yussen, S.R. & Flavell, J.H. (1972) The development of the distinction between perceiving and memorizing. *Child Development*, 43, 1365-81

Arnold, D.S. & Brooks, P.H. (1976). Influence of contextual organizing material on children's listening comprehension. *Journal of Educational Psychology*, 68, 711-16

August, D.L., Flavell, J.H. & Clift, R. (1984). Comparison of comprehension monitoring of skilled and less-skilled readers. *Reading Research Quarterly*, 20, 39-53

Ausubel, D.P. (1968). *Educational Psychology, A Cognitive View*. New York: Holt Rinehart & Winston

Baddeley, A.D. (1986). *Working Memory*. Oxford: Oxford University Press

Baddeley, A.D., Eldridge, M. & Lewis, V.J. (1981). The role of subvocalization in reading. *Quarterly Journal of Experimental Psychology*, 33, 439-54

Baddeley, A.D. & Lewis, V.J. (1981). Inner active processes in reading: The inner voice, the inner ear and the inner eye. In A.M. Lesgold and C.A. Perfetti (eds.), *Interactive Processes in Reading*. Hillsdale, N.J.: Lawrence Erlbaum Associates

Baddeley, A., Logie, R., Nimmo-Smith, I. & Brereton, N. (1985). Components of fluent reading. *Journal of Memory and Language*, 24, 119-31

Baddeley, A.D., Thomson, N. & Buchanan, M. (1975). Word length and the structure of short-term memory. *Journal of Verbal Learning and Verbal Behavior*, 14, 575-89

Baker, L. (1984a). Spontaneous versus instructed use of multiple standards for evaluating comprehension: effects of age, reading proficiency, and type of standard. *Journal of Experimental Child Psychology*, 38, 289-311

Baker, L. (1984b). Children's effective use of multiple standards for evaluating their comprehension. *Journal of Educational Psychology*, 76, 588-97

Baker, L. (1985). Working memory and comprehension: A replication. *Bulletin of the Psychonomic Society*, 23, 28-30

Baker, L. & Anderson, R. (1982). Effects of inconsistent information on text processing. *Reading Research Quarterly*, 17, 281-94

Baker, L. & Brown, A.L. (1984). Metacognitive skills and reading. In P.D. Pearson (ed.), *Handbook of Reading Research*. New York: Plenum Press

Baker, L. & Stein, N. (1981). The development of prose comprehension skills. In C. Santa & B. Hayes (eds.), *Children's Prose Comprehension: Research and Practice*. Newark, Delaware: International Reading Association

Barron, R.W. (1978). Reading skill and phonological coding in lexical access. In M.M. Gruneberg, R.N. Sykes & P.E. Morris (eds.), *Proceedings of the International Conference on Practical Aspects of Memory*. London: Academic Press

Barron, R.W. & Baron, J. (1977). How children get meaning from printed words. *Child Development*, 48, 587-94

Bartlett, F.C. (1932). *Remembering*. Cambridge: Cambridge University Press

Beck, I.L., Perfetti, C.A. & McKeown, M.G. (1982). Effects of long-term vocabulary instruction on lexical access and reading comprehension. *Journal of Educational Psychology*, 74, 506-21

Bereiter, C. & Scardamalia, M. (1982). From conversation to composition: the role of instruction in a developmental process. In R. Glaser (ed.), *Advances in Instructional Psychology*, Vol. 2. Hillsdale, N. J.: Lawrence Erlbaum Associates

Bishop, D. (1983). *Test for Reception of Grammar*. Department of Psychology, University of Manchester

Black, J.B. & Wilensky, R. (1979). An evaluation of story grammars. *Cognitive Science*, 3, 213-30

Bormuth, J.R., Manning, J.C., Carr, J.W. & Pearson, P.D. (1970). Children's comprehension of between- and within-sentence syntactic structures. *Journal of Educational Psychology*, 61, 349-57

Bowey, J.A. (1985). Contextual facilitation in children's oral reading in relation to grade and decoding skill. *Journal of Experimental Child Psychology*, 40, 23-48

Bradley, L. & Bryant, P.E. (1983). Categorising sounds and learning to read: A causal connexion. *Nature*, 301, 419-21

Bransford, J.D., Barclay, J.R., & Franks, J.J. (1972). Sentence memory: A constructive versus interpretive approach. *Cognitive Psychology*, 3, 193-209

Bransford, J.D. & Franks, J.J. (1971). The abstraction of linguistic ideas. *Cognitive Psychology*, 2, 331-50

Bransford, J.D. & Johnson, M.K. (1972). Contextual prerequisites for understanding: Some investigations of comprehension and recall. *Journal of Verbal Learning and Verbal Behavior*, 11, 717-26

Brown, A.L. (1975). The development of memory: Knowing, knowing about knowing and knowing how to know. In H.W. Reese (ed.), *Advances in Child Development and Behavior*, Vol. 10. New York: Academic Press

Brown, A.L. (1980). Metacognitive development and reading. In R.J. Spiro, B.C. Bruce & W.F. Brewer (eds.), *Theoretical Issues in Reading Comprehension*. Hillsdale, N.J.: Lawrence Erlbaum Associates

Brown, A.L. & Campione, J.C. (1978). Memory strategies in learning: Training children to study strategically. In H.L. Pick, H.W. Leibowitz, J.E. Singer, A. Steinschneider & H.W. Stevenson (eds.), *Psychology: From Research to Practice*. New York: Plenum

Brown, A.L. Palincsar, A.S. & Armbruster, B.B. (1984). Instructing comprehension-fostering activities in interactive learning situations. In H. Mandl, N.L. Stein & T. Trabasso (eds.), *Learning and Comprehension of Text*. Hillsdale, N.J.: Lawrence Erlbaum Associates

Brown, A.L. & Smiley, S.S. (1977). Rating the importance of structural units of prose passages: A problem of metacognitive development. *Child Development*, 48, 1-8

Byrne, B. (1981). Deficient syntactic control in poor readers: Is a weak phonetic memory code responsible? *Applied Psycholinguistics*, 2, 201-12

Calfee, R.C., Arnold, R. & Drum, P.A. (1976). A review of *The Psychology of Reading* by E. Gibson & H. Levin. *Proceedings of the National Academy of Education*, 3, 1-80

Campione, J.C. & Armbruster, B.B. (1984). An analysis of the outcomes and implications of intervention research. In H. Mandl, N.L. Stein & T. Trabasso (eds.), *Learning and Comprehension of Text*. Hillsdale, N.J.: Lawrence Erlbaum Associates

Canney, G. & Winograd, P. (1979). *Schemata for Reading and Reading Comprehension Performance*. Technical Report No. 120, Urbana: University of Illinois, Center for the Study of Reading

Carroll, J.B., Davies, P. & Richman, B. (1971). *Word Frequency Book*. Boston: Houghton Mifflin

Carver, R.P. (1987). Should reading comprehension skills be taught? In J.E. Readence & R.S. Baldwin (eds.), *Research in Literacy: Merging Perspectives*. Rochester, N. Y.: National Reading Conference

Case, R., Kurland, D.M. & Goldberg, J. (1982). Operational efficiency and the growth of short-term memory span. *Journal of Experimental Child Psychology*, 33, 386-404

Chabot, R.J., Petros, T.V. & McCord, G. (1983). Developmental and reading ability differences in accessing information from semantic memory. *Journal of Experimental Child Psychology*, 35, 128-42

Chi, M.T.H. (1976). Short-term memory limitations in children: Capacity or processing deficits? *Memory and Cognition*, 4, 559-72

Chomsky, C. (1969). *The acquisition of syntax in children from five to ten*. Cambridge, Mass.: MIT Press

Cirilo, R.K. (1981). Referential coherence and text structure in comprehension. *Journal of Verbal Learning and Verbal Behavior*, 20, 358-67

Clark, H.H. (1973). The language-as-fixed-effect fallacy: A critique of language statistics in psychological research. *Journal of Verbal Learning and Verbal Behavior*, 12, 335-9

Clark, H.H. (1977). Bridging. In P.N. Johnson-Laird & P.C. Wason (eds.), *Thinking: Readings in Cognitive Science*. Cambridge: Cambridge University Press

Clark, H.H. & Sengul, C.T. (1979). In search of referents for nouns and pronouns. *Memory and Cognition*, 7, 35-41

Clay, M.M. & Imlach, R.H. (1971). Juncture, pitch and stress as reading behaviour variables. *Journal of Verbal Learning and Verbal Behavior*, 10, 133-9

Coltheart, V., Laxon, V.J., Keating, G.C. & Pool, M.M. (1986). Direct access and phonological encoding processes in children's reading: Effects of word characteristics. *British Journal of Educational Psychology*, 56, 255-70

Corbett, A.T. & Dosher, B.A. (1978). Instrument inferences in sentence encoding. *Journal of Verbal Learning and Verbal Behavior*, 17, 479-91

Corrin, S. & Corrin, S. (1982). *More Stories for Seven-Year-Olds*. Harmondsworth: Penguin

Cromer, W. (1970). The difference model: A new explanation for some reading difficulties. *Journal of Educational Psychology*, 61, 471-83

Curtis, M. (1980). Development of components of reading skill. *Journal of Educational Psychology*, 72, 656-69

Daneman, M. (1987). Reading and working memory. In J.R. Beech & A.M. Colley (eds.), *Cognitive Approaches to Reading*. Chichester: Wiley

Daneman, M. & Carpenter, P.A. (1980). Individual differences in working memory and reading. *Journal of Verbal Learning and Verbal Behavior*, 19, 450-66

Daneman, M. & Carpenter, P.A. (1983). Individual differences in integrating information between and within sentences. *Journal of Experimental Psychology: Learning, Memory and Cognition*, 9, 561-84

Daneman, M. & Tardif, T. (1987). Working memory and reading skill re-examined. In M. Coltheart (ed.), *Attention and Performance*, Vol. 12: *The Psychology of Reading*. Hove: Lawrence Erlbaum Associates

Danner, F.W. (1976). Children's understanding of intersentence organization in the recall of short descriptive passages. *Journal of Educational Psychology*, 68, 174-83

Davis, F.B. (1972). Psychometric research on comprehension in reading. *Reading Research Quarterly*, 7, 628-78

van Dijk, T.A. (1972). *Some Aspects of Text Grammars*. The Hague: Mouton

van Dijk, T.A. & Kintsch, W. (1983). *Strategies of Discourse Comprehension*. New York: Academic Press

Dixon, P., LeFevre, J.A. & Twilley, L.C. (1988). Word knowledge and working memory as predictors of reading skill. *Journal of Educational Psychology*, 80, 465-72

Doctor, E. & Coltheart, M. (1980). Phonological recoding in children's reading for meaning. *Memory and Cognition*, 8, 195-209

Dommes, P., Gersten, R. & Carnine, D. (1984). Instructional procedures for increasing skill-deficient fourth graders' comprehension of syntactic structures. *Educational Psychology*, 4, 155-65

Donaldson, M. L. (1986). *Children's Explanations: A Psycholinguistic Study*. Cambridge: Cambridge University Press

Dooling, D.J. & Lachman, R. (1971). Effects of comprehension on the retention of prose. *Journal of Experimental Psychology*, 88, 216-22

Downing, J. (1984). Task awareness in the development of reading skill. In J. Downing & R. Valtin (eds.), *Language Awareness and Learning to Read*. New York: Springer

Ehri, L.C. (1979). Linguistic insight: Threshold of reading acquisition. In T.G. Waller & G.E. MacKinnon (eds.), *Reading Research: Advances in Theory and Practice*, Vol. 1. New York: Academic Press

Ehrlich, K. (1980). Comprehension of pronouns. *Quarterly Journal of Experimental Psychology*, 32, 247-55

Ehrlich, K. & Johnson-Laird, P.N. (1982). Spatial descriptions and referential continuity. *Journal of Verbal Learning and Verbal Behavior*, 21, 296-306

Flavell, J.H. (1970). Developmental studies of mediated memory. In H. Reese & L.P. Lipsitt (eds.), *Advances in Child Development and Behavior*, Vol. 5. New York: Academic Press

Fleisher, L.S., Jenkins, J.R. & Pany, D. (1979). Effects on poor readers' comprehension of training in rapid decoding. *Reading Research Quarterly*, 15, 30-48

Forrest-Pressley, D.L. & Waller, T.G. (1984). *Cognition, Metacognition and Reading*. New York: Springer

Fowles, B. & Glanz, M.E. (1977). Competence and talent in verbal riddle comprehension. *Journal of Child Language*, 4, 433-52

Frederiksen, J.R. (1978). Assessment of perceptual, decoding and lexical skills and their relation to reading proficiency. In A.M. Lesgold, J.W. Pellegrino, S.D. Fokkema & R. Glaser (eds.), *Cognitive Psychology and Instruction*. New York: Plenum

Gardner, H. & Winner, E. (1986). Attitudes and attributes: Children's understanding of metaphor and sarcasm. In M. Perlmutter (ed.), *Perspectives on Intellectual Development*, Vol. 19. London: Lawrence Erlbaum Associates

Garner, R. (1980). Monitoring of understanding: An investigation of good and poor readers' awareness of induced miscomprehension of text. *Journal of Reading Behavior*, 12, 55-63

Garner, R. (1981). Monitoring of passage inconsistency among poor comprehenders: A preliminary test of the 'piecemeal processing' explanation. *Journal of Educational Research*, 74, 159-62

Garner, R. (1982). Resolving comprehension failure through text lookback: Direct training and practice effects among good and poor comprehenders in grades six and seven. *Reading Psychology*, 3, 221-31

Garner, R. (1987). *Metacognition and Reading Comprehension*. Norwood, N.J.: Ablex

Garner, R. & Kraus, C. (1981-2). Good and poor comprehender differences in knowing and regulating reading behaviors. *Educational Research Quarterly*, 6, 5-12

Garner, R. & Reis, R. (1981). Monitoring and resolving comprehension obstacles: An investigation of spontaneous text lookbacks among upper-grade good and poor comprehenders. *Reading Research Quarterly*, 16, 569-82

Garner, R. & Taylor, N. (1982). Monitoring of understanding: An investigation of attentional assistance needs at different grade and reading proficiency levels. *Reading Psychology*, 3, 1-6

Garnham, A. (1979). Instantiation of verbs. *Quarterly Journal of Experimental Psychology*, 31, 207-14

Garnham, A. (1982). Testing psychological theories about inference making. *Memory and Cognition*, 10, 341-9

Garnham, A. (1983). What's wrong with story grammars. *Cognition*, 15, 145-54

Garnham, A. (1987). *Mental Models as Representations of Discourse and Text*. Chichester: Ellis Horwood

Garnham, A. & Oakhill, J.V. (1985). On-line resolution of anaphoric pronouns: Effects of inference making and verb semantics. *British Journal of Psychology*, 76, 385-93

Garnham, A., Oakhill, J.V. & Johnson-Laird, P.N. (1982). Referential continuity and the coherence of discourse. *Cognition*, 11, 29-46

Gates, A.I. & MacGinitie, W.H. (1965). Gates–MacGinitie Reading Tests. New York: Columbia University Teachers' College Press

Gazdar, G. (1981). Unbounded dependencies and coordinate structure. *Linguistic Inquiry*, 12, 155-84

Gitomer, D.H., Pellegrino, J.W. & Bisanz, J. (1983). Developmental change and invariance in semantic processing. *Journal of Experimental Child Psychology*, 35, 56-80

Gleitman, H. & Gleitman, L.R. (1970). *Phrase and Paraphrase*. New York: W.W. Norton & Co

Goldman, S. (1976). Reading skill and the minimum distance principle: A comparison of listening and reading comprehension. *Journal of Experimental Child Psychology*, 22, 123-42

Goldman, S.R., Hogaboam, T.W., Bell, L.C. & Perfetti, C.A. (1980). Short-term retention of discourse during reading. *Journal of Educational Psychology*, 72, 647-55

Golinkoff, R. (1975-76). A comparison of reading comprehension processes in good and poor comprehenders. *Reading Research Quarterly*, 11, 623-59

Golinkoff, R.M. & Rosinski, R.R. (1976). Decoding, semantic processing and reading comprehension skill. *Child Development*, 47, 252-8

Grice, H.P. (1975). Logic and conversation. In P. Cole & J.L. Morgan (eds.), *Syntax and Semantics*, Vol. 7: *Speech acts*. New York: Academic Press

Guenther, R.K., Klatzky, R.L. & Putnam, W. (1980). Commonalities and differences in semantic decisions about pictures and words. *Journal of Verbal Learning and Verbal Behavior*, 19, 54-74

Guttman, J., Levin, J.R. & Pressley, M. (1977). Pictures, partial pictures and young children's oral prose learning. *Journal of Educational Psychology*, 69, 473-80

Halliday, M.A.K. & Hasan, R. (1976). *Cohesion in English*. London: Longman

Hansen, J. & Pearson, P. D. (1983). An instructional study: Improving the inferential comprehension of good and poor fourth-grade readers. *Journal of Educational Psychology*, 75, 821-9

Harris, P.L., Kruithof, A., Meerum Terwogt, M. & Visser, T. (1981). Children's detection and awareness of textual anomaly. *Journal of Experimental Child Psychology*, 31, 212-30

Harris, P.L., Mandias, M., Meerum Terwogt, M. & Tjintjelaar, J. (1980). The influence of context on story recall and feelings of comprehension. *International Journal of Behavioral Development*, 3, 159-72

Haviland, S.E. & Clark, H.H. (1974). What's new? Acquiring new information as a process in comprehension. *Journal of Verbal Learning and Verbal Behavior*, 13, 512-21

Healy, J.M. (1982). The enigma of hyperlexia. *Reading Research Quarterly*, 17, 319-38

Henry, L.A. (1989). Rehearsal and the word length effect in young children's short-term memory. Paper presented at the British Psychological Society Annual Conference, April 1989

Hess, A.M. (1982). An analysis of the cognitive processes underlying problems in reading comprehension. *Journal of Reading Behavior*, 14, 313-33

Hess, T.M. & Radtke, R.C. (1981). Processing and memory factors in children's reading comprehension skill. *Child Development*, 52, 479-88

Hirsh-Pasek, K., Gleitman, L.R. & Gleitman, H. (1978). What did the brain say to the mind? A study of the detection and report of ambiguity by young children. In A. Sinclair, R.J. Jarvella & W.J.M. Levelt (eds.), *The Child's Conception of Language*. New York: Springer

Hirst, G. (1981). *Anaphora in Natural Language Understanding: A Survey*. Berlin: Springer

Hirst, W. & Brill, G.A. (1980). Contextual aspects of pronoun assignment. *Journal of Verbal Learning and Verbal Behavior*, 19, 168-75

Hitch, G.J. & Halliday, M.S. (1983). Working memory in children. *Philosophical Transactions of the Royal Society, Series B*, 325-40

Huey, E. (1968). *The Psychology and Pedagogy of Reading*. Cambridge, Mass.: MIT Press (originally published 1908)

Hulme, C.,Thomson, N., Muir, C. & Lawrence, A. (1984). Speech rate and the development of short-term memory span. *Journal of Experimental Child Psychology*, 38, 241-53

Hunt, E. (1977). We know who knows, but why? In R.C. Anderson, R.J. Spiro and W.E. Montague (eds.), *Schooling and the Acquisition of Knowledge*. Hillsdale, N.J.: Lawrence Erlbaum Associates

Hunt, E., Lunneborg, C. & Lewis, J. (1975). What does it mean to be high verbal? *Cognitive Psychology*, 7, 194-227

Huttenlocher, J. & Burke, C. (1976). Why does memory span increase with age? *Cognitive Psychology*, 8, 1-31

Huttenlocher, R.R. & Huttenlocher, J. (1973). A study of children with hyperlexia. *Neurology*, 23, 1107-16

Isakson, R.L. & Miller, J.W. (1976). Sensitivity to syntactic and semantic cues in good and poor comprehenders. *Journal of Educational Psychology*, 68, 787-92

Johns, J.L. (1984). Students' perceptions of reading: Insights from research and pedagogical implications. In J. Downing & R. Valtin (eds.), *Language Awareness and Learning to Read*. New York: Springer

Johnson, M.K., Bransford, J.D., & Solomon, S. (1973). Memory for tacit implications of sentence. *Journal of Experimental Psychology*, 98, 203-5

Johnson-Laird, P.N. (1977). Psycholinguistics without linguistics. In N.S. Sutherland (ed.), *Tutorial Essays in Psychology*, Vol. 1. Hillsdale, N.J.: Lawrence Erlbaum Associates

Johnson-Laird, P.N. (1983). *Mental Models: Towards a Cognitive Science of Language, Inference, and Consciousness*. Cambridge: Cambridge University Press

Jorm, A.F. & Share, D.L. (1983). Phonological recoding and reading acquisition. *Applied Psycholinguistics*, 4, 103-47

Kail, R.V. (1979). *The Development of Memory in Children*. San Francisco: W.H. Freeman & Co

Kail, R.V., Chi, M., Ingram, A., & Danner, F. (1977). Constructive aspects of children's reading comprehension. *Child Development*, 48, 684-8

Karmiloff-Smith, A. (1980). Psychological processes underlying pronominalization and non-pronominalization in children's connected discourse. In J. Kreiman & A. Ojeda (eds.), *Papers from the Parasession on Pronouns and Anaphora*. Chicago: CLS

Karmiloff-Smith, A. (1985). Language and cognitive processes from a developmental perspective. *Language and Cognitive Processes*, 1, 61-85

Kennedy, A. (1987). Eye movements, reading skill and the spatial code. In J.R. Beech & A.M. Colley (eds.), *Cognitive Approaches to Reading*. Chichester: Wiley

Kintsch, W. & van Dijk, T.A. (1978). Towards a model of text comprehension and production. *Psychological Review*, 85, 363-94

Kleiman, G.M. (1975). Speech recoding in reading. *Journal of Verbal Learning and Verbal Behavior*, 14, 323-39

Kolers, P.A. (1970). Three stages of reading. In H. Levin, & J.P. Williams (eds.), *Basic Studies in Reading*. New York: Basic Books

LaBerge, D. & Samuels, S.J. (1974). Toward a theory of automatic information processing in reading. *Cognitive Psychology*, 6, 293-323

Lesgold, A., Resnick, L.B. & Hammond, K. (1985). Learning to read: A longitudinal study of word skill development in two curricula. In G.E. MacKinnon & T.G. Waller (eds.), *Reading Research: Advances in Theory and Practice*, Vol. 4. New York: Academic Press

Levin, J.R. (1973). Inducing comprehension in poor readers: A test of a recent model. *Journal of Educational Psychology*, 65, 19-24

Levin, J.R. (1981). On functions of pictures in prose. In F.J. Pirozzolo & M.C. Wittrock (eds.), *Neuropsychological and Cognitive Processes in Reading*. London: Academic Press

Levy, B.A. (1978). Speech analysis during sentence processing: Reading and listening. *Visible Language*, 12, 81-101

Light, L.L. and Capps, J.L. (1986). Comprehension of pronouns in young and older adults. *Developmental Psychology*, 22, 580-5

Luria, A.R. (1976). *Cognitive Development: Its cultural and social foundations*. Cambridge, Mass.: Harvard University Press

McClelland, J.L. & Jackson, M.D. (1978). Studying individual differences in reading. In A.M. Lesgold, J.W. Pellegrino, S.D. Fokkema & R. Glaser (eds.), *Cognitive Psychology and Instruction*. New York: Plenum

McDowell, J.H. (1979). *Children's Riddling*. Bloomington: Indiana University Press

McFarland, C.E. & Rhodes, D.D. (1978). Memory for meaning in skilled and unskilled readers. *Journal of Experimental Child Psychology*, 25, 199-207

McNemar, Q. (1962). *Psychological Statistics*. (3rd edn). New York: Wiley

Mann, V.A., Liberman, I.Y. & Shankweiler, D. (1980). Children's memory for sentences and word strings in relation to reading ability. *Memory and Cognition*, 8, 329-35

Maria, K. & MacGinitie, W. (1987). Learning from texts that refute the reader's prior knowledge. *Reading Research and Instruction*, 26, 222-38

Markman, E.M. (1977). Realizing that you don't understand: A preliminary investigation. *Child Development*, 48, 986-92

Markman, E.M. (1979). Realizing that you don't understand: Elementary school children's awareness of inconsistencies. *Child Development*, 50, 643-55

Markman, E.M. (1981). Comprehension monitoring. In W.P. Dickson (ed.), *Children's Oral Communication Skills*. London: Academic Press

Markman, E.M. & Gorin, L. (1981). Children's ability to adjust their standards for evaluating comprehension. *Journal of Educational Psychology*, 73, 320-5

Mayer, R.E. (1979). Can advance organizers influence meaningful learning? *Review of Educational Research*, 49, 371-83

Mehegan, C.C. & Dreifuss, F.E. (1972). Hyperlexia: Exceptional reading ability in brain-damaged children. *Neurology*, 22, 1105-11

Merrill, E.C., Sperber, R.D. & McCauley, C. (1981). Differences in semantic encoding as a function of reading comprehension skill. *Memory and Cognition*, 9, 618-24

Meyer, B.J.F. (1977). The structure of prose: effects on learning and memory and implications for instructional practice. In R.C. Anderson, R.J. Spiro & W.E. Montague (eds.), *Schooling and the Acquisition of Knowledge*. Hillsdale, N.J.: Lawrence Erlbaum Associates

Moberly, P.G.C. (1979). *Elementary Children's Understanding of Anaphoric Relationships in Connnected Discourse*. Ann Arbor, Mich.: University Microfilms

Myers, M. & Paris, S.G. (1978). Children's metacognitive knowledge about reading. *Journal of Educational Psychology*, 70, 680-90

Neale, M.D. (1966). *The Neale Analysis of Reading Ability*. (2nd edn). London: Macmillan Education

Neale, M.D., McKay, M.F. & Childs, G.H. (1986). The Neale Analysis of Reading Ability – Revised. *British Journal of Educational Psychology*, 56, 346-56

Oakan, R., Wiener, M. & Cromer, W. (1971). Identification, organization and reading comprehension in good and poor readers. *Journal of Educational Psychology*, 62, 71-8

Oakhill, J. (1981), *Children's Reading Comprehension.* Unpublished D.Phil. thesis, University of Sussex

Oakhill, J. (1982). Constructive processes in skilled and less skilled comprehenders. *British Journal of Psychology*, 73, 13-20

Oakhill, J. (1984). Inferential and memory skills in children's comprehension of stories. *British Journal of Educational Psychology*, 54, 31-9

Oakhill, J. & Garnham, A. (1985). Referential continuity, transitivity, and the retention of spatial descriptions. *Language and Cognitive Processes*, 1, 149-62

Oakhill, J. & Garnham, A. (1988). *Becoming a Skilled Reader.* Oxford: Basil Blackwell

Oakhill, J., Shaw, D. & Folkard, S. (1983). Selective impairment of educationally subnormal children's delayed memory for text. *Nature*, 303, 800-1

Olshavsky, J. (1976-77). Reading as problem-solving: An investigation of strategies. *Reading Research Quarterly*, 12, 654-74

Omanson, R.C., Warren, W.M. & Trabasso,T. (1978). Goals, inferential comprehension and recall of stories by children. *Discourse Processes*, 1, 337-54

Palincsar, A.S. & Brown, A.L. (1984). Reciprocal teaching of comprehension-fostering and comprehension-monitoring activities. *Cognition and Instruction*, 1, 117-75

Pany, D., Jenkins, J.R. & Schreck, J. (1982). Vocabulary instruction: Effects of word knowledge and reading comprehension. *Learning Disability Quarterly*, 5, 202-15

Paris, S.G. (1975). Integration and inference in children's comprehension and memory. In F. Restle, R.M. Shiffrin, N.J. Castellan, H.R. Lindman, & D.B. Pisoni (eds.), *Cognitive Theory*, Vol. 1. Hillsdale, N.J.: Lawrence Erlbaum Associates

Paris, S.G. & Carter, A. (1973). Semantic and constructive aspects of sentence memory in children. *Developmental Psychology*, 9, 109-13

Paris, S.G., Cross, D.R. & Lipson, M.Y. (1984). Informed strategies for learning: An instructional program to improve children's reading awareness and comprehension. *Journal of Educational Psychology*, 76, 1239-52

Paris, S.G. & Lindauer, B.K. (1976). The role of inference in children's comprehension and memory for sentences. *Cognitive Psychology*, 8, 217-27

Paris, S.G., Lindauer, B.K. & Cox, G.L. (1977). The development of inferential comprehension. *Child Development*, 48, 1728-33

Paris, S.G. & Oka, E.R. (1986). Children's reading strategies, metacognition and motivation. *Developmental Review*, 6, 25-56

Paris, S.G. & Upton, L.R. (1976). Children's memory for inferential relationships in prose. *Child Development*, 47, 660-8

Pearson, P. & Gallagher, M. (1983). The instruction of reading comprehension. *Contemporary Educational Psychology*, 8, 317-44

Peeck, J. (1974). Retention of pictorial and verbal content of a text with illustrations. *Journal of Educational Psychology*, 66, 880-8

Perfetti, C.A. (1985). *Reading Ability.* Oxford: Oxford University Press

Perfetti, C.A., Finger, E. & Hogaboam, T. (1978). Sources of vocalization latency differences between skilled and less skilled young readers. *Journal of Educational Psychology*, 70, 730-9

Perfetti, C.A. & Goldman, S.R. (1976). Discourse memory and reading comprehension skill. *Journal of Verbal Learning and Verbal Behavior*, 15, 33-42

Perfetti, C.A., Goldman, S.R. & Hogaboam, T.W. (1979). Reading skill and the identification of words in discourse context. *Memory and Cognition*, 7, 273-82

Perfetti, C.A. & Hogaboam, T. (1975a). Relationship between single word decoding and reading comprehension skill. *Journal of Educational Psychology*, 67, 461-9

Perfetti, C.A. & Hogaboam, T. (1975b). The effects of word experience on decoding speeds of skilled and unskilled readers. Paper presented at the Psychonomics Society, Denver, November 1975

Perfetti, C.A. & Lesgold, A.M. (1977). Discourse comprehension and sources of individual differences. In M. Just & P.A. Carpenter (eds.), *Cognitive Processes in Comprehension*. Hillsdale, N.J.: Lawrence Erlbaum Associates

Perfetti, C.A. & Lesgold, A.M. (1979). Coding and comprehension in skilled reading and implications for reading instruction. In L.B. Resnick & P. Weaver (eds.), *Theory and Practice of Early Reading*, Vol. 1. Hillsdale, N.J.: Lawrence Erlbaum Associates

Perner, J. (1988). Developing semantics for theories of mind: From propositional attitudes to mental representations. In J.W. Astington, P.L. Harris & D.R. Olson (eds.), *Developing Theories of Mind.* Cambridge: Cambridge University Press

Peters, E.E., Levin, J.R., McGivern, J.E. & Pressley, M. (1985). Further comparison of representational and transformational prose-learning imagery. *Journal of Educational Psychology*, 77, 129-36

Poulsen, D., Kintsch, E., Kintsch, W. & Premack, D. (1979). Children's comprehension and memory for stories. *Journal of Experimental Child Psychology*, 28, 379-401

Prawat, R.S. & Kerasotes, D. (1978). Basic memory processes in reading. *Merrill-Palmer Quarterly*, 24, 181-8

Pressley,G.M. (1976). Mental imagery helps eight-year-olds remember what they read. *Journal of Educational Psychology*, 68, 355-9

Reid, J. (1972). Children's comprehension of syntactic features found in some extension readers. Occasional Paper, Centre for Research in Educational Sciences, University of Edinburgh

Revelle, G.L., Wellman, H.M. & Karabenick, J.D. (1985). Comprehension monitoring in preschool children. *Child Development*, 56, 654-63

Rosenshine, B.V. (1980). Skill hierarchies in reading comprehension. In R.J. Spiro, B.C. Bruce & W.F. Brewer (eds.), *Theoretical Issues in Reading Comprehension*. Hillsdale, N.J.: Lawrence Erlbaum Associates

Rosinski, R.R., Golinkoff, R.M. & Kukish, K.S. (1975). Automatic semantic processing in a picture-word interference task. *Child Development*, 46, 247-53

Rubin, A. (1980). A theoretical taxonomy of the differences between oral and written language. In R.J. Spiro, B.C. Bruce & W.F. Brewer (eds.), *Theoretical Issues in Reading Comprehension*. Hillsdale, N.J.: Lawrence Erlbaum Associates

Rumelhart, D.E. (1975). Notes on a schema for stories. In D.G. Bobrow & A. Collins (eds.), *Representation and Understanding: Studies in Cognitive Science*. New York: Academic Press

Rusted, J. (1984). Differential facilitation by pictures of children's retention of written texts. *Current Psychological Research and Reviews*, 3, 61-71

Rutter, P. & Raban, B. (1982). The development of cohesion in children's writing: a preliminary investigation. *First Language*, 3, 63-75

Schallert, D.L. (1980). The role of illustrations in reading comprehension. In R.J. Spiro, B.C. Bruce & W.F. Brewer (eds.), *Theoretical Issues in Reading Comprehension*. Hillsdale, N.J.: Lawrence Erlbaum Associates

Shultz, T.R. (1974). Development of the appreciation of riddles. *Child Development*, 45, 100-5

Shultz, T.R. & Pilon, R. (1973). Development of the ability to detect linguistic ambiguity. *Child Development*, 44, 728-33

Siegel, L.S. & Ryan, E.B. (1989). The development of working memory in normally achieving and subtypes of learning disabled children. *Child Development*, 60, 973-80

Silverberg, N.E. & Silverberg, M.C. (1967). Hyperlexia: Specific word recognition skills in young children. *Exceptional Children*, 34, 41-2

Sinclair, A. (1980). Thinking about language: An interview study of children aged three to eight. *International Journal of Psycholinguistics*, 4-7, 19-40

Sinclair, A., Jarvella, R.J. & Levelt, W.J.M. (1978). *The Child's Conception of Language*. Berlin: Springer

Smiley, S.S., Oakley, D.D., Worthen, D., Campione, J. & Brown, A.L. (1977). Recall of thematically relevant material by adolescent good and poor readers as a function of written versus oral presentation. *Journal of Educational Psychology*, 69, 381-7

Snodgrass, J.G. & Vanderwaert, M. (1980). A standardised set of 260 pictures: Norms for name agreement, image agreement, familiarity and visual complexity. *Journal of Experimental Psychology: Human Learning and Memory*, 6, 174-215

Snowling, M.J. (1980). The development of grapheme-phoneme correspondence in normal and dyslexic readers. *Journal of Experimental Child Psychology*, 29, 294-305

Spearitt, D. (1972). Identification of subskills of reading comprehension by maximum likelihood factor analysis. *Reading Research Quarterly*, 8, 92-111

Stanovich, K.E. (1982). Individual differences in the cognitive processes of reading: II. Text-level processes. *Journal of Learning Disabilities*, 15, 549-54

Stanovich, K.E. (1986). Cognitive processes and reading problems of learning-disabled children: Evaluating the assumption of specificity. In J.Torgesen & B. Wong (eds.), *Psychological and Educational Perspectives on Learning Disabilities*. New York: Academic Press

Stein, N.L. (1979). How children understand stories: A developmental analysis. In L.G. Katz (ed.), *Current Topics in Early Childhood Education*, Vol. 2. Norwood, N.J.: Ablex

Stein, N.L. (1982). What's in a story: Interpreting the interpretations of story grammars. *Discourse Processes*, 5, 319-36

Stein, N.L. & Glenn, C.G. (1979). An analysis of story comprehension in elementary school children. In R. Freedle (ed.), *Multidisciplinary Approaches to Discourse Comprehension*. Hillsdale, N.J.: Lawrence Erlbaum Associates

Steiner, R., Wiener, M. & Cromer, W. (1971). Comprehension training and identification for poor and good readers. *Journal of Educational Psychology*, 62, 506-13

Stenning, K. & Michell, L. (1985). Learning how to tell a good story: The development of content and language in children's telling of one tale. *Discourse Processes*, 8, 261-79

Taylor, B.M. (1982). Text structure and children's comprehension and memory for expository material. *Journal of Educational Psychology*, 74, 323-40

Tierney, R.J. & Cunningham, J.W. (1984). Research on teaching reading comprehension. In P.D.Pearson (ed.), *Handbook of Reading Research*. New York: Longman

Tizard, B. & Hughes, M. (1984). *Young Children Learning: Talking and Thinking at Home and at School*. London: Fontana

Torgesen, J.K. (1978-79). Performance of reading disabled children on serial memory tasks: A selective review of recent research. *Reading Research Quarterly*, 14, 57-87

Townsend, D.J., Carrithers, C. & Bever, T.G. (1987). Listening and reading processes in college- and middle school-age readers. In R. Horowitz & S.J. Samuels (eds.), *Comprehending Oral and Written Language*. New York: Academic Press

Tulving, E. and Bower, G.H. (1974). The logic of memory representations. In G. Bower (ed.), *The Psychology of Learning and Motivation: Advances in Research and Theory*, Vol. 8. New York: Academic Press

Tunmer, W.E. & Bowey, J.A. (1984). Metalinguistic awareness and reading acquisition.

In W.E. Tunmer, C. Pratt & M.L. Herriman (eds.), *Metalinguistic Awareness in Children*. New York: Springer

Tunmer, W.E., Nesdale, A.R. & Pratt, C. (1983). The development of young children's awareness of logical inconsistencies. *Journal of Experimental Child Psychology*, 36, 97-108

Tunmer, W.E., Pratt, C. & Herriman, M.L. (1984). *Metalinguistic Awareness in Children*. Berlin: Springer

Wagner, R. & Torgesen, J.K. (1987). The nature of phonological processing and its causal role in the acquisition of reading skills. *Psychological Bulletin*, 101, 192-212

Waller, T.G. (1976). Children's recognition memory for written sentences: a comparison of good and poor readers. *Child Development*, 47, 90-5

Wanner, E. & Maratsos, M. (1978). An ATN approach to comprehension. In M. Halle, J. Bresnan & G.A. Miller (eds.), *Linguistic Theory and Psychological Reality*. Cambridge, Mass: MIT Press

Weaver, P. (1979). Improving reading comprehension: Effects of sentence organization instruction. *Reading Research Quarterly*, 15, 127-46

Weber, R. (1970). A linguistic analysis of first-grade reading errors. *Reading Research Quarterly*, 5, 427-51

Wechsler, D. (1974). *Manual for the Wechsler Intelligence Scale for Children – revised*. New York: The Psychological Corporation

Weinstein, R. & Rabinovitch, M.S. (1971). Sentence structure and retention in good and poor readers. *Journal of Educational Psychology*, 62, 25-30

Wilks, Y. (1975). A preferential, pattern-seeking semantics for natural language interface. *Artificial Intelligence*, 6, 53-74

Wimmer, H. (1979). Processing of script deviations by young children. *Discourse Processes*, 2, 301-10

Wimmer, H. & Perner, J. (1983). Beliefs about beliefs: Representation and constraining function of wrong beliefs in young children's understanding of deception. *Cognition*, 13, 103-28

Winograd, P. & Johnston, P. (1982). Comprehension monitoring and the error detection paradigm. *Journal of Reading Behavior*, 14, 61-74

Wykes, T. (1981). Inferences and children's comprehension of pronouns. *Journal of Experimental Child Psychology*, 32, 264-78

Yalisove, D. (1978). The effect of riddle structure on children's comprehension of riddles. *Developmental Psychology*, 14, 173-80

Yussen, S.R. (1982). Children's impressions of coherence in narratives. In B.A. Hutson (ed.), *Advances in Reading/Language Research*, 1, 245-81

Yussen, S.R., Mathews, S.R. & Hiebert, E. (1982). Metacognitive aspects of reading. In W. Otto and S. White (eds.), *Reading Expository Material*. London: Academic Press

Zabrucky, H. & Ratner, H.H. (1986). Children's comprehension monitoring and recall of inconsistent stories. *Child Development*, 57, 1401-18

Author index

Subject index

For EU product safety concerns, contact us at Calle de José Abascal, 56–1°,
28003 Madrid, Spain or eugpsr@cambridge.org.

www.ingramcontent.com/pod-product-compliance
Ingram Content Group UK Ltd.
Pitfield, Milton Keynes, MK11 3LW, UK
UKHW010039140625
459647UK00012BA/1487

* 9 7 8 0 5 2 1 1 2 5 7 9 6 *